Leaders for a New Era

Leaders for a New Era

Strategies for Higher Education

Edited by

MADELEINE F. GREEN

American Council on Education • Macmillan Publishing Company
NEW YORK
Collier Macmillan Publishers
LONDON

The American Council on Education/Macmillan Series on Higher Education

Macmillan Publishing Company
866 Third Avenue, New York, N.Y. 10022

Collier Macmillan Canada, Inc.

Library of Congress Catalog Card Number: 87–28265

Printed in the United States of America

printing number
1 2 3 4 5 6 7 8 9 10

Library of Congress Cataloging in Publication Data

Leaders for a new era.

(The American Council on Education/Macmillan series on higher education)
Includes bibliographies.
1. Universities and colleges—United States—Administration. 2. Leadership. 3. College administrators—Training of—United States. I. Green, Madeleine F. II. Series.
LB2341.L264 1988 378.73 87–28265
ISBN 0-02-912470-0

Contents

Introduction 1

PART ONE: **The Context** 9

1. Leaders and Their Development
   Madeleine F. Green 13
2. Toward a New Leadership Model
   Madeleine F. Green 30

PART TWO: **New Leaders and New Models** 53

3. Department Chairs: Leadership in the Trenches
   John B. Bennett 57
4. In Support of Faculty Leadership: An Administrator's Perspective *Patricia R. Plante* 74
5. Developing Faculty Leadership: A Faculty Perspective *Rose-Marie Oster* 87
6. Women as Leaders *Donna Shavlik* and *Judith G. Touchton* 98
7. Strategies for Developing Minority Leadership
   Reginald Wilson and *Sarah E. Melendez* 118
8. Building Leadership Teams *John J. Gardiner* 137

PART THREE: Strategies and Resources 155

9. Administrative Careers: Multiple Pathways to Leadership Positions *Kathryn M. Moore* 159
10. Selecting Campus Leaders *Madeleine F. Green* 181
11. Professional Development Programs: Options for Administrators *Jack H. Schuster* 201
12. Leadership Development: A Participant's Perspective *Daniel H. Perlman* 225

Conclusion: An Action Agenda 249

Index 255

Introduction

Colleges and universities by their own proclamation are in the business of developing leaders for society. Discussions of how the curriculum and the cocurriculum influence the development of leadership among undergraduates are taking place with renewed frequency and intensity, and institutions are preoccupied with fostering in their students a commitment to civic responsibilities and leadership. More than a hundred formal "leadership studies" programs are offered on campuses around the country. But what attention does higher education pay to developing leaders for this vast, hundred-billion-dollar enterprise of twelve million students and four hundred thousand full-time faculty on three thousand campuses?

Ironically, the academy has paid little systematic attention to developing its own leaders. People are its most important resource, and yet, while we are vitally concerned about deferred maintenance of the physical plants, we ignore the more terrible toll that can be exacted by the deferred maintenance of human resources. Colleges and universities are highly labor-intensive; a typical campus may devote as much as sixty percent of its operating budget to personnel. Yet we invest little in the development of these valuable human resources, and, when times get tight, faculty and administrative development funds are among the first casualties.

While a number of efforts to identify and train leaders have been launched in the last twenty years, both on the national level and on individual campuses, these programs hardly constitute a comprehensive effort to improve the leadership of a major force in American society. Higher education's relative lack of interest in developing administrative leadership is hardly accidental. Its traditions value faculty rather than administrative achievements; its culture sees administration as a necessary evil requiring little special aptitude or preparation. For many academics, administration is a temporary assignment in a faculty career.

Getting a Handle on Leadership

One reason for higher education's relative neglect of this important investment in its health, a particularly important concern for this book, is the slipperiness of the whole topic of leadership and the special problems presented by the higher education context in which it is exercised. In spite of the many books providing tips and wisdom on how to be an effective leader, a definitive theory of leadership has yet to be set forth. Seventy-five years of analysis and research have yielded mountains of scholarly production and many insights but no conclusions as to what constitutes effective leadership. And even models of effective leadership that can be constructed do not necessarily lead us to an understanding of how to get from here to there, or in other words, how to *develop* leadership talent. Indeed, higher education still struggles with the question of whether leaders are born or made, and if leadership can be taught at all, how it can be done. As one researcher put it: "After over forty years of empirical investigation, leadership remains an enigma" (McCall, p. 1). The literature on leadership is vast; heroic efforts by Stodgill (1974) and later Bass (1981) to synthesize the existing literature reviewed some three thousand titles on the subject. Researchers are still trying to sort through the many existing approaches and to discern patterns and unifying structures, and yet neat paradigms and precise definitions elude us. Warren Bennis's observation made almost thirty years ago is distressingly valid today: "Of all the hazy and confounding areas in social psychology, leadership theory undoubtedly contends for top nomination. And, ironically, probably more has been written and less known about leadership than about any other topic in the behavioral sciences" (pp. 259–60 cited by McCall, p. 3). And indeed, writing in 1985 with Nanus, Bennis (p. 4) expressed no new optimism about arriving at a clear understanding of leadership:

> Decades of academic analysis have given us more than 350 definitions of leadership. Literally thousands of empirical investigations of leaders have been conducted in the last seventy-five years alone, but no clear and unequivocal understanding exists as to what distinguishes leaders from non-leaders, and perhaps more important, what distinguishes *effective* leaders from *ineffective* leaders and *effective organizations* from *ineffective* organizations.

The subject of leadership has been described and analyzed from many perspectives—sociology, psychology, business, history, and education. There is often little relationship among these various approaches, leaving the student of leadership to make connections among the disparate, and often contradictory, research and discussions. Yet there are certain recurring themes, and it is possible to arrive at some general definitions of leadership, as well as ways of thinking about the subject that provide at least a coherent frame of reference.

Leadership is commonly thought of as a *process*, a *transaction* between an individual leader (or possibly a group of leaders) and followers. Furthermore, that transaction takes place in a given context that shapes the nature of the transaction. Thus, the various elements of leadership—the leader, the followers, the relationship between them, and the context—can be examined singly or in combination. For example, the leader himself or herself can be the subject of scrutiny, with the examination focusing on the traits or characteristics of the individual that might be correlated with effective leadership. Or the relationship between the leader and followers can be studied and the transactions noted between the two that facilitate or impede leadership. Alternatively, analysis can focus on the context or circumstances, such as the cultural or historical conditions that give rise to leadership at a particular time or, again, the nature of the organization in which leadership is exercised.

Discussions of leadership in the first half of this century focused largely on "the great man" theory, attempting to identify the personality traits of successful leaders. These discussions were then broadened to consider the behaviors of leaders as reflected by two dimensions of leadership style—"task" versus "people" (consideration) orientation. These two axes gave rise to numerous other descriptors of style and attempts to define the combinations of people and task orientation that are most effective. Current theories have emphasized the importance of situation or context. The "great man" theory of leadership and the search for the most effective leadership style have given way to an examination of leadership in a specific context, and scholars now recognize that different situations require different leaders, who in turn use various leadership behaviors and styles in differing environments.

A second important theme in the literature on leadership concerns the nature of the relationship between the leader and the followers or constituents. Leader and followers have shared goals; this element distinguishes leadership from authoritarianism or coercion. According to Maccoby, "Leaders succeed when they embody and express, for better or for worse, values rooted in the social character of group, class, or nation." Burns describes leadership as deriving its strength from the congruence of the goals of the leader and followers. He defines leadership

> as leaders inducing followers to act for certain goals that represent the values and the motivations—the wants and the needs, the aspirations and expectations—of *both leaders and followers*. And the genius of leadership lies in the manner in which leaders see and act on their own and their followers' values and motivations.

Developing New Leadership Models

This book carries through it the assumption that there is no single model of an effective leader, and that leaders are very much a product of their particular era, culture, and organizational setting. In short, leadership is contextual. While this belief is widely shared by analysts and researchers, the literature is replete with advice on how to be a good leader, delivered with certainty not warranted by the many factors that shape leadership according to time, place, and circumstance. *Leaders for a New Era* is not a "how-to-be-an-effective-leader" manual for present and aspiring leaders. Rather, it is a guide to identifying, developing, and selecting leaders who will lead in different capacities, with different backgrounds, different styles, and different skills.

Also, the authors explicitly or implicitly recognize that leadership is not the sole province of administrators, although they are formally designated as leaders in the academy. Indeed, many administrators are not leaders at all, and many leaders are to be found in the faculty ranks and in the lower echelons of the administrative hierarchy. These concepts are explicitly explored in the chapters on faculty leadership and department chairs. While it is important to recognize and applaud the dispersion of leadership throughout an institution, it would be foolish to maintain that administrators are not vital to the direction of an institution or that they are not leaders. Thus, one assumption underlying the chapters dealing with new groups of leaders—women and minorities—is that their influence can be most strongly felt if they are duly anointed in positions of leadership such as presidencies and deanships.

The authors also challenge the current conventional wisdom calling for the empowerment of leaders, especially presidents, enabling them to provide the kind of forceful leadership required to take higher education through these difficult times and to transcend the constraints placed on them by diminished resources, meddlesome coordinating boards, and state legislatures as well as by incessant conflicting demands of various constituencies. This book takes a different approach, postulating that these constraints are unlikely to vanish. At worst, they will increase as the public and the consumers clamor for more accountability; at best they will lessen slowly through the efforts of leaders to sensitize the public about the nature of higher education and through skillful leadership efforts. Several of the authors assert a nonheroic concept of leadership, one that can be developed in a variety of individuals and in teams. Gardiner's chapter emphasizes the importance of developing an effective presidential team, with the chief executive officer lowering his or her own profile to serve as catalyst and "servant" in building this team. The dominant vision of leadership in the book is that it is shared, dispersed throughout the institution, and diverse in nature. The authors propose that leadership and its development are essential at all levels of the institution and are not the province of a single powerful individual or even of a few. Executive leadership is indispensable, to be sure, but insufficient by itself; empowering college presidents and senior officers will simply not solve the problems of colleges and universities. The Lone Ranger leader is a model ill-suited to the new era we face in higher education.

Thus, it is time to pay careful attention to the cultivation of leadership talent throughout the academy—in the faculty and in department chairs as well as in the areas of the institution that support the academic core. Accordingly, Plante's and Oster's chapters on faculty leadership and Bennett's on the department chair make important points about where leadership resides and how it can be fostered. Faculty and chairs make the crucial decisions about curriculum and personnel; they are the guardians of academic quality. Arguably, their leadership is the most important in the institution to the quality of the education delivered.

Because the book focuses on developing new groups and patterns of leadership, it deliberately omits discussions of presidential and trustee leadership as such. This omission does not mean that their leadership is unimportant; indeed their commitment to developing more inclusive and shared models of leadership is indispensable, and thus, many of the recommendations set forth in the various chapters are directed to them. *Leaders for a New Era* postulates that while leadership is everyone's business on a campus, senior administrators and boards have the responsibility to make it happen.

Underlying these studies is the premise that this new era in higher education will benefit not only from leadership that is shared throughout the institution, but also from greater diversity. Majority (that is, nonminority) men have occupied leadership positions up to the present and have shaped how we think about institutions and about leadership itself; they have established norms of organizational behavior that have yet to be opened up seriously to different styles or values. In short, the contributions of women and minorities to a collective vision of higher education and its leadership have yet to be made. New perspectives, different values and experiences brought to leadership by these underrepresented groups will undoubtedly reshape some of the conventional wisdom about leadership. Only by intensifying its efforts to remove the powerful obstacles put in their paths to leadership, by focusing on their leadership development needs, and by improving the search process can higher education diversify its leadership to create truly new models. These issues are addressed by Shavlik and Touchton in their chapter on women, by Wilson and Melendez in their chapter on minorities, and by Green in her chapter on the search process.

The uniqueness of this volume is its focus on *leadership development*. It begins with the development of a conceptual framework in the first two chapters, which are necessarily the most theoretical. Beginning with a review of literature to anchor the analysis of leadership development, they set the context with a discussion of leadership roles and responsibilities and the changing higher education environment. An examination of what leaders actually do, and in what context, sets the stage for the second chapter to address the questions of how to prepare leaders for these roles and how to enhance their effectiveness. The profound changes in higher education and the new roles for leaders described in Part 1 suggest that new models of leadership and new sources of leadership talent are in order. The chapters in Part 2 focus on potential leaders who have a great deal to contribute to higher education but who have traditionally been ignored or undervalued. The value of shared leadership—majority men sharing their power with women and minorities, administrators sharing their authority with faculty, and individuals sharing their skills with members of the team—is common to all the chapters. The dispersion of leadership throughout the institution is a second common theme in this section, and two chapters are devoted to empowering faculty and department chairs to exercise leadership from the grass roots.

Part 3 examines how we select and train leaders. New models of leadership will require altered career paths and improved ways of selecting and training leaders. Moore discusses the structure of administrative careers in Chapter 9 and analyzes the implications of these patterns for leadership and leadership development. In Chapter 10, Green looks at how the search process might be used to select a more diverse group of administrative leaders and to expand our thinking about leadership and institutional change. The final two chapters describe and analyze existing leadership development programs and activities. Schuster inventories the existing major programs, their purposes, and their outcomes. Perlman provides a personal perspective as a participant, reflecting on the impact of these programs on his own career and his ability to function as an institutional leader.

Leaders for a New Era presents many different ways to consider how institutions can develop the human resources that exist in such abundant supply on their campuses. Higher education will reap the benefits of this important investment. It is a book for campus leaders—faculty, administrators, and trustees—and it is intended as an encouragement to give leadership development the attention it deserves as an investment in the future of higher education.

REFERENCES

BASS, B.M. *Stodgill's Handbook of Leadership: A Survey of Theory and Research.* New York: The Free Press, 1981.

BENNIS, W.G. "Leadership Theory and Administrative Behavior: The Problem of Authority." *Administrative Science Quarterly, 4* (1959), 259–301.

BENNIS, W.G., and NANUS, B. *Leaders: The Strategies for Taking Charge.* New York: Harper & Row, 1985.

BURNS, J.M. *Leadership.* New York: Harper & Row, 1978.

Maccoby, M. *The Leader: A New Face for American Management.* New York: Simon and Schuster, 1981.

McCall, M.W. *Leaders and Leadership: Of Substance and Shadow.* Greensboro, N.C.: Center for Creative Leadership, Technical Report No. 2, 1977.

Stodgill, R.M. *Handbook of Leadership.* New York: Macmillan, 1974.

PART ONE

The Context

We begin with an attempt to clarify the murky issues surrounding leadership. Leadership is hard to define; we know it when we see it, but it is hard to predict. Further complicating matters is the absence of consensus as to what constitutes effective leadership; there is no formula. Thus, it is no surprise that we are also uncertain about how to develop it. In spite of the complexity and frequent obscurity of the subject, some guiding principles emerge from a look at what leaders do, in what environment, and how leadership development activities relate to both of these important considerations. Thus, before launching a discussion of what kind of leaders higher education needs and how their growth might be deliberately fostered, we start by constructing a framework within which to examine leadership and its development in the higher education context.

Context is a key word here, for leadership is contextual. It does not exist without followers or constituents, separate from an organization or group, or divorced from its environment or moment in history. Thus, an examination of leadership and its development logically begins with a discussion of context. What is the current climate of higher education that forms the context for the exercise of leadership? How has it changed, if at all, over the years? And how have these changes affected leadership? The opportunities and constraints presented by the environment shape the kind of leadership that higher education needs and will accept. Thus, in order to examine *how* we are to go about developing leaders, we must first look at the nature of the enterprise they are leading.

A second important foundation is an understanding of what leaders actually *do* and of which leadership tasks are especially important in higher education. This examination will help answer the question: What are we preparing leaders to do? Since leadership tasks are not necessarily concrete or easily defined, the question of how leaders might be prepared to undertake them becomes problematical. How, for example, does one prepare to serve as the symbol of an college or university? Or to develop the ability to sort through an endless barrage of information and integrate the important elements of the knowledge explosion? While we can talk with a degree of certainty about teaching people such management skills as reading a budget or learning enough about preventive law to stay out of court, the development of the more intangible leadership skills is a great deal more elusive.

The first chapter, *Leaders and Their Development*, sets the stage for considering these issues. Ironically, this book about leadership development begins with an examination of why higher education has traditionally been an inhospitable environment for leadership development efforts. Author Madeleine F. Green analyzes higher education's reluctance to undertake systematic efforts to develop leaders and its traditional antipathy toward management. She examines the various sources of this resistance—the fluid and ambiguous nature of higher education institutions, historic faculty antipathy for administration, and the academic culture that considers administration a necessary evil. However, these obstacles have not totally prevented the higher education community from engaging in deliberate efforts to identify and train leaders. The chapter presents a framework for understanding leadership development activities by describing the different kinds of experiences, both planned and unplanned, that contribute to leadership development. Since educators can exert control only over planned leadership development activities, they are the focus of the book.

The first chapter concludes with a discussion of the goals of formal leadership development activities: identification of new leaders, skill development, broadening of leadership vision, and personal and professional renewal.

Chapter 2, *Toward a New Leadership Model,* examines the changing higher education context and proposes new models of leadership that this new environment will require. It traces the recent shift from the "managerial" era of the past ten to twelve years to the current environment stressing accountability and quality. In the managerial decade effective and efficient management became a high priority for institutional leaders and led to the development of a number of formal leadership development programs. The author postulates that we are now in the postmanagerial era, in which good management is a necessary but not sufficient condition for effective leadership. The current era of continuing financial difficulties, of a changing student population, and of a changing society has increased external constraints, and a national focus on accountability and quality form the current context that will require new models of leadership.

While the frustrations of higher education in the recent past seem to have spawned a wish for heroic leaders, Green asserts that powerful individuals, visionaries who can move institutions singlehandedly, are more a fantasy than a realistic solution in today's environment. An examination of the various tasks of leaders reveals that the requirements of leadership today and tomorrow will require not only vision and courage, but much skill in communicating ideas, selling them to various constituencies, catalyzing others to action, and building teams. A leader without constituents or followers has no one to lead. A higher education leader who cannot mobilize the many different constituents toward a common agenda cannot lead.

In short, to understand the realities of the new environment is to understand also the need for the new models of leadership. This first section sets the stage for thinking differently about who leads higher education and how.

1

Leaders and Their Development

MADELEINE F. GREEN

An understanding of leadership development in higher education must begin with an analysis of higher education itself. What kind of individuals and organizations are leaders leading? What are the organizing principles, traditions, and values that will provide the context for the exercise of leadership? Indeed, higher education provides a unique context for the exercise of leadership. While leadership in colleges and universities has some basic similarities to leadership in the corporate environment, in the political arena, or even in a religious context, the most useful insights will derive from a discussion of the uniqueness of the educational context. Higher education scholars have conceptualized the enterprise in many different ways: as bureaucracies, as hierarchies, as municipalities, and as political democracies, to name a few. And inevitably, discussions of leadership are shaped by these various visions of how colleges and universities function.

At one end of the spectrum is the vision held by Cohen and March (1974, p. 81) of the university as an "organized anarchy." "Institutions are vague and confused about their goals," and it is extremely difficult to exercise leadership in an organization that is so confused about its purposes. Bennis (1976, p. 26) agrees with

Madeleine F. Green is vice president of the American Council on Education and director of ACE's Center for Leadership Development.

this vision, contending that the university "is society's closest realization of the pure model of *anarchy*, that is, the locus of decision making is the individual." Other models are less extreme, acknowledging real limitations on leadership in academe, but also allowing for the exercise of leadership within the constraints of external regulation, as well as traditions of faculty autonomy, shared governance, and decentralized decision making. Walker (1979), for example, attenuates the Cohen and March view with his model of "polycentric" authority, where power and leadership are dispersed throughout the campus, and various interest groups exert veto power over each other as they bargain and constantly shift the balance of power; the university operates like a "political democratic community" (p. 8), and its leaders can lead only with the consent of the governed. Administrators have neither the heroic powers that derive from a hierarchical and homogeneous organization, nor are they as powerless as Cohen and March contend.

A Historic Resistance to Leadership

While the amount of authority and power attributed to institutional leaders varies with the conceptual model of the university, few would contend that the autocratic president "who can make decisions, subject to a few checks and balances, and can expect to have them carried out" (Kerr and Gade, 1986, p. 125) is the dominant model. The last few years, however, have generated a number of calls by leaders and higher education commentators for more decisive and unfettered leadership. The Commission on Strengthening Presidential Leadership concludes its report (1984, p. 99) as follows: "Over the past 20 years, the strength of the presidency in most, but by no means all, institutions of higher education (particularly the public institutions) has been weakened." This trend has weakened higher education, and so, "strengthening presidential leadership is one of the most urgent concerns on the agenda of higher education in the United States (p. 102)."

In spite of these calls for strengthened leadership, higher education today provides an environment that constrains the exercise of unfettered leadership. Some of these constraints are external, but many derive from the internal traditions and values of the academy. One such constraint concerns the academy's image of itself, its tradition of collegiality and civility. Power resides in many different areas of the institution and with different individuals. The exercise of leadership involves power—a loaded term, to be sure. According to a widely used typology developed by French and Raven (1959), power derives from many sources: from threats and punishments (coercive power), from the ability to bestow recognition or rewards (reward power), from the acceptance of the group (legitimate power), from knowledge and expertise (expert power), and from the admiration of the followers (referent or charismatic power). Since colleges and universities are characterized by decentralized decision making, a tradition of faculty independence, and the pressures of many different constituents, leaders must rely heavily on legitimate power, which depends on shared values and goals. Legitimate power depends, in other words, on the acceptance of the followers. According to Fisher (1984, p. 36): "Legitimate power is maintained . . . not so much by its originating sanctions, but rather by the degree to which the group continues to adhere to the common and unifying bonds that produced the legitimate leader in the first place." As other commentators put it: "Followers give legitimacy to the leadership role. If people do not believe that a leader has the authority to exert influence or if they cannot accept whatever authority a leader has, there cannot be successful leadership" (Rosenbach and Taylor, 1984, p. 135). But that acceptance is hard to come by in colleges. The resistance to leadership from faculties is historic, and unless conditions are truly awful, most faculty members prefer simply to be left alone by the administration. In perilous times, faculty attitudes may change. As Walker observes, "university communities are more tolerant of seemingly high-handed administration when the university is faced with threats from inside or outside" (p. 19). But this is the exception, not the rule.

Conflict between faculties and administrators has been exacerbated in recent years. The increasing legalization of this relationship, either through collective bargaining agreements or through agreements formalized in faculty handbooks, has served to protect the rights of faculty, but also to reinforce a labor/management mentality. Kerr and Gade (1986, p. 46) observe that "faculty attitudes [are] often viscerally anti-administration or at least not pro-administration. Higher education is one of the few segments of American society where class conflict seems to be endemic."

Faculty antipathy for administrators stems in part from a value system that devalues the overt exercise of power; the desire for power or its cultivation seems incompatible with academic norms. In short, to seek or wield power is somehow unseemly, and so the wise administrator or faculty leader consistently and consciously deemphasizes power. The power that administrators do hold is usually invoked with restraint, and academic protocol discourages overt reminders of a hierarchical structure such as referring to one's chair or dean as one's "boss." The undisguised exertion of authority is far more common and acceptable outside of academe, resulting in increased accountability for individual decisions and actions and greater acknowledgment of the potential of the manager to use the authority invested in him or her by the organization.

Management and Leadership in the Academic Culture

By the same token, the culture of higher education dictates that administration, or management, is a necessary evil, supporting however clumsily the true center of a college or university—teaching and learning. Administration, in short, is not a very lofty art. Often we hear of the administrator who took the job only under duress, intending to return to the classroom at the first available opportunity. The true member of the academic community is expected to long for the classroom and the library. Management connotes the mundane, the operational, the ability to get things done toward the accomplishment of a predetermined goal. Leadership, on the other hand, provides shape, direction, and meaning, and is therefore far more intellectually respectable. Many commentators on leadership have carefully enunciated the differences between *management* and *leadership*. Max Weber (Gerth and Mills, 1958, pp. 247–48) distinguishes charismatic domination from bureaucratic domination, describing charismatic leaders as beyond worldly ties and existing outside of bureaucratic structures and routine occupations. Other writers differentiate leadership from *headship* (Holloman, 1984). Persons in headship positions are appointed by a higher level of the organization and are placed in supervisory positions in order to achieve the objectives of those who appointed them. Zaleznik (1984) finds that leaders and managers have different personality types and differing psychological profiles.

Nevertheless, effective leaders are often described as individuals of great personal strength who are "visionaries" or "pathfinders". Leaders take the long view, see the "big picture," and are able to project beyond the boundaries of the here-and-now to set a course for an organization. They are the creators, the energizers. Bennis and Nanus (1985, p. 21) define "leading" as "influencing, guiding in direction, course, action, opinion". In the most positive sense, they are "transforming" leaders who "*engage* with others in such a way that leaders and followers raise one another to higher levels of motivation and morality" (Burns, 1974, p. 20). These characteristics are often cited as distinguishing leaders from managers or power holders.

This distinction is especially important to higher education scholars. Mayhew (1979, pp. 74–75) differentiates between management and leadership in these terms: "Management means bringing all relevant information together concerning an issue, reflecting on it in rational ways, and making judgments and plans about issues. . . . Administrative leadership is the presence of an enlightened vision of what an institution is and can become and the ability to persuade others to accept the vision."

Argyris and Cyert (1980, p. 63) emphasize the distinctions between leadership and management as follows:

> There are significant differences between management and leadership, and both qualities will be necessary if presidents are to be effective in the 1980's. Management is the art of allocating resources within the organization in a manner designed to reach the goals of the organization. . . . It is possible to be an effective manager without being an effective leader. . . . Leadership is the art of stimulating the human resources within the organization to concentrate on total organizational goals rather than on individual subgroup goals. . . . The art of leadership is to convince the participants to modify their goal so that they conform with those of total organization and to put their efforts into helping the total organization achieve their goals.

It is less important to come to any conclusion about the similarities and differences between the two than to understand the symbolic differences that are meaningful for higher education. The devaluation of administration makes aspiring to a career in administration intellectually suspect. And—of great importance to the topic of leadership development—it prevents the institution of higher education from paying systematic attention to training administrators and to their career development. An acceptable career pattern is simply to "fall" into administration, learn on the job, and then be called to the next level of responsibility by virtue of having done reasonably well. If administration is not valued, then preparation for it will not be either. Waggman (1984, p. 3) writes, for example, of the prototypical fear of many professors in the arts and humanities that they could "be infested with a 'managerial mentality.' This aversion to 'management' appears no less pronounced among scientists and most other academic specialists who believe that the work of real scholars is scholarship, not the adjudication of mindless budgetary battles." An interesting attitudinal indicator of the disregard of academicians for the field of higher education management is reflected in the relatively low prestige enjoyed by the discipline of education, and by the accepted tradition that the Ed.D. and Ph.D. in education are generally not the most desirable credentials for academic administrators in four-year institutions.

How Are Leaders Developed?

Given this historic reluctance to pay serious attention to developing higher education leaders, it is no wonder that the programmatic efforts are relatively few and the research scarce. Most of the research on management and leadership development has been generated by organizations outside of higher education—corporations, research centers, and government agencies, much of it focusing on corporate leadership. Academic research emanating from business schools concentrates as well almost exclusively on the corporate world. The research on college and university leadership is sparse. And while the higher education literature is rich in discussion of *leadership,* it has paid little attention to *leadership development.* The same is true of the literature on corporate leadership; it focuses largely on the end product rather than on the process (McCauley, 1986); that is, it explores the nature of successful executives and organizations, and not on the experiences or interventions that contributed to that success. Often, works on leadership will conclude with a few pages on management or executive development (Bennis and Nanus, 1985; Maccoby, 1981; Cleveland, 1985) but there is little systematic study of the subject.

Yet there are a few studies focused specifically on leadership development that can shed light on useful approaches for higher education. McCauley's study (1986) describes a recent research project on management development conducted by the Center for Creative Leadership, which clustered important developmental experiences into several broad categories—job assignments, other people, hardships or setbacks executives had endured in their jobs, and formal training. McCauley points out that most managers learn on the job; the more challenging the position, the more they learn (p. 3). Challenge gives individuals the stimulation to perform well, and the stress involved may also teach them valuable coping skills. Additionally, the visibility that accrues to those who perform well may also enhance their careers. But challenging positions may pose a chicken-and-egg problem: managers need challenging assignments to receive the opportunities required to hone their skills and be visible. But only the visibly promising receive assignments that will continue to further their development. Job assignments that provide a breadth of experience are also viewed by managers as important to career development. Exposure to different aspects of the organization is helpful in developing an understanding of the total operation. This exposure can be achieved by rotating positions in different functional areas, or with assignments that confer broad responsibility, such as projects that cut across different parts of the organization, or by staff positions that enable managers to see the organization from the perspective of the top leadership. Most often, job assignments are made on the basis of organizational demands and priorities. The development experiences that accrue to the individuals are an added bonus, but hardly the central point of the assignment. McCauley concludes (p. 3) that "based on current research, it would be difficult to design a formal program of job assignments for developing managers." While managers attribute learning to job assignments, the research is not clear as to specifically what is learned from various assignments nor how long a person should spend at a particular job to reap the benefits of that experience.

A second source of learning is other people—colleagues, subordinates, superiors, and mentors. Mentors have received a great deal of attention in the popular and in the higher education literature, but there is little empirical research on mentors. Mentoring relationships can take on many different forms—from an intense personal relationship between a senior person and a junior one, in which the mentor has an important influence on the career of the protégé, to a less intimate mentoring model in which the mentor serves as a coach, sponsor, or role model. Mentor-protégé relationships are frequently spontaneous and informal rather than deliberate parts of a development program. These informal mentoring arrangements are potentially the most powerful, when a person recognizes the talent of a more junior colleague, and then invites that colleague to work under his or her tutelage. Moore (1984, pp. 209–222) finds that the opportunity for learning, feedback from the mentor, visibility in the organization, and access to the mentor's network are all important benefits derived from the mentor-protégé relationship.

Some organizations, such as the Jewel Tea Company, Merrill Lynch, and Honeywell, use formally assigned mentors to assist in the development of junior managers. The little systematic evaluation of formal mentoring programs that do exist shows, not surprisingly, that the quality and intensity of these relationships vary, and that the majority of the participants judged these relationships as worthwhile. The mentoring relationships helped the younger people learn new technical skills, become socialized into the organization, and develop career-planning skills (Kram, 1983, 608–625; cited by McCauley, p. 11). The research on mentoring is corroborated by the experiences of the ACE Fellows Program (described in Chapter 11), which has relied on the formal designation of a mentor for each Fellow. Fellows' and mentors' appraisal of their experiences show a similar diversity of experiences. The important chemistry between mentor and protégé is changed when the relationship results from an assignment to a mentor as part of a formal program, rather than a spontaneous selection.

Bosses are another important source of learning—as role models (positive or negative) and as sources of feedback. Bosses can provide challenging assignments and can influence a manager's career advancement by representing that person upward in the organization. Peers provide not only information and resources to help managers do their jobs but informal feedback as well. They may also be a source of information about job possibilities and may provide advice on career strategies. Most frequently, however, learning derived from these personal relationships is secondary to the primary purpose of the relationship. Constructing a leadership development program around what is learned from other people would require focusing on precisely what individuals can learn from bosses and peers and how these learning experiences might be structured.

People also learn from failures, and a few studies point out that learning to recognize one's limitations can be a potentially positive outcome of a failure or a demotion. Setbacks can cause individuals to reexamine their behaviors or assumptions; but this area has been studied very little.

The fourth area—training—has received the most attention and certainly the greatest investment. It is estimated that corporations spend forty to sixty billion dollars per year (Eurich, 1985, pp. 6–7). By comparison, higher education's expenditures, though hard to quantify, would undoubtedly be extremely modest in comparison. While the research does show that "learning often does take place in training programs" (McCauley, 1986, p. 16), few have studied whether this learning gets transferred to work situations. Studies of top-level executives reveal that they place training low on the list of factors contributing to their success or effectiveness (Margerison and Kakabadse, 1984; Glickman et al., 1968, cited by McCauley, p. 16). In spite of their low ranking, executives still see management training as useful for informing managers about certain topics (McCauley, 1986, p. 16). She hypothesizes that these individuals, "when explaining their own success [may] play down the importance of events in which they were not a significant actor." Training programs cover a wide variety of topics—from specific skills required at various management levels to broadening the executive's understanding of the organization, the external context, and personal revitalization.

Developing Leaders in Higher Education

Leadership development has for the most part been an informal process in higher education. Academic leaders—deans, vice presidents, and presidents—have generally risen through the academic ranks, learning administration as they go. Historic resistance to management and management development described earlier, as well as faculty antipathy to administration, have made formal leadership and management training programs and courses a relatively recent phenomenon. The first systematic efforts to identify and train new leaders began in the 1960s, an era of dramatic increases in the numbers of colleges and universities and students attending them. The demand for faculty was enormous, and the need for administrators grew at least in proportion to the growth in the size of faculties. The tremendous expansion of higher education spawned new administrative positions and the recognition that systematic preparation for these complex jobs was desirable. While higher education was not yet rushing to embrace the idea of academic administrators as managers of the collegiate enterprise, the notions that administration is indeed a complicated undertaking and that preparing for administrative responsibilities is legitimate were gaining acceptance.

This climate of growing interest in administrative training led to the development in the mid-sixties of several programs that were to continue to this day: the American Council on Education Fellows Program, the Institute for College and University Administrators (ICUA), first sponsored by Harvard University, then by the American Council on Education. A few years later, the Claremont Summer Institute provided a ten-day program for administrators; during the same period, the Association of American Colleges began offering programs for deans, and Harvard began its six-week (later four-week) summer program, the Institute for Educational Management. The real burgeoning of seminars and workshops began in the mid-seventies, when financial and other managerial pressures became undeniably urgent.

Formal programs, though only one approach to administrative development, are the most visible and therefore susceptible to description and analysis. Although informal efforts are hard to quantify, one can speculate that they are potentially an even more important resource in the identification and development of new leaders. A variety of formal programs now exists with different purposes and for different audiences. Presumably, each was created to respond to a set of needs or problems perceived in the supply, preparation, or effectiveness of college and university administrators. Most programs have multiple goals, which can be generally categorized as follows: identification of new leaders, development of management skills, enhancement of leadership abilities, and promotion of leadership vitality. Identifying and clarifying these overlapping components of leadership development is a first step toward understanding the existing array of activities and their purposes, as well as toward identifying gaps and needed strategies.

Identifying New Leaders

Many of the early efforts in leadership development, as well as some current programs, address the need to identify promising new leaders. Twenty years ago, increasing the pool was a priority in a rapidly expanding industry. Today, the academy still needs to search actively for the best leaders and especially to encourage the identification of potential women leaders, minority leaders, and individuals who would bring diverse talents and backgrounds to leadership positions.

Higher education's efforts in this area are episodic, and no tradition exists as in the corporate world of grooming individuals for the next position. Nonetheless, several national efforts do exist, as well as a number of programs sponsored by large university systems. On the national level, the ACE Fellows Program, the now defunct Hispanic Fellows Program, the National Identification Program of ACE's Office of Women in Higher Education, and the efforts of ACE's Office of Minority Concerns function specifically to identify individuals with promise of assuming greater responsibility. Identification of new leaders is an important component of other national programs, too, such as the Summer Institute for Women in Higher Education, cosponsored by Bryn Mawr College and Higher Education Resource Services (HERS), and such as Harvard's Institute for Educational Management; the very fact of participating in these programs usually indicates the individual's interest in career advancement and support by the participant's institution. The competitive nature of the ACE and Harvard Programs makes the identification aspect a very important one for these activities. Among the campus-based efforts are the programs of the California State College and University System and the City University of New York, which select promising faculty and mid-level administrators to serve as interns.

An important question arising from efforts to identify new leaders is what happens once a promising individual has been "identified." Visibility resulting from participation in one of the programs mentioned above may not necessarily result in career advancement, and the credential of having participated may not necessarily open doors. This is especially true of individuals who are "trapped" in fields such as counseling, student affairs, continuing education, and affirmative action. The search process works against people with nontraditional credentials, who would not necessarily bring to a position the typical experience or academic credentials that a search committee might expect. It is well known that mobility between academic administration, student affairs, and administrative affairs is quite limited and that the general behavior of search committees is to look for very closely related academic preparation and administrative experience. Thus, leaps across "sectors" in an institution or over too many rungs on the administrative ladder are highly unusual in academe.

The various national and on-campus programs that are designed to identify new leadership talent, or that do so as a by-product of its training function, have brought higher education a long way toward recognizing the need to single out promising individuals and to groom them for future responsibility, but unless colleges and universities can open up the search process and the prevailing lock-step notions of career development, some of these excellent identification efforts will be wasted.

Management Development

The job of the administrator has become increasingly technical and complex. Academic officers are not only intellectual leaders, shaping the curriculum and translating the institutional mission into a meaningful educational program, but they are also budget officers, long-range planners, and personnel specialists. Administrators outside of academic affairs are specialists in a variety of sophisticated areas and require a systematic knowledge of management. While administrators learn mostly on the job, nevertheless courses, seminars, and workshops can be a far more efficient means of delivering a concentrated dose of needed information or skills.

Thus, management development focuses on enabling administrators to do a better job, to acquire the knowledge and skills that enable them to understand the domain in which they operate, and to master the information they must command. Workshops on legal issues, computers, grants administration, and the like address these crucial information needs. Another kind of management development experience focuses on the "people" side of management, and programs on leadership styles and management techniques provide opportunities to reflect on how one accomplishes goals with and through others. The vast majority of existing programs, even those with a strong "identification" emphasis, have a considerable management development component, and these focus on information and techniques useful to administrators.

Leadership Enhancement

Leadership goes far beyond effective and efficient administration. While few would contend that the vision, the sensitivity to issues and people, or the drive integral to leadership are acquired through specific programs, certain structured opportunities can be provided to enhance personal and intellectual growth.

"Leadership enhancement" and "management development" often overlap. Their differences are exaggerated here for clarity. The two terms are roughly analogous to the conventional definitions of "leadership" versus "management" discussed earlier. These distinctions lead to a definition of "leadership enhancement" as broadening one's perspectives, expanding one's vision beyond a particular position or institution, and integrating information and experience to shape the course of institutions. The higher the level of responsibility, the greater the need to raise one's sights, to understand the interelationship of all the parts, and to place the institution in the larger social context. Cleveland (1985) presents a model of "the get-it-all-together" leader, whose job is not to be an expert or a specialist but a generalist, who can sift through the barrage of information and make decisions that are consistent with the needs, values, and future of the organization. "Breadth," he says, "is a quality of mind, the capacity to relate disparate facts to a coherent theory, to fashion tactics that are part of a strategy, to act today in ways that are consistent with a studied view of the future" (p. 8). Maccoby (1981) similarly highlights the need for integration and the ability of the leader to keep his or her sights fixed on goals and to work for a consensus on both goals and values. Maccoby notes that "technical skills may be necessary, but all leaders must be able to articulate goals and values" (p. 231).

Vision and personal values are hardly the exclusive domain of chief executive officers. While the notions of "leadership enhancement" and broad vision are crucial to college presidents, they are applicable to other administrators as well. Administrators must be able to make connections between their particular function and the mission of the institution, and beyond that, with the world at large. Certainly, if department chairs know more about the overall workings of an institution, they will be more effective. At the same time, their work will be more meaningful and more rewarding. Similarly, business officers who understand academic programs and issues will make more informed decisions, addressing the health of the whole enterprise rather than the isolated financial dimension.

This intellectual breadth, the ability to digest information, and to make meaningful connections are really a product of lifelong experiences and habits. Maccoby (1981) argues for humanistic study as preparation for leadership; he sees the Bible, comparative religion, ethical philosophy and literature as vehicles to explore the inner life and thus to help leaders define their own values and personal vision. "Without [such an education], a would-be leader tends to confuse his or her own character with human nature, guts with courage, worldly success with integrity, the thrill of winning with happiness" (p. 232). Cleveland (1985, p. 167) suggests that our educational system must foster integrative thinking at all levels. Yet the educational system treats knowledge in compartments and encourages study, especially at the higher levels, of specialized slices of knowledge. In addition, an education emphasizing civic responsibility, self-knowledge, and a global perspective are all important educational preparation for leadership. If this foundation is present, then leaders can benefit from occasional participation in programs at various points in their career, but these cannot substitute for a well-formed mind and personal value system.

But just as learning is a lifelong process, so is leadership development. In an effort to keep broadening their executives' horizons, new corporate executive development programs focus on the external environment, helping participants to make important connections between their organizations and the larger world context. In the higher education arena, the Christian A. Johnson Endeavor Foundation provides a program for presidents and trustees, discussing enduring themes of the liberal arts through readings in "the great books" and providing an opportunity for reflection and observation totally removed from the business of running an institution. Similarly, a new program for presidents offered in 1985 by the American Council on Education, entitled "The 6,000 Minute Sabbatical," dealt with larger social issues that affect contemporary American life. Not surprisingly, many administrators do not turn to higher education programs or the company of their administrative colleagues for "leadership enhancement." Rather, they achieve these goals through their associations with others outside of higher education, or with experts in various fields who provide opportunities for stimulation and mind-stretching. "Leadership enhancement" occurs in different ways for different individuals, and some would argue that it is more self-generated and eclectic than susceptible to programed efforts.

Leadership Vitality

The academy has been quicker to recognize the need to nurture faculty vitality than to foster the continued growth of its administrators. Administrators, like faculty, need to grow in their work and find new challenges and new sources of satisfaction. Long hours, seemingly endless mountains to climb, and conflict as a way of life will sap the energy and enthusiasm of even the most dynamic administrator (Brown, 1979).

When opportunities for faculty and administrative mobility were greater, a prime source of revitalization was the challenge of a new position. But now, burnout is as much or more a problem for administrators as for faculty, and opportunities for professional and personal renewal are of prime importance to maintaining leadership vitality. Again, leaders choose a variety of routes to stay energized, including but not limited to keeping up in one's discipline, attending professional meetings to stay in touch with administrative colleagues and to keep up with current issues, and taking sabbaticals. For some, developing outside interests helps balance their working life and provide personal satisfaction. Whatever the strategy used, administrators must work at staying creative and enthusiastic about their work and their institutions.

"Leadership vitality" raises the question of how career paths relate to personal development. Certain mindsets about career paths prevail in spite of ample evidence that only some chairs become deans, and few deans become presidents. The tightening pyramid and the current no-growth climate suggest that leadership vitality is an important question, and the issue of career steps after a tour of duty in administration that may have lasted from three to thirty years is certainly a pressing one. What are the alternatives to the strictly "onward and upward" career trajectory? The question of life after the presidency certainly preoccupies college presidents; the next steps for chief executive officers and senior administrators who have grown distant from their faculty origins is an important question in leadership.

Conclusion

Many experiences contribute to the development of organizational leaders. Some of them are deliberate, others are part of the natural progression of gaining experience and seasoning in the workplace. The latter group of experiences are impossible to structure and control. But there are a number of deliberate steps that can be taken to identify leaders and attend to their skill level and their understanding of their responsibilities and the nature of the enterprise. While there is a lot that we do not know about leadership development, we do know that people can learn new skills and new behaviors. To accept the notion that leadership is an undefinable art is to give up too easily; to believe that there are formulas for success is naive. Exploring the relationship among all the changing variables—the individuals, the context, and the moment—is a much more productive approach.

REFERENCES

ARGYRIS, C., and CYERT, R. *Leadership in the 1980's*. Cambridge, Mass.: Institute for Educational Management, 1980.

BENNIS, W.G. *The Unconscious Conspiracy: Why Leaders Can't Lead*. New York: AMACOM, 1976.

BENNIS, W.G., and NANUS, B. *Leaders: The Strategies for Taking Charge*. New York: Harper & Row, 1985.

BURNS, J.M. *Leadership*. New York: Harper & Row, 1974.

BROWN, D. *Leadership Vitality: A Workbook for Academic Administrators*. Washington D.C.: American Council on Education, 1979.

CLEVELAND, H. *The Knowledge Executive: Leadership in an Information Society*. New York: E.P. Dutton, 1985.

COHEN, M.D., and MARCH, J.G. *Leadership and Ambiguity: The American College President*. New York: McGraw-Hill, 1974.

COMMISSION ON STRENGTHENING PRESIDENTIAL LEADERSHIP, CLARK KERR, DIR. *Presidents Make a Difference: Strengthening Leadership in Colleges and Universities*. Washington, D.C.: Association of Governing Boards of Universities and Colleges, 1984.

EURICH, N.P. *Corporate Classrooms: The Learning Business*. Princeton: Carnegie Foundation for the Advancement of Teaching, 1985.

FISHER, J. *Power of the Presidency*. New York: American Council on Education and Macmillan Publishing Company, 1984.

FRENCH, J.R.P., and RAVEN, B. "The Bases of Social Power." In Cartwright, D., ed. *Studies in Social Power*. Ann Arbor: University of Michigan, Institute for Social Research, 1959.

GARDNER, J.W. *The Tasks of Leadership*. Leadership Papers/2. Washington, D.C.: Independent Sector, 1986.

GERTH, H.H., and MILLS, C.W., eds. *From Max Weber: Essays in Sociology*. New York: Oxford University Press, 1958.

GLICKMAN, A.S.; HANS, C.P.; FLEISHMAN, E.A.; and BAXTER, B. *Top Management Development and Succession*. New York: Committee for Economic Development, 1968.

HOLLOMAN, C.R. "Leadership and Headship: There is a Difference." In Rosenbach, W.E., and Taylor, R.L., eds. *Contemporary Issues in Leadership*. Boulder: Westview Press, 1984, pp. 109–116.

KERR, C., and GADE, M.L. *The Many Lives of Academic Presidents: Time, Place, and Character*. Washington, D.C.: Association of Governing Boards of Universities and Colleges, 1986.

KRAM, K.E. "Phases of the Mentor Relationship." *Academy of Management Journal*, 26 (1983), 608–625.

MACCOBY, M. *The Leader: A New Face for American Management*. New York: Simon and Schuster, 1981.

MARGERISON, C., and KAKABADSE, A. *How American Chief Executives Succeed*. New York: American Management Association, 1984.

MAYHEW, L. *Surviving the Eighties: Strategies and Procedures for Solving Fiscal and Enrollment Problems.* San Francisco: Jossey-Bass, 1979.

MCCAULEY, C.D. *Developmental Experiences in Managerial Work: A Literature Review.* Greensboro, N.C.: Center for Creative Leadership, Technical Report Number 26, 1986.

MOORE, K.M. "The Role of Mentors in Developing Leaders for Academe." In Rosenbach, W.E., and Taylor, R.L., eds., *Contemporary Issues in Leadership.* Boulder: Westview Press, 1984, 209–222.

ROSENBACH, W.E., and TAYLOR, R.L., eds. *Contemporary Issues in Leadership.* Boulder: Westview Press, 1984.

WAGGMAN, J.S. "Development Programs for Academic Administrators," *Administrators Update,* 5 (1984).

WALKER, D. *The Effective Administrator: A Practical Approach to Problem Solving, Decision Making, and Campus Leadership.* San Francisco: Jossey-Bass, 1979.

ZALEZNIK, A. "Managers and Leaders: Are They Different?" In Rosenbach, W.E., and Taylor, R.L., eds., *Contemporary Issues in Leadership.* Boulder: Westview Press, 1984, 86–103.

2

Toward a New Leadership Model

MADELEINE F. GREEN

A Changing Context

Analyzing leadership in the context of the higher education environment is a multifaceted effort. Changing times are an especially important variable, for effective leadership in one era may be entirely inappropriate or ineffective in another. It is also important to recognize institutional differences as a factor, for with more than three thousand institutions, each changing over time in different ways, higher education is not a monolith. Diversity is the hallmark of the American system. Just as there is no recipe for institutional effectiveness, there is no single model of leadership. And definitions of effectiveness and of leadership requirements inevitably change over time.

Kerr and Gade (1986) provide an incisive summary of the changing context of higher education and the accompanying change in the nature of leadership. They describe the period 1964—1970 as dominated by the challenge of student revolts, with internal conflicts of faculty versus faculty, students versus administration, and faculty versus administration. External conflicts of that era pitted the faculty against the board and the campus against the community. The next significant challenge was posed by the OPEC crisis and recession of 1973–1975 and was characterized by minor conflicts, as was the succeeding era (1980–1985), which saw a slowing growth in student enrollments. The authors predict that in the coming decade, which will see an overall decline in student enrollments, the major source of conflict will be faculty against faculty and faculty against administration. They maintain that the predominant type of president is and has been over time the managerial leader, who is "concerned with the efficient pursuit of what is already being done, of what some constituency wants to have done, or of what circumstances may require to be done." Managerial leaders are contrasted with "pathfinding leaders" who are the visionaries, the agents of change, and are "concerned with the long-run effectiveness of the total organization as opposed to the short-run effectiveness and the performance of tasks" (Kerr and Gade, p. 70).

Effective management, efficiency, and financial control have been a veritable obsession of higher education administrators for the past fifteen years, and with good reason. Beginning with the recession of the early seventies, colleges and universities were gripped by severe financial pressures, and Kerr and Gade's depiction of that era and its propulsion of leaders to assume a managerial mode certainly rings true.

The seventies were a paradoxical era of growth and decline. Enrollments grew by forty percent between 1970 and 1980; there was a net gain in the number of colleges and universities. Yet at the same time, inflation and fuel costs ravaged budgets, faculty salaries declined so that faculty salaries dropped by 20 percent in constant dollars, states slashed their appropriations, and federal aid to students declined. Compounding these financial stresses were growing federal regulation, increased litigation, and greater intervention in campus autonomy by system offices and state boards. These conditions put severe constraints on leaders' abilities to move swiftly or decisively on any issue. Also, administering an institution became increasingly cumbersome as well as complex, and specialists in various administrative areas proliferated. The person managing the institution's daily cash flow could hardly be the same as the institutional researcher or the administrator of a multimillion dollar financial aid budget. In short, higher education was experiencing more management by more individuals.

The managerial era brought with it the recognition that management and management development indeed had a legitimate place in higher education. Images of leadership also changed with the times, and the conventional wisdom deemed it important that academic leaders be good managers as well. While the elite institutions were never greatly preoccupied with the managerial qualities of their deans or presidents, they still aspired to be well run. For the rest of higher education, struggling mightily to acquire and conserve resources, good management was vital to the very existence of the institution. Academic officers and presidents were subject to the often-conflicting demands of educational leadership and resource management and found themselves disconcertingly preoccupied with the latter. For many, the job of college president had changed from that of educational leader presiding over growth and a seemingly unlimited future for higher education to that of the fund-raiser, financial manager, and politician in an endless quest to obtain scarce new dollars and spend them wisely. The academic officer's job, too, became more involved with money and procedures and less with academic issues.

As management became vitally important in the 1970s, management development became respectable and even valued by some. That decade saw the growth of seminars, workshops, and other training efforts to help administrators get up to speed on the complexities of their jobs. The number was still manageable enough to be compiled in a directory of professional development opportunities published for several years by the Academy for Educational Development and then from 1978 to 1981 by the American Council on Education. By the mid-eighties the number of programs was so enormous that compiling such a directory was a herculean task.

As the idea of professional development caught on, and the complexity of the management tasks of administrators increased, so programs focusing on financial and personnel management, legal issues, and other informational areas began to proliferate. One has only to peruse the *Chronicle of Higher Education,* which now devotes a separate section to workshops and conferences, to recognize that administrators are still preoccupied with their managerial roles and in need of assistance in fulfilling them.

The Managerial Era

More than a decade of hard times and imperiled institutions gave rise to calls for bold new leadership and especially for visionaries and pathfinders, who could develop new directions, inspire others to share the vision, and work toward its implementation. Leaders facing difficult choices, limited resources, and the static created by divergent constituents rarely have news or solutions that please everyone. The harder the times, the more intense is the wish for leaders who can transcend the limitations placed on them by circumstances, articulate a vision that unites the college community, and lead the community out of perilous times. In short, the wish for heroic or pathfinding leadership flourishes when organizations founder.

Adversity often breeds the wish to find a savior, a heroic individual who can make bold and difficult decisions and cure the institution's ills. Indeed, the call for stronger presidential leadership has been issued with urgency by many; Fisher (1984), the Commission on Strengthening Presidential Leadership (1984), and Kerr and Gade (1986) call for powerful and imaginative leaders who can transcend the constraints of their office. Fisher sees weak leaders as sorry characters, battered by the forces of boards, legislatures, accrediting agencies, and others into being "mediators," "support mechanisms," "chairs," "apostles of efficiency," "managers of human resources," and "energy maximizers" (p. 16). He buttresses his call for powerful leaders by citing such well-known commentators on the presidency as Joseph Kauffman, David Riesman, Frederic Ness, and Richard Cyert, all of whom describe the many forces that weaken the presidency and who posit the need for courageous new leaders.

The Commission on Strengthening Presidential Leadership (1984) interviewed more than eight hundred current and past presidents, board members, and others, and concludes that "strengthening presidential leadership is one of the most urgent concerns on the agenda of higher education in the United States. It makes a great difference who the presidents are and what the conditions are that surround their contributions;" the presidency "has often unnecessarily and unwisely been diminished" by the many constraints that have been placed on leaders over the past twenty years (p. 102). The report issues a series of recommendations to governing boards and public policymakers that would minimize these constraints and allow presidents more autonomy to provide effective leadership. Its message is clear: untie the presidents' hands so they can lead.

And indeed, in spite of academe's general unwillingness to accept strong leadership, adversity made some institutions more hospitable to it. The specter of cutbacks and financial distress, or even of institutional doors closing, drove out more leisurely discussions typical of the academy and accelerated the pace of decision-making on pressing matters. The era of hard-nosed management in a climate of trying economic circumstances spawned a resurgence of the model of the "take-charge" leader, a reality on some campuses, a wish on others, and an anathema on yet others.

Another type of leader brought forth by the seventies was the so-called entrepreneurial leader (Peck 1983). While Peck applies this description to presidents, it is equally applicable to senior officers. According to Peck, entrepreneurial leaders flourish in small private colleges, characterized by an approach to the future that is "informal, intuitive, and opportunistic (p. 18). Entrepreneurial leaders, as Peck defines them, keep their eye out on the environment and are quick to spot trends and their potential for the institution. It is not surprising that such leadership flourishes in small private institutions, which because of their size and governance systems are relatively quick to act. They are free of some of the constraints of public institutions and small enough to have a manageable turnaround time. These leaders move the status quo "not so much by the exercise of autocratic power as by an exercise of will" (p. 22). The seventies and early eighties saw some institutions on the brink of closure, and while some colleges went under, others were "turned around" by imaginative and entrepreneurial presidents. Some of these institutions changed their mission to be more responsive to career-oriented consumers, others changed their curriculum to balance the liberal arts and the vocational, and still others courted adult and nontraditional students with different and flexible programing. Such institutions were frequently led by entrepreneurial leaders, who looked for opportunities presented by the environment and could bring about institutional adaptation.

The Postmanagerial Era

The vast majority of college and universities survived the difficult times of the past decade, and most have grown accustomed to a constant level of fragility and uncertainty. It is now a given that higher education will never return to the loose management controls and ad hoc decision-making of earlier eras. Today, good management is a necessary but not sufficient condition of leadership. There is consensus that institutions must be well managed and that hard financial times will continue, if not worsen, for the foreseeable future. No institution or leader can minimize the importance of good management.

But new concerns that pose altogether different problems for leaders have arisen and have claimed the attention of the entire higher education community. The preoccupation of the 1970s and early 1980s with money and management now shares center stage with issues of quality, institutional effectiveness, and some very fundamental questions about whom higher education is serving and how well. These new concerns were reflected in the spate of reports on educational quality, including Bennett (1984), National Institute of Education (1984), Association of American Colleges (1985), and Newman (1985). National reports rarely anticipate issues; rather, they crystallize and focus discussions already underway. The improvement of undergraduate education and demonstrable standards are common themes to these reports, which reflect the growing malaise of educators as well as consumers and lawmakers with the nature and quality of American higher education.

The national concern for quality and standards has captured the attention of governors and legislators, and many states have become involved in assessment and standard-setting that was once the domain of individual institutions. State-mandated entrance requirements and tests at various points during the undergraduate experience have called into question the ability of faculty and institutional leaders to make the crucial decisions affecting academic standards. Thus, the ability of leaders to shape the academic course of their institutions is even further endangered, and external interference is becoming a greater, not a lesser threat.

As the twentieth century ends and the twenty-first begins, diversity will be important to higher education in a number of ways. Our higher education system is losing ground in providing access to minorities. The last decade has seen an increase in minority high school graduation, but decreased college-going by blacks. Many of the gains in minority participation since the 1960s have been lost, and unless leaders can propose creative strategies for admissions, better retention, and public commitment to the issue, this slippage will continue.

Also, the student body will continue to change in other ways, with more women, more adult, and more part-time students. Women already constitute more than half of all undergraduates, and part-time students outnumber the full-time learners. The median age of college students is twenty-six, and only two million of the twelve million students in higher education are full-time resident undergraduates of traditional college age. Leading more heterogeneous institutions requires different leadership skills—people with negotiating skills, more breadth, and greater understanding of different groups and interests. In short, as student bodies change, so must institutions and their leaders.

Today's and tommorow's higher education environment is also marked by intense competition among institutions—for students, for research monies, for federal dollars. In all likelihood, intensifying the competition will damage institutions, with a few getting stronger, and the rest exhausted by the struggle. New cooperative solutions will be a requirement. And as colleges and universities look at the importance of primary and secondary education to their own success, as well as to noncollegiate providers of postsecondary education, such as businesses, government, and the military, alliances, cooperation and compromise will take on even greater value and significance regarding leadership.

Thus, the late 1980s and the 1990s will bring a changed environment for leadership. Good management will continue to be vital but campuses and society will look to academic leaders to clarify their institutional missions, to articulate an academic vision, and to be accountable for the quality of their programs and graduates. They will have to do all in an atmosphere of growing external controls, decreased institutional autonomy, and generally scarce resources.

Leaders for the Future

Given the difficulty of the balancing act that academic leaders must perform, it is no surprise that they believe that they would be more effective if the constraints on the office were lessened and they had greater freedom to act. Nor is it surprising that only on rare occasions are faculties willing to accept strong executive leadership and most often are apt to reject it out of hand. These classic tensions, rooted in the academic culture of professional autonomy and affecting decisions at every level of the institution and in every corner, have been exacerbated by the profound changes that have occurred in higher education in the last twenty years.

Strengthening the hands of leaders may not be the answer for the coming decades. Many of the trends cited as limiting executive leadership are here to stay. Faculties are unlikely to dissolve their unions; coordinating boards will not abdicate the powers they have gained; and students and other constituents will not be as heterogeneous as they were two decades ago. And indeed, the ability of presidents and senior administrators to exercise leadership will depend on a variety of external circumstances beyond their control. Most important is the nature of the institution. Kerr and Gade (1986) argue that research universities, prestigious land grant and other public doctorate-granting universities, institutions with a very strong specialized mission (evangelical protestant colleges, Hispanic colleges, and Catholic institutions), as well as less-selective liberal arts colleges that are struggling to survive are favorable climates for aggressive leadership. Community colleges with fractionalized constituencies and a politically controlled board, historically black institutions left weakened by a decade of cuts and loss of students to predominantly white institutions, and comprehensive institutions that take a back seat to the flagship institutions and which are subject to heavy state control through personnel policies and central boards, are less likely to foster "pathfinding" leadership, they maintain.

Thus, the debate about pathfinding or charismatic leaders as opposed to managerial ones is to a certain extent academic. First, since the research gives no evidence that either is more effective, we can probably only say that both work in different circumstances. Second, given the complexity and constraints of the current higher education environment, this single variable tells us little about other leadership behaviors and sheds no light on the question of leadership development. A discussion of leadership and its development in the postmanagerial era turns more profitably on an understanding of leadership skills and behaviors in the changing context of higher education.

What, then, will institutional leaders actually *do* in the late twentieth century? While identifying the tasks of leadership may not automatically elucidate the appropriate preparation of individuals for those tasks, it is nevertheless a rational point of departure. The tasks of leaders do not necessarily change over time or in different circumstances, but the relative importance of the various tasks do. John Gardner (1986) identifies nine tasks that are eternal functions of leadership: envisioning goals, affirming values, motivating, managing, achieving workable unity, explaining, serving as a symbol, representing the group, and renewing. Certainly, all of these are applicable to college presidents and institutional leaders. A modification of Gardner's lists yields five tasks that are particularly important in the current era. Two of them, namely, serving as a symbol and achieving workable unity, are drawn directly from Gardner's list. In addition to these, serving as a team leader, as an information executive, and as a future agent are particularly important in today's world.

Leadership Tasks in the Postmanagerial Era

Symbolic Leader

Symbolism is without doubt an eternal aspect of leadership. It is especially important to the chief executive officer, but is also valid for any person in a position of authority. College presidents are the living symbol of their institutions. They embody the values and aspirations of the college and its constituents, who project on to them their hopes and goals. While leaders are hardly blank slates upon which a wishful image is inscribed, some of the symbolism may in truth have little to do with the nature or the particular agenda of the leader. For example, consider the new president or dean who comes to a campus that has been slipping academically over the years. The quality of the students has declined as the college dipped farther and farther into the applicant pool, and the college community has formulated a new agenda to improve the academic quality of the curriculum and its students. The new leader was selected primarily because of his academic credentials and the hope that he could lead the institution to fulfilling its agenda of improving academic quality. Invested with these hopes and a strong shared agenda, the president or dean becomes the symbol of academic reform and forward movement. Until he *disproves* that he can do it, or refuses to take on the task, the new leader embodies the communal educational vision. Part of the power of the "honeymoon" period of the new administrator is this symbolism factor at work. In time, the vision may fragment, or the reality of getting things done may anger various individuals or groups on campus, and in that event the symbolism will weaken.

On some campuses, the sense of community and unity is strong. The shared value system of church-related colleges or historically black institutions may invest the leader with the collective energy and shared goals of the campus, empowering him or her to act on the communal agenda. To the extent that the communal agenda holds together, the leader retains the symbolic power invested in him or her by the campus community. The symbolic role of the leader on such a campus also heightens the possibility of the transformational leadership—through that special rapport with the constituents, the leader can inspire them and lead them toward a vision that goes beyond the preservation of the status quo.

At other institutions, where consensus is minimal, the symbolic nature of leadership is quite different. There, the leader will serve on some occasions as a symbol of the collective vision, but since the vision is often as fragmented and varied as the constituencies, he or she will more often symbolize different things to different people. The president might symbolize a prudently managed enterprise to the trustees, an intellectually vital one to the faculty, and a socially conscious one to the students. The fragmented campus is the more typical one, and leaders have few opportunities to transcend this fragmentation to serve as a symbol of the collective will. Finding those opportunities to strengthen the collective vision and to articulate shared goals is a challenge to leaders today. In spite of adversity's unfortunate aspect, it frequently serves to unify diverse campus groups and to make people aware of the need for cooperative action. Such times strengthen the hand of leadership by allowing the community to project a unified wish for solutions onto the leader, permitting him or her to act on their behalf.

But since the realities of a pluralistic campus society often prevent such a drawing together, it is important for leaders to understand the opportunities and limitations of symbolic leadership. An important axiom of leadership is "Don't take it personally," meaning that much of the criticism (as well as praise) is directed toward the leader as symbol, not the leader as person. There are times when an act of symbolic leadership will be effective and well received (a sound intellectual address by the president at convocation) and others when it may have no effect or a negative one (the groundbreaking for a new computer science building when the arts and science budget has just been slashed and the college of education closed).

The symbolic aspect of leadership is perhaps the most difficult to teach directly, and may be the most susceptible of all the leadership tasks to learning by example and on the job.

Coalition Builder

Campuses are fragmented in a number of ways. Faculty, students, parents, legislators, alumni, and the community have different expectations and different agendas. Within the campus community, departments and schools compete for students, resources, and centrality to the institutional agenda. Academic, administrative, and financial operations tend to work in isolation without a full understanding of, or commitment to, a larger institutional agenda. To the extent that the leader views the campus as a political community with varied interest groups and diffused power, his or her job will be to build coalitions and consensus. Gardner (1986, p. 16) points out that fragmentation of society into groups in contemporary American life is a fact "rooted in the pluralism of our society." That reality is even more acute on academic campuses, which have a tradition of decentralized decision-making, faculty autonomy, and the different priorities and pressures of various interest groups.

Kerr and Gade (1986, p. 143) point out that in an environment of rival interest groups and a high level of conflict, "fewer decisions can be made because of more veto power; . . . those decisions that can be made are made more slowly due to extensive consultation and confrontation." In short, they question whether leaders can get *anything* done in this environment. One obvious solution is to work to remove the obstacles to presidential leadership. But in the likely event that the environment can be changed only minimally, another strategy is to focus on the kinds of leadership behaviors that will work and the ways they can be learned.

In this environment, conflict resolution may be the most important skill for an academic leader. Evidently, it requires leaders to listen carefully, to provide a forum for civilized discussion, to de-escalate conflict, and to communicate well with all parties. Conflict resolution can be learned, and is particularly well taught through simulations, analysis, and feedback. Experience is also a wise teacher in this arena, and especially it hones the more intangible skills required to deal with conflict: knowing when conflict is useful and productive, knowing when it is imperative to de-escalate and resolve, knowing when to assume a high profile and when to manage conflict quietly behind the scenes.

Even when shared values and a common agenda do not exist on a campus, symbolic leadership can be invoked to help create them. Some common ground can be found in any institution—service to students, service to the community, the pursuit of excellence. By identifying unifying themes and nurturing their development through highly visible and symbolic acts, leaders can foster a stronger sense of community. These opportunities may be dispiritingly few and far between, and the pull of diversity and disunity is always a countering force. The challenge of finding these opportunities and maximizing the beneficial effects of symbolic leadership is considerable.

More frequently, coalition building requires a leader to take a low profile, working quietly to build alliances, instructing various interest groups about the vantage point of others, and serving as a conduit among the parties. A conduit is antithetical to a symbol, requiring a divestment of ego, a willingness to submerge one's own visibility to build bridges and move toward consensus in an unobtrusive way. The role of leader as arbiter and manager of conflicts, consensus builder, and orchestra leader is a nonheroic one. Articulating a vision and infusing others with enthusiasm is only one element of academic leadership. Making it happen in spite of the agendas of various factions requires a varied repertoire of leadership skills.

Team Leader

The factionalism of external groups is mirrored by the many separate functional interests within the campus. Academic leaders must build coalitions internally as well as externally. Within the organizational structure of a college or university, the academic, financial, and administrative units exist independent of each other, with only a dim recognition of their interdependence and their common goals. The specialists produced by the managerial era are highly knowledgeable in their own areas, but often uneducated about the operations of the rest of the campus and the relationship of the parts to the whole. Financial aid officers are classic examples of highly expert professionals, with responsibility for enormous amounts of money, but frequently little integration into campus decision-making. Yet financial aid is central to the development of an institutional budget and to understanding the behavior of students as they stop out, drop out, or have academic difficulties.

Needless to say, the problems of compartmentalization and tunnel vision are often proportional to the size of the campus. Smaller campuses may permit personal relationships to overcome disciplinary or administrative boundaries, but rarely do they disappear. A major task of a leader on any campus is to minimize the separate agendas of the various parts of the institution and create a common one, raising people's sights to the institutional agenda as opposed to a departmental or narrowly administrative one. On an operational level, this is accomplished by a group of senior officers who preside over the various functions. The job of the president is to select well (a difficult assignment, to be sure) and to help those officers not only to manage their units well but to work together as a team for the collective good. An officer below the presidential level must create the same feeling of unity within a division or department. To build and nurture a team is both a management and a leadership task. To put a team in place requires a realistic assessment of institutional or divisional needs, an analysis of the strengths needed to complement the skills and style of the team leader and other members, and a good selection process. These skills can be learned by leaders in a variety of ways, on the job, from mentors, and from formal training programs. There is also a strong requirement of self-understanding as one builds a team, admittedly an elusive part of leadership development. For example, leaders must be clear in their own minds how much stylistic diversity they really can tolerate. The conventional wisdom tells administrators to balance the team with styles and strengths that complement the team leader and the other team members. But in reality, the leader may find it difficult to tolerate too stark a value difference or stylistic approach and may need at least as much harmony as diversity. Understanding one's real attitude toward such matters is an important foundation for team building.

Some skills required to lead a team are the same as those required to build coalitions: conflict resolution, communications, and the effective use of symbolic power. Other skills are tied more directly to relationships among individuals rather than groups. An effective team requires the leader to delegate meaningfully and to develop team members so that they will grow and improve. In short, leadership development is a primary responsibility of a team leader. The cliché that a leader can stand or fall on the effectiveness of his or her subordinates speaks to the vital importance of the growth of individual team members. Team leaders are facilitators, teachers, and mentors, and developing others is crucial to their success.

Another skill required of the team leader is the ability to process and screen information, related, of course, to the role of leader as executive in an information society. Leaders are dependent on their subordinates, and indeed on a host of people in the institution, for manageable amounts of useful information that will inform decision-making. Good executives rely on team members to provide information in a usable form and in a timely way so that they are neither overwhelmed with information nor deprived of it. A crucial aspect of information management in a team situation is knowing enough about the various operations to ask the right questions and elicit the appropriate information. Academic leaders must be highly informed generalists who can elicit and integrate the relevant information about financial aid, about admissions, and about public relations, all of which will feed into the total picture of decision-making.

By understanding the range of skills required to be a team leader, individuals can seek experiences as they move up the administrative ranks that will allow them to develop these skills. Chairing a major committee or a self-study prior to an accreditation visit can be valuable training experiences for a faculty member or department chair. Serving as a representative of the faculty union can develop conflict resolution skills; an associate deanship can be an invaluable apprenticeship for future responsibilities. Similarly, deans and presidents seeking to develop future leaders can seek out individuals with leadership promise and use these opportunities to train them. Formal training programs can also teach team leadership through case studies, simulations, and feedback on one's behaviors.

Knowledge Executive

Coined by Harlan Cleveland (1985), this term describes effective leaders in the current information society as "get-it-all-together" generalists, characterized by their breadth, by their ability to see connections, and by their ability to extract and integrate relevant bits of information. His model goes beyond the cognitive skills of an intelligent person able to process information wisely and make good judgments, and speaks to intellectual curiosity, interest in other people and their viewpoints, and the willingness to take risks and responsibility for one's actions.

Hiring good people and turning them completely loose is a high-risk strategy for an academic leader. A president who is not very well informed about academic programs, enrollment trends, or the budgetary picture, or a chief academic officer who ignores student affairs or admissions will find himself or herself in trouble on one of these fronts. It is not enough to know the bottom line; leaders must know how they got there and what the alternatives are for getting someplace else. Only the leader with a generalist's mastery of the various operational areas will ask good questions and develop the breadth of knowledge to make those vital connections. Of course, the larger and more complex the institution, the more superficial the chief executive or chief academic officer's knowledge will be. Nonetheless, it is hard to decide whether to sell a university hospital when one is only dimly aware of its financial operation and implications for the total budget or of the importance of that hospital to the community and its place in total health care picture.

The ability of the generalist to make connections, to see the forest beyond the trees, is crucial to good team leadership. The team leader serves as the unifying force, as the one to educate team members about the relationship of the parts to the whole. Only the team leader has the perspective of the entire task or institution.

Paradoxically, few leaders have as part of their development a structured opportunity to see the larger picture. By moving up the academic ranks, one sees progressively larger slices of the institution, but even then, one is largely confined to a particular area. Movement within academic, business, student, or external affairs limits one's horizons to that slice of the institution. Presidents and chief academic officers may understand the dynamics of heading a department, but they have little opportunity along the way to learn about institutional finance, fund-raising, or enrollment management. If breadth of vision is essential to a chief executive officer, than surely it makes sense to learn as much about the enterprise as possible *before* assuming the top position. Of course, people have learned on the job for time immemorial, but that approach hardly seems efficient or effective. Businesses and the military have a long tradition of rotating people through various aspects of the operation. Top executives in business are likely to have had a stint in sales and marketing, served in staff positions to a senior officer, and worked in the production end at various points in their career. Internships are one way to expose individuals to a broad range of institutional activities. This exposure is the cornerstone of the ACE Fellows Program, as well as of several programs developed on individual campuses providing internships in the offices of the president and chief academic officer.

Unwritten rules about career progression in colleges and universities also hamper the development of needed breadth. Faculty become department chairs, deans, chief academic officers, and then presidents, and rarely deviate to positions in finance or development. And if they do, there is always the worry that they will be forever banned from returning to the academic administrative ranks once they have left the sacred order. For reasons that are more plausible, individuals with the bulk of their experience outside of academic administration (though they may have quite respectable academic credentials) are not viable candidates for those positions. Faculty-dominated search committees are unlikely to be receptive to a person who has not been through all the required rites of passage of tenure, professorship, and progressively responsible positions in academic administration. The argument that leaders of faculty can have credibility only if they have proved themselves as academicians has merit. (And even if one is skeptical of that argument, the power of that belief system is irrefutable.)

Similar taboos apply to staff positions. Conventional wisdom tells aspiring administrators to avoid the position of "assistant to." But what better perch to observe the workings of all the schools and departments than the office of the vice president for academic affairs or what better view of the entire institution than the president's suite? And what more propitious circumstance to develop a mentor-protégé relationship than through a staff position? Indeed, a staff position can be an ideal learning experience, a vantage point to observe institutional processes and dynamics, a chance to learn administration without being on the firing line from the very beginning, and the opportunity to observe an experienced (and, one would hope, effective) administrator at work.

Current career tracks and the resulting lack of exposure to the totality of an institution make the knowledge executive's job as a generalist that much harder. But breadth of knowledge about the enterprise one leads is only one dimension of that important leadership quality. As Cleveland also points out, and as critics of our educational system have been charging for years, our entire system with its narrow disciplinary or professional focus works against the kind of intellectual breadth needed by leaders. The movement to reform undergraduate education certainly takes us a few steps in that direction; the renewed emphasis on liberal learning, on interdisciplinary studies, and on broad analytic and communication skills is certainly a good sign. Cleveland (1985, p. 165) observes that "if complexity is growing faster than anything else in the United States, then the education of men and women to manage complexity should be the fastest-growing function in American higher education. It isn't, not yet." If liberal education does indeed teach the intellectual skills to manage complexity, to explore the inner life, and to develop a value system that will enable students to make informed choices throughout their lives, then liberal education is arguably the best preparation for future leaders. Maccoby (1981, p. 232) argues:

> The study of the Bible, comparative religion, ethical philosophy and psychology, and great literature leads one to explore the inner life, particularly the struggle to develop the human heart against ignorance, convention, injustice, disappointment, betrayal, and irrational passion. Such an education prepares one to grapple with his fear, envy, pride and self-deception. It raises questions about the nature of human destructiveness and the legitimate use of force. Without it, a would-be leader tends to confuse his or her own character with human nature, guts with courage, wordly success with integrity, the thrill of winning with happiness.

Future Agent

Leaders must always have an eye on the future. Higher education has undergone periods of transition in the past, and it is once again in a period of profound change. To some extent, we know now what the future holds. An end to the decline in the supply of traditional college-age students awaits us in the middle of the next decade, as does a shortage of faculty members as a wave of retirements hits higher education. The minority students that constitute a majority of many school systems will be higher education's pool of students at the end of the century. Advancing technology, the shift of world power, and the growing importance of the third world are but a few trends that will shape the world in which higher education exists.

Given the significant changes within the academy and in the external environment, leaders must understand this ferment and see its implications for the future of the institution. What does it mean for a women's college that some institutions have 70 percent women in their student body even though they have been traditionally coed? What does it mean for an urban institution serving first-generation college students that the minority dropout rate in that city's high schools is 50 percent or that a large proportion of the elementary school students live in families below the poverty line? How will the reform movement in the secondary schools change an institution five or ten years hence? What is the role of a community college in addressing the needs of workers who will be displaced in the coming decade? The future agent looks outward, foresees trends, anticipates issues, and when possible acts rather than reacts.

Future agents are knowledge executives (generalists who can see the forest beyond the trees) and coalition builders (building alliances with the many constituencies that are part of this dynamic future). They are intellectually curious enough to scan the horizon with interest and discrimination, and sufficient risk-takers that they will act on an idea without the benefit of conclusive data or a proven track record. For once those data are available, the leader is living in the present, not the future.

Being a future agent combines cognitive skills and certain traits and behaviors. In the cognitive realm, broadly educated generalists are well equipped to look beyond the immediate, to let their minds roam into the future and to conjure up possibilities. But it is hard to imagine how one might train to be a future agent to live in the world of possibilities and ideals or how one might develop a talent for risk-taking. The question of how one becomes a future agent brings us right up against the age-old question of whether leaders are born or made.

Developing New Leaders

The answer to the question Are leaders born or made? seems to be a resounding and unequivocal *both*. Leadership is a combination of individual traits, learned behaviors and skills, and historical circumstances, which coexist and change in highly complex and still dimly understood ways. Which of these are susceptible to being developed in light of the tasks of leadership discussed above?

The most difficult aspect of leadership development turns on individual personalities or traits. Changing one's own psychological characteristics or attitudes is indeed difficult, and an intellectual understanding of oneself does not necessarily lead to the desire or the ability to change. Some of one's ability to be effective as a symbolic leader, coalition builder, team builder, and knowledge executive depends on who one is, that is, what kind of individual one is, rather than what one knows. How does one learn to be more tolerant? more patient? more charismatic? to submerge one's ego needs when the situation calls for it? to recognize one's limitations and compensate for them?

The ability to relate to different groups, to build teams and coalitions requires a well-developed set of human relations skills. And a prerequisite to understanding others and one's relationship to them is an understanding of oneself. Developing self-awareness is a lifelong task, and is accomplished in a variety of ways. For those who are willing to listen for overt and covert messages, feedback on one's behaviors comes in a variety of ways from family, friends, and and colleagues. The person who quipped, "If you want to know what kind of manager you are, ask your spouse," spoke wisely. Giving and receiving feedback in the workplace is difficult for most people. But an individual with a trusting relationship to colleague, supervisor, or mentor can learn invaluable lessons by soliciting candid feedback from them. Feedback in the work place deals with behaviors, not personalities. It is the psychiatrist's task to examine the origins and dynamics of an individual's personality. Those explorations are best left out of the workplace or training programs. It is the supervisor's or mentor's task to observe positive and negative behaviors and to give honest and prompt feedback.

Behaviors are manifestations of personality traits that can be observed and controlled. Assuming, of course, that one is willing to learn and change unproductive behaviors, feedback is a valuable learning tool. A trusted colleague who will share the observation that his co-worker literally turned his back on another person at a meeting as the level of disagreement mounted, or that another's habit of consistently interrupting women, but never men, can, if delivered in a reasonably nonjudgmental way, will provide valuable information about negative behaviors. The Center for Creative Leadership teaches several thousand executives every year how to give and receive feedback as a key aspect of leadership training. Participants observe each other throughout an intensive weeklong program and record behaviors, both positive and negative, and then practice giving feedback at the end of the week. The exercise has the twofold outcome of enabling managers to receive candid feedback in a nonthreatening environment and to hone the technique of observing behaviors, delivering feedback as well as receiving it. The emphasis on feedback is strengthened by an extensive battery of psychological testing administered to each participant. A session of several hours interpreting those tests and relating them to one's work performance is a highly effective method of gaining additional insights and perhaps providing the motivation to examine and change certain behaviors. Of course, the motivation to see oneself clearly and to receive honest feedback must be present to begin with. Sometimes it takes a significant failure to motivate an individual in those directions. And even if the will is there, behavioral change is hard to sustain, and there is a strong pull to lapse back into comfortable lifelong patterns and behaviors of which we are unaware.

Much of leadership development takes place on the job, as we have observed. An ongoing relationship with a supervisor or mentor may be the most effective way for people to become sensitized to their own styles, behaviors, and impact on others. This kind of teaching is part of the responsibility that leaders have to develop new talent by focusing attention to the human side of administration.

Intellectual development will be a special leadership need in the late twentieth century and the next one. For if the task of college and university leaders will be increasingly as generalists and knowledge executives, we will need to rethink the way they are prepared. Advancing through the ranks has served leaders in academe and elsewhere over time, but leaving development to career progression alone is a difficult route to take. Deliberate exposure to the many facets of institutions will help prepare leaders to preside over complex enterprises with many different operational subsets. Internships and campus workshops can educate a variety of people about the totality of the institution. Also, assignments that increase one's scope of responsibility and contact with various parts of the university are all useful leadership development experiences. And going beyond the institution, leaders and future leaders need broad exposure to higher education in all its diversity and complexity, to the social issues that shape this country and its educational institutions, and beyond the American borders.

The origins of lifelong intellectual development begin early in the educational system. Certainly colleges and universities must continue and intensify their efforts with the undergraduate experience. While many institutions are laboring mightily to develop a coherent and intellectually integrated core curriculum, the pull toward fragmentation by the disciplines is great. Graduate education, with its intense specialization and frequent irrelevance to the undergraduate curriculum that it is preparing professors to teach is certainly part of the undergraduate problem. It needs to be changed significantly if it is to prepare integrative thinkers as well as scholars and disciplinary specialists. The temptation for professors to recreate the graduate experience with their undergraduates is too great, and without a reform of graduate education, undergraduate reform will be incomplete. The rewards for specialization continue into the faculty ranks, where interdisciplinary studies are often a group of professors teaching their own disciplines side by side. Cleveland (p. 166) observes wryly that team-teaching is "the favored academic device for avoiding interdisciplinary thought." Promotion and tenure tend to reward specialized research rather than interdisciplinary thought that may not have a proper home in an established journal.

Leaders who survive the constricting ways of the system still have their continued development to attend to. They must put it high on their agendas to make it happen, since it is all too easy for any overworked administrator to drown in administration and to be consumed by the tasks at hand. Time for reading and reflection or attendance at a program that will pull one away from the concerns of day-to-day management are useful to expand one's vision and recharge one's batteries. Such renewal may take the form of a vacation with a pile of good books, attendance at a seminar, or a week in the woods with one's thoughts.

Conclusion

To the extent that higher education has paid attention to leadership development in the last twenty years, our efforts have largely been devoted to the business of administration and helping administrators master the technical information they need to know to be effective in their jobs. In short, higher education responded well to the needs of professional development in the managerial era. And certainly managerial concerns and the need for management development will continue. But leaders whose environment is rapidly changing, whose institutions will increasingly reflect the diversity and fragmentation of society, and who will be required to lead higher education through a period of public criticism and intense self-examination, will need some different skills and qualities. They will need to be prepared beyond management competency to perform the tasks of coalition and team-building and to serve as knowledge executives and future agents. Some of this preparation will begin early in life with an integrative education and the development of lifelong learning patterns. Other approaches will involve one-on-one learning situations that will enable leaders to assess their own abilities and actions with mentors and other teachers. And some will be specially designed programs for leaders, designed to keep open their windows on the world.

An important shift in leadership development efforts will be an emphasis on the effectiveness of the organization, as opposed to the individual. While the two are clearly related, most current efforts and programs focus on the individual. Individual administrators attend workshops and seminars, learn new skills, and recharge their batteries, but return to the same environments, the same problems, and the same colleagues who have not had the benefit of these experiences and insights. If teams and work groups are indeed the cornerstone of the effective institution in the information society, as Gardiner maintains in Chapter 8 of this volume, then the development of teams as functioning units and of individuals as team members will have to be far more central to leadership development. Academics are trained as "solo flyers," as scholars, researchers, and even teachers. Gaining the strengths of team participation, of collaboration, of information sharing—qualities that make the group greater than the sum of its parts—requires a different mindset and heightened interpersonal skills. Developing the individual and the group in a delicate and dynamic balance is a leadership development agenda for the future.

NOTE

1. I would disagree with Kerr and Gade's point that those historically black institutions that were weakened by loss of students and money during the last decade are not conducive to aggressive leadership. Indeed, a shaky institution should be all the more receptive to strong leadership to help save it, and the strong spirit of commitment and community would buttress that leadership.

REFERENCES

Association of American Colleges. *Integrity in the College Curriculum: A Report to the Academic Community.* Washington, D.C.: Author, 1985.

Bennett, W. *To Reclaim a Legacy.* Washington, D.C.: National Endowment for the Humanities, 1984.

Cleveland, H. *The Knowledge Executive: Leadership in an Information Society.* New York: E.P. Dutton, 1985.

Commission on Strengthening Presidential Leadership, Clark Kerr, dir. *Presidents Make a Difference: Strengthening Leadership in Colleges and Universities.* Washington, D.C.: Association of Governing Boards of Universities and Colleges, 1984.

Fisher, J. *Power of the Presidency.* New York: American Council on Education and Macmillan Publishing Company, 1984.

Gardner, J.W. *The Tasks of Leadership.* Leadership Papers/2. Washington, D.C.: Independent Sector, 1986.

KERR, C., and GADE, M.L. *The Many Lives of Academic Presidents: Time, Place, and Character.* Washington, D.C.: Association of Governing Boards of Universities and Colleges, 1986.

MACCOBY, M. *The Leader: A New Face for American Management.* New York: Simon and Schuster, 1981.

NATIONAL INSTITUTE OF EDUCATION. *Involvement in Learning: Realizing the Potential of American Higher Education.* Washington, D.C.: Author, 1984.

NEWMAN, F. *Higher Education and the American Resurgence.* Princeton: Carnegie Foundation for the Advancement of Teaching, 1985.

PECK, R.D. "The Entrepreneurial Presidency." *Educational Record, 64* (1983), 18–25.

ROSENBACH, W.E., and TAYLOR, R.L., eds. *Contemporary Issues in Leadership.* Boulder: Westview Press, 1984.

BIBLIOGRAPHY

ARGYRIS, C., and CYERT, R. *Leadership in the 1980's.* Cambridge: Institute for Educational Management, 1980.

BENNIS, W.G. *The Unconscious Conspiracy: Why Leaders Can't Lead.* New York: AMACOM, 1976.

BENNIS, W.G., and NANUS, B. *Leaders: The Strategies for Taking Charge.* New York: Harper & Row, 1985.

BURNS, J.M. *Leadership.* New York: Harper & Row, 1974.

COHEN, M.D., and MARCH, J.G. *Leadership and Ambiguity: The American College President.* New York: McGraw-Hill, 1974.

FRENCH, J.R.P., and RAVEN, B. "The Bases of Social Power." In Cartwright, D., *Studies in Social Power.* Ann Arbor: University of Michigan, Institute for Social Research, 1959.

GERTH, H.H., and MILLS, C.W., eds. *From Max Weber: Essays in Sociology.* New York: Oxford University Press, 1958.

HOLLOMAN, C.R. "Leadership and Headship: There Is a Difference." In Rosenbach, W.E., and Taylor, R.L., eds., *Contemporary Issues in Leadership.* Boulder: Westview Press, 1984, 109–116.

MAYHEW, L. *Surviving the Eighties: Strategies and Procedures for Solving Fiscal and Enrollment Problems.* San Francisco: Jossey-Bass, 1980.

WAGGMAN, J.S. "Development Programs for Academic Administrators," *Administrators Update, 5* (1984).

WALKER, D. *The Effective Administrator: A Practical Approach to Problem Solving, Decision Making, and Campus Leadership.* San Francisco: Jossey-Bass, 1979.

ZALEZNIK, A., "Managers and Leaders: Are They Different?" In Rosenbach, W.E., and Taylor, R.L., eds., *Contemporary Issues in Leadership.* Boulder: Westview Press, 1984, 86–103.

PART TWO

New Leaders and New Models

In order to be practical as well as analytic, this book must get beyond the mere assertion that new models of leadership are required for the new era we face. It addresses the question of who these new leaders will be, how leadership should differ in the future, and how leadership development efforts can contribute to realizing new visions of leadership. Thus, this section presents alternatives to the traditional hierarchical models of management and heroic leadership. It identifies sources of strength and potential leadership that have historically been underutilized. Because we tend to equate leadership with positions of administrative authority in higher education, it is not surprising that most of the higher education literature concerning leadership deals with the presidency. As an easily discernible group, presidents lend themselves to study. Presidents are the anointed leaders of colleges and universities; thus, their role in managing and guiding the entire enterprise is essential. But leadership is not necessarily exercised by administrators, nor are chief executive officers the only institutional leaders to shape an institution; leaders are found at all levels, and their contributions must be not only acknowledged, but also nurtured.

This volume singles out two important campus groups that require more attention as potential leadership forces: the faculty and the department chairs. Though they have the least formal power in conventional terms of the pecking order, faculty and department chairs have the greatest impact on the core of an institution, namely, teaching and learning. In Chapter 3, John B. Bennett focuses on department chairs, who arguably have the potential for the greatest impact on the quality of an institution. The approximately eighty thousand existing department chairs are in a position to shape curriculum, improve teaching, and positively affect the lives of students. While the academy has historically paid little attention to the development of the department chair, a number of successful approaches do exist and are described in this chapter.

From her perspective as college president and former chief academic officer, Patricia R. Plante discusses in Chapter 4 the importance of faculty participation in decision-making and how faculty talents can best be cultivated and used. Rose-Marie Oster, now a faculty leader and formerly a dean, looks at faculty as leaders in Chapter 5, analyzing the historic roots of faculty–administrator tensions and calling for a new model of shared leadership. This new model envisions a faculty that is empowered, perhaps always living in a state of creative tension with administrators, but at the same time, sharing the responsibilities and rewards of leadership. Oster concludes with recommendations on how faculty leadership can be encouraged through the development of individuals and through creating an institutional climate that is conducive to shared leadership.

New models of leadership entail sharing it not only with those who occupy nonpowerful positions in the hierarchy, but also with groups who have heretofore been exluded from decision-making roles. Higher education has been dominated by majority men throughout its history. Although women and minorities have made some inroads during the last decade as a result of concerted efforts at affirmative action, they are still vastly underrepresented in leadership positions. Sexism and racism, though they are often very subtle and even unconscious, are still with us in academe. The voice and the perspective of women and minorities are largely absent in most institutions and in much of the national dialogue. Thus, the contributions of women and minorities as leaders who create new directions for higher education institutions, and as scholars and commentators who reflect about their past and their future, have been quite limited; yet the increasing diversity of higher education makes the inclusion of women and minorities as leaders essential. Shavlik and Touchton's chapter on problems faced by women leaders and questions surrounding their identification and development is a vital piece that will broaden our definition of who shall lead.

The question of minority participation in higher education at all levels has reached crisis proportions. The dearth of minority leadership, addressed by Wilson and Melendez in Chapter 7, is a complex issue. Historic and continuing discrimination are compounded by the drying up of the pipeline, with a lower percentage of minority high school graduates going to college, and a woefully inadequate supply of minority Ph.D.s. Addressing the problem of developing minority leaders for higher education requires strategies to increase minority participation at every level, according to the authors, as well as continuing efforts to identify promising minority leaders on campuses and to equip them for success.

Leadership, then, must be shared in several ways. The growing fragmentation of higher education, as of the rest of society, demands leaders who can build coalitions and forge a consensus. The growing diversity of colleges and universities requires that their leadership reflect this diversity and that the perspectives of women and minorities be brought to bear on all phases of institutional life. And finally, the ever-increasing complexity of the information society dictates that no individual can lead an institution without the support and synergistic energy of a team. As John J. Gardiner points out in Chapter 8, team leadership requires a willingness to share power, to submerge one's ego, and to attend to the personal and professional growth of others. An effective team leader is the antithesis of a lone ranger, as much a servant of others as a hero.

The six chapters in Part 2 draw attention to some of the more notable ways of broadening and redefining traditional concepts of leadership. Each chapter specifies strategies for leadership development and provides practical suggestions for transforming visions into realities.

3

Department Chairs: Leadership in the Trenches

JOHN B. BENNETT

Arguably the most important leaders on campus, department and division chairs are located at just that point within the institution where academic services are actually delivered . . . or not. Of course others within the institution also play indispensable roles. Institutions need chief operating officers, someone must pay attention to donors and legislators, student affairs must be tended, and a variety of other constituencies and functions must be served. Nonetheless, if the chairs are not doing their jobs, the educational mission of the institution is truly jeopardized.

For the quality of the core academic success of the institution depends upon the quality of the chairpersons—their dependability, their resourcefulness, their appreciation of academic values, and their insight into the abilities and weaknesses of their colleagues; in short, their ability to manage and lead. The degree to which the institution succeeds or fails in meeting its fundamental objectives turns upon the ability of the chair to shape a vital curriculum, to encourage teaching effectiveness, and to support faculty professional growth and improvement. The terms "shape, encourage, support" are suggestive of the kind of leadership required of effective department chairs. Their direct or coercive power is limited.

John B. Bennett is vice president for academic affairs and dean of the faculty at Siena Heights College. He is former director of the Departmental Leadership Program at the American Council on Education.

They must lead their colleagues, who indeed consider themselves peers, by example, persuasion, and consensus-building. In many ways, the leadership exercised by department chairs embodies the model of leadership described throughout this volume. Conflicting constituencies, role ambiguity, and external constraints are the hallmark of the chair's position. While these are certainly characteristic of deanships and presidencies, the constraints of the chair's position are even greater and provide greater challenges to the exercise of leadership.

While the chair's role is pivotal, and the opportunities for leadership considerable, academe has ironically paid little attention to the selection or the development of chairpersons. Often chairs are selected for reasons that have little to do with management or leadership skills. They may have just published a book or achieved some other academic honor; they may be perceived as belonging to the "right" political group or, at least, not to the wrong one; it may be their "turn" for a rotation into the responsibilities of the position; or, as happens not infrequently, no one else may be willing. Rarely, however, are individuals identified as department chairs because of management experience or abilities.

As Green points out in Chapter 1, the academy has historically devalued administration and deemed administrative ambition as unseemly. In fact, at some institutions prior management experience is viewed as a liability, if not an actual disqualification, for the job. Many faculty have a deep-seated suspicion of anything connected with management and regard it as incompatible with academic values. Similarly, individuals who may express an interest in the position of chairperson can be eliminated from consideration by their colleagues precisely because of that interest. Those who have no interest or talent are then too often dragooned into accepting the position. And once in office, too many chairpersons are left to their own devices to get the job done and to grow in it.

While the role of the chair is of critical importance and is an opportunity to exercise leadership, it is also difficult. Development of chairpersons requires addressing the problems inherent to the position. Among the problems they frequently cite are these:

1. No help is available from one's predecessor in learning the ropes or in dealing with institutional bottlenecks or procedures. Nor is much institutional orientation or assistance typically provided.

2. Then, once in the position, chairs often find inadequate role definition so far as the faculty handbook and department bylaws are concerned. This deficiency is compounded for many by widely differing expectations for the chair by department faculty.
3. Continuing problems with communication are common—either it is lacking, delayed, or beset by conflict, and it culminates with the complaint that there is almost always insufficient feedback from both faculty and the administration regarding performance.
4. Constraints placed by lack of money and time are large and growing. Economic recessions take a direct toll on chairpersons, as institutional financial resources shrink abruptly. But even with adequate financial resources, sufficient time remains a problem for many chairpersons.
5. An imbalance is often perceived between responsibility and authority in a situation characterized by rampant individualism. As one wag put the matter, being a department chair is easy—it's no different from herding a bunch of frogs.
6. Finally, some chairs experience the position as having a negative impact upon their own career possibilities and development. And it is true that some institutions do take advantage of chairs, holding out one set of expectations and another, unrelated, set of rewards. For instance, too often for purposes of promotion and salary advancement institutions will hold chairs to expectations impossible to fulfill by very reason of the time and energy expenditure required to be a good chair.

Role Ambiguity

So the position is not an easy one. It has role ambiguity built into it. Divided allegiances and assaults upon personal identity come with the territory. On the one hand, coming out of the faculty ranks, the chairperson remains a faculty member, views himself or herself that way, and is often so regarded by other, full-time, administrators. On the other hand, the chairperson is no ordinary faculty member, but has instead a special set of institutional responsibilities for other faculty—often longtime colleagues. From each of these perspectives, the chair is still expected somehow to represent both sets of interests. It is not uncommon to hear this role ambiguity referred to as the "Janus-like" character of the position—the requirement to look in two directions simultaneously (Bennett, 1982, pp. 54–57).

Several illustrations of the structural ambiguity of the position of department chairperson can be provided. For example, independent of institutional type, chairs again and again report considerable discomfort regarding the requirement to evaluate faculty or to deal with unsatisfactory behavior. Statements of this discomfort should come as no surprise, for close colleague relationships are part and parcel of the chairperson's position in a way not often paralleled among academic deans or presidents. Risking the disruption of familiar and long-established ties is not easy, particularly when there may be no obvious institutional reward or support for doing so. Yet doing so is crucial to effective departmental leadership.

On the other hand, chairs typically recognize the importance to the profession and to the institution of providing leadership in evaluation and performance counseling. After all, these activities are best done locally, by those in the best position to know the relevant circumstances. Difficult though it may be, it is far better to have philosophers, rather than upper-level administrators, making judgments about other philosophers—at least up to a point. It is the wise academic dean who knows where that point is.

Another example of the structural ambiguity of the position of chairperson is at hand in budget battles. Institutions may not be quite so clear in their statements of expectations, but most do in fact look to chairpersons to provide leadership to the discipline or disciplines in the department or division, and at the same time to provide assurances that the demands of the larger institutional context are observed. Not infrequently, especially with today's reduced funds for higher education, advancing the interests of the discipline can run counter to the opposing institutional needs to reallocate resources away from the department or division. The chairperson is expected to do both things—clearly a difficult task and one that can make great demands upon individual resources and credibility.

And these difficulties have been aggravated for some chairs recently by such developments as the addition of responsibilities for coordinating faculty and courses for night school and evening classes, for off-campus centers, and for continuing education, as well as for weekend colleges. These developments have occurred as institutions have struggled to adjust to changes in their market constituencies. So in addition to monitoring the integrity of the department daytime offerings, the chair often finds himself or herself having to respond to new administrative offices with their flurry of memoranda and deadlines.

Specialized accrediting agencies add their own unique pressures, as do federal, and now state, regulatory initiatives. As if these trends were not sufficient, the ever-increasing resort to litigation can diminish the pleasure once found in a professional self-regulatory role. And throughout these recent developments, rarely have any additional support staff resources been provided.

Chairs who work at institutions with collective bargaining agreements face additional complexities—for there is a downside no matter where they are placed. If by the agreement they are considered part of management, issues of personal identity and resentment of separation from faculty colleagues can loom large. Faculty suspicions about intentions and motivations seem to be magnified and can stand in the way of advancing either departmental or institutional interests.

If chairs are part of the unit, they are more likely to retain the spirit of collegiality and close relationships with colleagues. However, the typical drawback is that those responsibilities smacking of supervision then become harder to discharge, if in fact they are viewed as part of the portfolio at all. Thus faculty evaluation is often slighted, and some institutions find themselves having to create new positions of assistant deans to attend to this function.

In addition to the complications introduced by collective bargaining, many chairs today also face the fallout from the national trend toward greater turnover in the position. As more faculty members serve as chairpersons, there are more former chairpersons in each department or division. Some of these individuals will be unhappy at their exclusion from formal influence and will try to interfere. Other departments will have as well the occasional dean who insists upon special treatment or one who, having stepped down, resents the new egalitarianism.

The Chairs' Position: Rewards and Frustrations

Clearly, there are rewards, too, in the department chair's position. Surveys conducted as part of the American Council on Education's workshops for department chairs revealed that chairs had varied reasons for accepting the position. Among the reasons cited are the ability to provide direction to the curriculum; the opportunity to recognize those who have contributed significantly but quietly to students, colleagues, or the institution itself; the chance to apply one's own particular combination of intellectual and interpersonal skills to resolve conflicts or to revitalize a tired research program. In short, most department chairs do see the position as an opportunity to "make a difference." On some occasions, however, damage containment rather than opportunity beckons—as one person put it, "I would rather chair than be chaired."

Just as motives for assuming the position vary, so do customs regarding selection, term of office, and compensation. There are still department heads—those identified and appointed by the administration, often without term and sometimes without any periodic review. Most, though, are chairs, who owe their selection at least in part to colleagues; sometimes through outright election, more often through faculty consultation and administrative ratification. Some, though not many, arrangements are rotational in character, the chairmanship passing from senior faculty member to senior faculty member, usually accepted only reluctantly with a reference to "its being one's turn." Wise administrators, however, will try to minimize this attitude by encouraging (and allowing) chairs to exercise leadership and by providing incentives for assuming the position.

Terms of office vary nationally, with most being either three or five years in length. Some institutions have one-year terms, others have two- or four-year stints, and still others provide indefinite tenure. Three- or four-year terms strike me as probably best, as they acknowledge that the new chair may require a considerable period of time to become effective and yet they also require the department to consider at appropriate lengths whether the chair's particular leadership style is still right for the department as conditions and people change.

Some ask whether there should be limits on the number of terms that an individual should be permitted. It is difficult to answer this in the abstract, though the stamina and creativity of some of those who continue through several terms is surely a factor to consider. An interim period for rest may be best for the individual and for the department.

There is a breadth of institutional practice regarding compensation. An occasional institution will expect its senior faculty to assume the duties of the chair as part of their faculty responsibilities and will provide neither additional salary nor released time to the bargain. Some of the rotating arrangements are of this sort. Clearly, such an arrangement is a disincentive to strong departmental leadership. Most institutions are more generous, though, or more willing to recognize that the institutional reward system should reflect institutional expectations regarding accomplishment.

A common arrangement is to provide released time by means of a schedule that reflects the range of effort likely to be involved. Thus, other things being equal, a large department is more likely to consume a chair's time than is a smaller one; a department requiring facilities management or clinical assignments or supervision is more demanding than one without these features. Formulas range from one-quarter time released from teaching obligations to a teaching load of only one course per year.

Stipends also vary, usually also reflecting institutional judgments about the burdens involved. A number of institutions place their chairs on twelve-month contracts, thereby assuring that someone will be around during most of the summer. Others will provide a monthly stipend (sometimes also adjusted for scope of responsibilities). Stipends range from fifty dollars at the low end to well over five hundred at the high end.

Occasionally someone will indicate that he or she sought the position of chair because of the perks of the job, but that is rare indeed. In fact, most incumbents find that being chair works against some of the very values that attracted them to higher education in the first place. For instance, the price of being an effective department or division chairperson may be to give up the freedom that many faculty enjoy from the ordinary budget and time pressures.

Indeed, never having enough time is one of the frequent complaints of chairs—a fact reflected in their interest in time management techniques. Likewise, the chairperson may initially have entered higher education because of the relative opportunity it provides to set one's own schedule. And it is just this flexibility that the new chairperson finds is the first thing to go. One must consult, and consult widely, and that can be done only by accommodating the schedules of others.

Transitions to Leadership

As we have seen, because the department chair is the first position in academic administration, and the individual is still very much tied to his or her faculty identity and role, the position is fraught with ambiguity. The move to the chair's position also represents a difficult transition, namely, the first major step out of one's professional identity as a teacher and scholar. The transition requires that the chair take on an additional identity, that of manager and leader. And in that leadership role, the chair must see the possibility of making things happen, of shepherding growth or change. If this does not happen, the chair is merely a caretaker, and institutions have lost a real opportunity for leadership at a crucial level.

Thus, the movement from faculty member to leader among peers actually requires several transitions—often of greater magnitude than one might initially anticipate. The chair must shift from one who is trained, socialized, and rewarded for being a specialist to one who sees the larger need to be a generalist within the department. One may have been trained as an organic chemist or a specialist in Renaissance English or in doing the sort of philosophy that phenomenologists do. But as a chair one had better be willing to look equally hard at inorganic chemistry, at Victorian English, and at metaphysics or linguistic analysis. A new breadth and judiciousness are required of the chairperson, a role for which earlier academic life may not have fully prepared one. Certainly when one thinks of earlier rewards, they are likely to have been for narrow specialization, not for being a generalist.

At the same time that this new judiciousness is required one must be paying a lot more attention to detail than was initially bargained for. The alternative is to have the registrar, the dean, and ultimately the department faculty themselves banging on the door with increasing impatience. And all the while the chair's own efforts to maintain teaching effectiveness and scholarly productivity are likely to flag. Heavy inroads are often made upon the time and the energy required for the chair to excel in all of these areas.

A second area of radical change is the shift from being an individualist to running a collective. In the first state one has relative control over one's own time and schedule. As observed above, though, the chair finds others controlling his or her pace as the need for consultation with and availability to colleagues becomes more consuming. Woe to him or her who forgets the need for extensive consultation. One way or another this lesson will be learned.

Another part of the shift away from being an individualist is the need one finds to share credit with others even for ideas that may well have been quite clearly one's own. Some find this requirement to be especially difficult. Certainly it violates much of graduate school socialization. There, and throughout one's faculty career, one is rewarded for advancing good ideas and for claiming them, not for presenting them as someone else's. Yet, the successful chair is one who has discovered how to enlarge the ownership of ideas regarding new directions for the department, and this enlarged ownership does not fit easily with an emphasis upon private claim.

Finally, most chairs today are confronted by the need to shift away from loyalty primarily, if not exclusively, to the discipline and to colleagues in that discipline and alternatively to move to a larger measure of loyalty to the wider institution. At some institutions, this shift requires that one become an advocate, however muted, of changes that will not favor the immediate interests of the department or division, or of colleagues. Here again the role ambiguity of the chairperson can be a heavy burden.

This burden is most evident in those institutions facing enrollment difficulties or financial downturns. In these situations the disappointment of faculty colleagues with their chair can turn into outright hostility toward him or her. The chair then becomes a lightning rod for their broader frustrations regarding career stability or advancement.

Leadership Opportunities for Chairs

The responsibilities of academic leaders at all institutional levels change with the changing context of higher education. The challenges of curriculum and personnel have taken on new dimensions and will define a new role for chairs as the "custodians of standards." It is to the chairs that the academic dean or provost turns, and should turn, for assurances that the departments are where they should be.

Departments need to change as institutions and the larger society change—to reflect shifts in student experience, capacity, interests, and needs and to reflect developments in the discipline itself as well as changes in faculty strengths and abilities. To be the "custodian of standards" means assuring oneself and then others that the curriculum is what it should be given these developments in the discipline, in the student body, and in faculty capacity. It means assuring oneself that the faculty are assigned judiciously and that individual talents are aligned with instructional needs and opportunities. And of course being able to provide these assurances often requires that one in fact first bring the department some significant distance.

In some departments and areas, being able to provide these assurances will mean that one has also to become an entrepreneur—seeking new or better students as well as other opportunities and resources outside the institution. In some instances, this will mean establishing and then maintaining relationships with high schools; in other cases, with local and regional businesses. It may mean new responsibilities for securing equipment or research support. It may also mean monitoring the externally funded research of department faculty so that inappropriate and clandestine arrangements are uncovered and terminated.

No less a part of being a "custodian of standards" is providing leadership with regard to personnel. From the faculty perspective the chair is looked to as advocate for departmental and disciplinary interests, especially as these interests are understood from the perspectives of the individual faculty members themselves. Thus, they are likely to see departmental needs as the same as their own. For them, being an advocate for the department means being an advocate for each of them. This is a natural expectation, especially given the traditions of faculty individualism and autonomy so cherished at most institutions.

But being a "custodian of standards" can mean some quite different things so far as advocating faculty interests are concerned. At one extreme, there is the traditional role of mentoring the junior faculty member. Usually both parties have similar expectations about what is important and appropriate. After all, the junior faculty member is often looking to the chair for tips about the institutional culture and about what is really required to secure tenure in that institution. Similarly, the newcomer is likely to appreciate guidance about committees and about publication and service expectations.

And, of course, in addition to providing guidance, the chair needs also to do what he or she can to provide personal assistance. This may be a bit harder, as it can entail having to persuade other, more senior members of the department that long-standing or preferred courses or class times or more interesting committee assignments should go instead to someone who really has yet to prove himself or herself in the same way that a tenured faculty member has done.

The chair has to worry not only about the junior faculty member, though. The professoriate is aging rapidly, and the chairperson has to reflect seriously upon the import of this development. And here any coincidence of perspectives is usually a lot less likely to occur. The older faculty member may not be so easily persuaded that the chair really has his or her best interests at heart when the chair is insisting that continued professional and personal growth requires surrendering the Shakespeare course taught all these years and honed to easy perfection, or giving up other comfortable routines and expectations. This is not easy and indeed may be the most important challenge facing department chairs today as the professoriate continues to age.

Other problems with the aging professoriate that are all too familiar for some include the alcoholic professor. Different problems of chronic ill health can surface, an especially poignant and difficult species being mental deterioration and disability. Almost all chairpersons will recognize the variety of afflictions visited upon the maturing middle class of today—marital disruptions, disappointments with children, and the inevitable compromises that come with the realization that the bright promise of youth will never be realized.

A third task facing chairpersons today is the need to start planning immediately for the recruitment of the next generation of faculty. At the same time that most chairs are looking at how to keep middle-aged faculty vital, other chairs are looking beyond the next few years to a period of dramatic turnaround for the college job market. A recent *New York Times* article tells us that "by the turn of the century at least 100,000 of the country's 450,000 full-time professors—those hired in the late 1950's and the 1960's to teach the babyboom generation—will retire" (Fiske, 1986, p. 1).

Some institutions see this sea change approaching much more rapidly than others. Columbia University, for instance, will have more than a third of its tenured professors reach the now-mandatory retirement age of seventy by 1995. Because of its own financial struggles during the 1970s and the unduly harsh hiring limits it imposed at that time, Columbia is a bit ahead of other major universities in contemplating retirements. "Taking into account early retirements, resignations and deaths, half (its) senior faculty could be gone by 1995 and two-thirds by 2000" (Fiske, 1986, p. 38). As time flows in the life of a university, 1995 is not that far away.

Of course the prospect of significant vacancies presents a rare opportunity to advance equity concerns and to reshape the department, its programs, and its academic directions.[1] In the interim, though, most of the innovation, revitalization, and newness that we will see will come from the chairperson.

This reality makes all the more important the responsibility that the chair has for promoting continued faculty professional growth and development. The trick is to harmonize or integrate individual development and departmental development. Variations of a growth contract have been used with great success. The key point is to facilitate the individual's initiative in identifying appropriate next steps in his or her career activities. Without the individual's own personal involvement in this process, continued professional development is unlikely to flourish. Rather, unless they take charge of their own professional growth, professors are likely to stagnate.

Of course, it may be that not all of an individual's proposals can be accommodated in any growth contract. At such points, the chairperson needs to negotiate with the faculty member those activities to which institutional support can be given—be it computer or library resources, teaching assistants, laboratory equipment, or released time for curriculum development. In any case, it is the process of individual initiation and ownership that is most important, and, so long as it is balanced, any project that will advance the strengths of the individual or of the academic unit should be hailed even if support cannot be provided.

In this context faculty evaluation must be seen as part of the larger process of faculty development or professional and personal growth. Faculty evaluation is the foundation of faculty development—the point from which plans for the future are made. It is the basis upon which new directions are identified. Without conscious attention to current strengths and weaknesses, improvement is haphazard, uneven, and fitful, if possible at all. Accordingly, periodic review of senior faculty performance is centrally important, however fitful it may currently be at some institutions (Bennett and Chater, 1984, pp. 38–41). Surely the mark of a strong institution and of a mature and collegial profession is regular attention by peers to ways in which performance can be strengthened.

Developing the Chairperson

How can institutions do a better job in assisting in the development of chairpersons? Help can be provided in two ways. We have noted the difficulties in making the transition from faculty member to chairperson, and the pressures that accompany assuming a new perspective on the institution and a new role vis-à-vis one's departmental colleagues. In light of the importance of the chair to the daily decisions affecting institutional quality, chairpersons should receive as much assistance as possible as they adjust to their new positions.

First, it is crucial that deans and presidents see the chair's position as a leadership role. Without that support, chairs cannot be effective; leaders must be empowered by other leaders as well as by their constituents. In an atmosphere of institutional support for departmental leadership, faculty will be much more likely to accept the leadership role of the chair and to recognize the job as important to the quality of teaching and learning.

Beyond the general empowerment of chairs by institutional leaders, there must be some general shared notion of the possibilities and limits of the chairperson's position. Most frequently, institutions tend to do this implicitly, but this is often a source of difficulty and conflict for chairs who do not understand the boundaries of their positions.

The chairs must be educated by institutional leaders about the nature of their roles. How does the dean or the vice president see the role of the chair? What authority and responsibility are delegated to chairs and what decisions are made by other administrators? Although ambiguity of role and expectation will always make the chair position less than clear-cut, it is possible to define at least the general expectations of important constituencies.

Workshops for department chairs can be helpful here. Participants new to the position or even those anticipating becoming chairpersons find an increased sense of self-confidence upon hearing experiences reported by those with several years in the job. Such reports usually focus upon problems solved as well as those eluding solution. Experienced chairpersons can be assisted by colleagues' sharing of strategies or offering of stories about how similar problems were resolved elsewhere or how they can be coped with if complete solutions are not available.

In general, the success of such workshops can be attributed in large part to the role they play in helping chairs to break out of the isolation in which they otherwise work. This is true independent of whether the workshop is conducted solely for chairs within one institution or for participants from several institutions. Usually, though, activities conducted for a group or consortium of institutions provide the additional values that come from learning how things are done elsewhere and how one's own department and institution compare with others.

It is also important for chairs to be familiar with relevant institutional procedures. How is the budget built? What are the relevant documents and timetables? The new chair should be quickly acquainted with personnel policies, equipment procurement, and other practices relevant to his or her responsibilities. Handbooks with such information are especially helpful to both new and experienced chairs.

While management experience or aptitude is generally not required for appointment to the chair position, once on the job new chairs often recognize a need for management training to help them be more effective. A number of professional development programs and resources for these leaders in the trenches have been created in recent years. . The demand for publications, workshops, and other resources indicates a real interest in developing these important academic managers. Among the resources recently established for the professional growth of chairs is the American Council on Education's Department Leadership Institute, launched in 1980, which offers chairpersons development programs in two- or four-day formats, in regional meetings or on-campus settings. Since 1984, the Center for Faculty Evaluation and Development at Kansas State University has offered annual conferences for chairpersons. New book-length materials have recently appeared, as have two newsletters with national circulation.[2] These resources supplement substantially the occasional disciplinary or system efforts that traditionally have been all that was available to assist chairs in their professional growth.[3]

The workshops in particular have been important developments, for they represent several values. The very fact that an institution sponsors such an activity is itself evidence, usually long overdue, that it appreciates the central importance of the chairpersons. Such workshops also help chairs to break out of the isolation in which so many work. Too often chairs labor independently of each other, not recognizing that most face many of the same problems (of which some are indeed intractable, but others do have some solutions, and in any case all can be approached in better and in more viable ways if chairs will but share with each other their successes and failures). Chairs *can* be resources to one another, and workshops designed specifically for them enable that process to occur more often and more readily.

Also, workshops are a useful vehicle for teaching the management skills so needed by department chairs. Topics such as budget preparation, proposal writing, long-range or strategic planning, and affirmative action lend themselves to short informational workshops conducted either by resource persons from within the institution or by outside consultants. A further option is the many top-ical workshops provided by associations, consortia, and other institutions.

Another useful strategy for helping the new chairperson be more effective is formally to designate a mentor. Some institutions have devised mentor systems for new chairpersons, the idea being that more experienced individuals are in the best position to provide help both of a general nature and in regard to institutional idiosyncrasies. Overlapping terms in the case of the larger, more complex departments is another possibility; a month or two of two fully salaried chairpersons can facilitate a more complete and efficient firsthand sharing of problems and solutions without either chair's feeling that unreasonable demands are being made.

Once chairs have settled into their roles and are more confident with their supervisory and managerial duties, other forms of professional development may take on equal importance. That is not to say that the development of management and human relations skills should not be continuous, for new issues constantly arise and leadership skills constantly need to be reevaluated and honed. However, because the department chair functions at the crucial juncture between faculty and senior administrator, the development of an institutionwide perspective is particularly important to a chair's effectiveness. This form of "leadership enhancement," to use Green's terminology in Chapter 1, helps the chairperson to understand the wider context of decision-making. He or she is thereby better equipped to balance institutional goals and priorities with understandable loyalty to the department.

A greater sense of investment in building and maintaining the institution's agenda can only help diminish the legendary departmental turf battles. A regular meeting of the chairs with the deans, vice president, and president can contribute to both the education of chairs and the cooperative efforts at institutional agenda-building. Retreats with flexible agendas are also useful and can build personal relationships in a relaxed setting that will benefit both individuals and the institution.

Going beyond the institution, chairs will benefit from exposure to issues and practices common to other higher education institutions. At national or regional workshops, chairpersons benefit from seeing how things are done elsewhere and from finding out that the grass may be no greener on other campuses. But new and different approaches are bound to be shared and even simple "tricks of the trade" can provide a helpful new perspective for experienced chairpersons.

Similarly helpful are opportunities to learn more about higher education in general, providing a context for understanding the relationship of departmental to institutional and of institutional to national issues. Subscriptions to journals and newsletters, invited speakers from outside, and attendance at national meetings can provide this "window on the world."

Certainly battle fatigue can be a big problem for chairs, as for other administrators. Attention must be paid to ensuring their continued vitality and enthusiasm. Since chairs always have one foot in the faculty ranks and the other in the administrative world, continued leadership vitality should be addressed on both these fronts. Continued involvement in the discipline, attendance at professional conferences, giving of assistance to pursue research, and adequate rewards for development of the chair's faculty persona are important to foster the faculty accomplishments with which most chairs strongly identify. When the chair role is strictly overload, an impediment to being a full-time faculty member, the chair will simply have to choose. The development of a good department chair involves nurturing *both* the faculty and the administrative parts of his or her existence, and rewarding performance in both.

At the other end of the relationship, a few institutions have devised specific sabbatical policies for those who have spent some time in especially demanding positions. Made available prior to the return to full-time faculty status, such sabbaticals can be quite useful in counteracting the toll on scholarship and teaching effectiveness that a demanding stint as chairperson can exact. Similarly, research institutions might think about ways to involve chairs in funded research projects upon the completion of their terms of office.

Conclusion

Department chairs have probably the most important and the widest range of leadership development needs of any group of administrators. Ironically for educational institutions, their developmental needs have usually been ignored—despite the clear and vital impact that department chairs have had upon the vitality of the institution and its success. Yet, the role ambiguity they typically feel makes them need complex forms of support, so that they can function and be accepted both as faculty members and as administrators.

Senior-level administrators need to attend to these developmental needs as effectively as possible. Chairs, after all, are also the spawning ground for a good number of other academic administrators. Investment in the present will provide rich returns both now and in a widening future.

NOTES

1. For an indication of some of the things a chairperson can do to advance the presence and concerns of women and minorities, see Lois VanderWaerdt, "Women in Academic Departments: Uneasy Roles, Complex Relationships," *The Department Advisor* (Summer, 1985), 1–5.
2. For books, see Allan Tucker, *Chairing the Academic Department*, 2d ed. (New York: ACE/Macmillan Publishing Company, 1984); David B. Booth, *The Department Chair: Professional Development and Role Conflict*, AAHE-Eric Higher Education Research Report 10, 1982; and John B. Bennett, *Managing the Academic Department: Cases and Notes* (New York: ACE/Macmillan Publishing Company, 1983). The two newsletters are the *The Department Advisor*, available from P.O. Box 12635, Denver, Colorado 80212, and the *The Academic Leader*, available from 607 North Sherman Avenue, Madison, Wisconsin 53704.
3. For a partial list of disciplinary activities for chairpersons, see Mary Ann F. Rehnke, "A Primer for Department Chairpersons," *AAHE Bulletin* (June, 1982), 13–15.

REFERENCES

BENNETT, JOHN B. "Ambiguity and Abrupt Transitions in the Department Chairperson's Role." *Educational Record* (Fall, 1982), 54–57.

BENNETT, JOHN B., and CHATER, SHIRLEY S. "Evaluating the Performance of Tenured Faculty Members." *Educational Record* (Spring, 1984), 38–41.

FISKE, EDWARD B. "College Scrambling to Avert a Possible Faculty Shortage." *New York Times*, March 16, 1986.

4

In Support of Faculty Leadership: An Administrator's Perspective

PATRICIA R. PLANTE

As novelists and other students of human behavior have observed repeatedly over the years, small rebellions and neglects and incidents often carry disproportionately large consequences. And only those who have never sat on the banks of a northern river in early spring, when the sudden and deafening loosening of ice succeeds a barely perceptible crack, find the phenomenon either unnatural or surprising.

In a contemporary college/university management world that takes great pride in its systems analyses, its financial forecastings, its marketing strategies, and its many other sophisticated modes of operation, a fissure, unresponsive to the ministrations of data bases and in any event often so small as to draw little notice, is ignored in favor of more immediately and obviously threatening structural defects. This cleft that under all but the best of economic and social conditions might well lead to eventual serious damage on any campus is the neglect of one aspect of faculty development, namely, the encouragement and support of faculty leadership. Administrators who defer maintenance in this area have chosen, often

Patricia R. Plante is president of the University of Southern Maine.

with indolence if not malice aforethought, to position their institutions in a danger zone.

In a world where intellectualism reigns with the approval of virtually everyone, any attempt to improve a condition or to reform a system begins not unexpectedly with theoretical discussions of meaning and informative gathering of data. Hence, now that the question of leadership in academe for a variety of historical, sociological, and economical reasons is drawing ever-increasing attention, the debate over definition of terms and analysis of inferences is gaining momentum. Such a pleasurable exercise threatens, however, to remain academic in its multiple senses. While one should examine with care the premises underlying all definitions of leadership, and one should analyze with equal attention useful figures attesting to progress or lack thereof, one should also guard against substituting examination and analysis for thoughtful action. And higher education's present love affair with data gathering is in some instances skirting numerology. Signs of data wallowing are everywhere. Some data, but for its entertainment value, is useless: 39.5 percent of all white male assistant registrars assumed this position at a median age of twenty-seven years and four months. Some, in the leadership advice category, is annoyingly simplistic: five items to include in a letter of nonreappointment—as if leadership were not a complex human matter incorporating dreams and rituals and myths.

The only practical problem with a definition of leadership is the obligation some feel to reach consensus as to its precise meaning. The only real problem with the immediate initiation of efforts that would encourage its development is the tendency to wait for computer printouts to shore up decisions that are perfectly secure and freestanding to begin with. Administrators who have become convinced that the development of faculty leadership is an important element of faculty development and who wish to support its promotion need only agree that leaders in academe seek, most frequently without prompting, creative paths to excellence and persuade others to follow these paths with enthusiasm.

Obstacles to the Development of Faculty Leadership

In some human endeavors, precision is simply not the queen of virtues. Many a poet who could not to anyone's satisfaction define poetry has nevertheless written memorable verse. So too faculty on campuses all over America are at this very moment leading decision-making without worrying about lines of authority or about flowcharts or about narrative descriptions or numerical assessment of responsibility. The task of immediate importance is to take more effective measures to encourage and to support all faculty who wish to participate in decision-making regarding all matters affecting a college/university's welfare so that they may be able to do so with ease. Let the debates over the proper definition of leadership and over the interpretation of data surrounding positions of power run their parallel courses. But let us not delay acting until the discussions have ceased and the computers have turned their fickle attention elsewhere, for by that time everyone may have become too bored with the topic to care. Joseph Epstein (1987) has wisely reminded us that, "just as primitive societies have no knowledge of the concept of vulgarity or poor taste, neither, one gathers, do they have bores. You need to attain a certain level of civilization to develop serious bores."

However, even with good will and clearheadedness and even after having set aside lexical games as frequently if not always unproductive and self-indulgent, obstacles to faculty leadership development are not easily overcome. Two are especially difficult to score against.

Limitations on Faculty Decision-Making

Ironically, the American Association of University Professors has, since 1940 when it issued its statement of principles on academic freedom and tenure, done such commendable work in promoting and defending the legitimate rights of faculty as the primary decision-makers in certain areas of the academic domain that professors have been encouraged to gallop freely in certain corrals and have been deterred from entering others without anyone's objecting to the fencing. Thus are faculty on most campuses given considerable opportunity for leadership in matters that form the academic heart of the enterprise: decisions regarding appointment, nonreappointment, tenure, and promotion of colleagues; curriculum and graduation standards; conditions of employment such as workload and evaluation systems. However, few faculty, especially in large universities, are involved in formulating policies regarding matters that affect the lives of students outside the classroom and that help form the culture of a campus in fundamental ways: strategic planning for the entire institution; improvement of the physical plant; fund-raising and institutional advancement; student recruitment, financial aid, and retention; management of residence halls; preparations of presentations to the various governing boards, members of the legislature, and the community at large. In addition, and in this case in spite of, the A.A.U.P.'s 1972 policy on the role of faculty in budgetary matters, few but the highest level of administrators are given an opportunity to link the allocation of funds to principles that undergird an institution's mission statement.

As if agreeing that good fences did make good neighbors, administrators in many universities do not expect to find an alien faculty at budgetary hearings and strategic planning sessions, and in return they themselves avoid trespassing across faculty territory. As reported and regretted by Clark Kerr and others, many university presidents spend little time on academic affairs, and all in higher education could name even academic vice presidents and deans who survive by bowing excessively low before the territorial imperative.

Thus have certain areas on campuses come to be known as appropriate for managerial overseeing by an administration not intellectually prepared to advance the knowledge of plasma physics and other zones marked as elevated enough to merit the attention of those engaged in promoting the life of the mind. And thus also can such a division between administrators and faculty lead to a college/university's lack of inner consistency, for no meaningful all-inclusive planning in the complex social context of the eighties can take place while these fences are allowed to stand. The challenge of the demolition work will, of course, depend upon the type, the size, and even the location of a college/university.

Oscar Handlin, Carl M. Loeb University Professor at Harvard University, in perhaps an unintended salute to the trespass of these forbidden borders (1987, p. 218) has recently reminded faculty that libraries are too important to leave to librarians, for, "since they usually count themselves as members of the administration, they tend to align themselves with presidents, deans, and provosts and too readily acquiesce in budgetary constraints." Examples of what may now be called this traditional attitude abound.

Persistence of the Idealized Professorial Image

A second significant obstacle to the development of faculty leadership clings with the tenacity of a barnacle to faculty self-image.

Colleges/universities were not created for the purpose of administering them. After the financial forecasting, after the office automation, after the marketing plans, after all of that and so much more, everyone knows that the heart of the enterprise beats in the classrooms, laboratories, and libraries: witness the number of deans who would return to teaching "if only one could." Academe still reveres the monk in his cell bending over an illuminated manuscript even if updated in pin-striped suit he now jets across continents to conferences and seminars. One simply does not meet biologists and poets and anthropologists who began their professional lives yearning to write retention plans. Many still succumb to the reasoning that faculty members who lead campus efforts other than those tied to the strictly and narrowly academic are undercover administrators, and since administrators are not worthy of undue respect, faculty leadership development is viewed as an endeavor of questionable merit.

Three thousand one hundred "custom-made" mission statements to the contrary, a universal academic culture often dismisses traditional concepts of leadership as the domain of administrators who seek happiness through power. Faculty, on the other hand, paint self-portraits that reveal tolerant, independent, contemplative, self-directed types who are not easily influenced, who possess unusual insight and perspicacity, and who are comfortable in a slightly anarchical world. Not a one would trade a good infielder for an excellent manager.

Consequently, a president, a provost, or a dean who sincerely wishes to pay more than lip service to the notion of shared governance and who is philosophically convinced that lines of authority in academe are appropriately lines of persuasion must go over, under, or around these two major obstacles described above. The way to begin is by *not* engaging in certain behavior patterns that have traditionally camouflaged authoritarian intents even from those who practice them with what they may have come to believe to be pure motives.

Pitfalls in Developing Faculty Leadership

Some of the expectations administrators have of faculty behaviors are misguided, the product of stereotyping, thoughtlessness, or occasionally paranoia. Suggestions for avoiding four major errors in developing faculty leadership follow.

First, faculty should never be asked to undertake clerical duties that can be done by staff. Administrators in their salad days often mistakenly attempt to involve faculty in certain campus projects by asking them to perform undemanding tasks that teach little and that provide even less opportunity for decision-making. Experience should quickly teach them, if some historian or philosopher does not reach them even more quickly, that one who respects the importance of faculty teaching and scholarship does not interrupt either one frivolously. However, when such requests are prompted not by inexperience and misguided good will but by a desire to appear to want to share power in a world that does not take kindly to autocracy, the action is dishonest as well as unwise. No one will long be deceived by an administrator who unilaterally decides which departments will be allotted additional faculty positions but is open to sharing the task of examining transcripts to be certain that seniors have met all graduation requirements. Faculty will respond generously when given an opportunity to seek solutions to problems worthy of their considerable talent and expertise but will justifiably resent the time stolen from their studies and their students for matters that might well be handled by staff. No one should confuse busy work with the acquisition of knowledge, including the knowledge of leadership.

Next, faculty should never be asked to attend meetings that are without a specific and vital purpose. Faculty who are serious about their own intellectual growth and that of their students do not need recreational directors. And it is patronizing indeed to conclude that they will be flattered when invited to attend meetings whose purpose is neither to share significant information nor to reach a decision regarding a matter that is of some importance. To one who nurtures contemplative leanings, as many faculty do, no sense of self-worth is enhanced and no feeling of membership in a serious enterprise is promoted by being asked to interrupt work on a manuscript or on the preparation of a class to join administrators who, out of heavy-handed good intentions or, worse yet, out of a calculated attempt to appear open and nonautocratic, think it "time to touch base with the faculty." These shaggy-dog assemblies, like shaggy-dog stories, lead nowhere but to a sense that somehow one has missed the point. Surely, the leading of colleges/universities through the difficult and complex eighties and nineties cannot consist of trivializing questions over cups of Maxwell House.

After attending a number of such gatherings, faculty who may have started out wishing to participate in shared governance react in predictable fashion. Some pay the same attention to future invitations as they do to junk mail; some lose confidence in the administrators who host these get-togethers and become increasingly anxious; some, long attached to the institution, continue to attend, but become ever more impatient and contentious; and, finally, some come to view the campus as simply a pied-à-terre that allows them certain comforts and privileges when they are in town.

Third, faculty should never be arbitrarily denied entrance into any area of decision-making. Just as presidents, provosts, and deans should never conclude that academic decisions belong exclusively to the faculty, so too should they never designate fiscal affairs, university advancement, or any of the multiple support service areas nontrespassing zones. It matters a great deal in strategic planning, that is, in the most effective use of an institution's resources for the purpose of attaining its dreams, to be certain, say, that courses are not duplicated in the departments of management and computer and information sciences or in those of sociology and anthropology and history. An academic vice president or a dean should be knowledgeable enough to recognize excess and brave enough to discourage it. Similarly, policies, say, governing financial aid, faculty-student ratios, allocation of discretionary funds, priorities in capital projects, and much more have a significant and long-term impact on a college/university. Faculty should be given opportunities to remain informed and to express opinions on all matters that affect their lives and those of their students.

Clearly, faculty should not be asked to prepare requests to allow companies to bid on replacing roofs and boilers. However, some well-intended efforts regarding certain aspects of campus life that might at first blush seem to belong exclusively to one division may upon reflection affect many—who will understandably resent having to cope with consequences not of their making. Take the following instance.

The personnel department in a medium-size public university, exasperated by a seemingly unending flow of demands for the upgrading of secretarial positions in academic departments, obtains permission from the administrative vice president to impose a moratorium on all promotions of secretaries and to begin a thorough study of their duties and responsibilities. The undertaking is to include desk audits. The chairs of the forty departments and the faculty are informed, but not consulted. The initiative is to begin in January and the results to be made known in early spring. No one objects: a sizable majority, convinced that their secretary is superior to all other secretaries and remembering with gratitude the nights she worked overtime to meet grant application deadlines, anticipate the long-overdue correction of the injustice of her unrewarded excellence; the others dismiss the project as another instance of pop management.

The exercise concludes in mid-April and the members of the personnel department, having sincerely and conscientiously made every effort to remain objective and just, are astonished to discover that the faculty response might not have differed had they planted explosives in the campanile. Their announcement of the study's conservative conclusions during spring break is viewed as a cowardly administrative ploy to perform a dastardly deed while the faculty is away; their point system, that keeps virtually every secretary *in situ* for life, is indefensible and is evidence of both simplemindedness and pettiness; their descriptive justifications support nothing but the well-known fact that the new breed of campus administrators understands nothing about the culture of academe and the needs of professors.

The vice president for administration hopes that we pass this way but once; the personnel officers busily defend themselves; the secretaries weep and threaten to leave; and the chairs and faculty write letters of outrage that demand immediate action from the provost and the president. One is reminded of a cartoon by Sempé that appeared in the *New Yorker* some years back. What is clearly the last scene of a grand opera has the hero collapsing at the feet of the dying heroine and light from a small gothic window illuminating a scene of general desolation. A bejewelled dowager in the audience turns to her companion and whispers: "What a shame! With a little professional help early on, all this could have been avoided." Well, in this instance, perhaps not *all*—but anyone with an understanding of shared governance that wisely involves its faculty in the solution of problems could most certainly have avoided *some* of the unfortunate consequences of what began as a project conceived as the exclusive domain of one division.

Fourth, faculty should never be forced to participate in an administration's plans to promote faculty leadership. To insist that someone "lead" is about as reasonable as to insist that someone be charming. Leadership supposes self-propulsion. However, what administrators might well do is to encourage flight and to maintain the runways properly while ever keeping in mind that many may simply not be interested in traveling. To assume that a faculty member who turns down an opportunity to add to his or her leadership experience by chairing the university senate or by directing the business outreach program is alienated or uncaring or lazy or filled with self-doubt is presumptuous. Faculty who are happy as scholar-teachers and who carry their fair share of a campus community's civic obligations must be allowed their own Waldens.

Ironically, some administrators in their eagerness to prove themselves egalitarians unconsciously use their power of office to impose decision-making on some who have chosen the academic life precisely because they find management in all its forms uncongenial and contemplation in all its manifestations attractive. These same administrators, in their real or imagined desire to share power, not only frequently create the impression that no one is at the helm, but, what is perhaps even worse, give signs of having so little respect for the important calling of a scholar-teacher that they find it beyond imagining that all faculty are not waiting to be "elevated" to the role of a dean or vice president and are not eager to be provided experiences that might eventually place them on those summits.

Formal leadership development efforts such as the American Council on Education's Fellows Program and the Summer Institute for Women in Higher Education Administration at Bryn Mawr may be useful and perhaps even invaluable for faculty who wish to become deans and vice presidents. However, the end of faculty leadership development is not the transformation of faculty into administrators, and one should examine closely a rhetoric that implies values inimical to the primary mission of any college/university: to discover, to preserve, and to share knowledge and wisdom. Faculty who decide to seek administrative posts are not "moving up" nor positioning themselves for "career advancement" though they may well be eager for a change of responsibilities.

In providing campus-based faculty development leadership opportunities, administrators must forever keep in mind the central purpose of such efforts and the philosophical conviction that gives it form. The aim is not to metamorphose physicists and literary analysts into deans and development officers but to share with them a vision of their institution's destination and to search with them for the most honest and most honorable routes to travel by.

Ways of Encouraging Shared Leadership

Assuming that one respects the central role of the faculty on any campus by not engaging them in clerical duties disguised as leadership assignments; by not interrupting their important work with trivial meetings meant to lead to no exit; by not excluding them from any realm of significant decision-making; and by not, through word or deed, implying that the good, the brave, and the beautiful leave small offices for larger ones, how is the faculty leadership voice amplified?

Though presidents, academic vice presidents, and deans must be allowed their style, it is difficult to imagine any of these administrators persuading a faculty that they subscribe to the importance of shared governance unless three elements form part of their mode of operation. Administrators who sincerely wish to promote faculty leadership development keep their faculty well informed; seek their faculty's advice on all significant issues, especially those involving personnel and fiscal matters; and use their faculty's initiatives as part of the institution's strategic planning.

Just as a scientist's years of advance study prepare him or her not only to detect the unusual but to deal with the unknown when it appears, so too a well-informed faculty is able to respond intelligently and wisely to the vagaries of fortune and the changing economic, political, and social influences that constitute a college/university's varied challenges. The ability to adapt is one of the virtues most needed in the complex world of contemporary higher education, but a faculty that is not prepared to anticipate change will greet it with defensiveness and hostility.

The tone with which administrators share information with faculty cannot be divorced from the information itself when we consider the benefits that accrue in such an educational process. It is essential that this tone be characterized by honesty and openness, of course, but just as importantly it must convey the conviction that the challenges to be met are not the property of the administration alone or of the faculty alone, but of the institution to which everyone belongs.

Two years ago, an academic vice president who came to the conclusion that a six-member technically oriented academic department's declining enrollment could not be reversed and therefore, he had one of three slopes to climb: he could ignore the high cost per credit hour, fold the expense in the three-hundred-page budget of the medium-size university, and place his name under the heading "Survivor" in the taxonomy of administrators; he could make a list of all the undeniably good managerial reasons for eliminating the department, and then write its members an "I have reluctantly come to the conclusion" letter followed by an "I only wish it were otherwise" gathering; or he could call a meeting of the appropriate dean, the six members of the department faculty, and a few of the faculty in leadership positions (say, the officers of the university senate, the chair of the retrenchment committee, the president of the local A.A.U.P. chapter) and ask for a united creative effort to solve a university problem.

The academic vice president chose the third option. A solution surfaced only after dozens of formal and informal conferences; only after the faculties of two other growing departments had been involved in examining the possibility of inviting some of the faculty in the shrinking department to join their own; and only after the faculty development committees had discussed ways and means of helping their colleagues. The final plan submitted, not by the vice president but by the faculty, to the university senate for its approval included closing the department and relocating and/or supporting the affected faculty through faculty development programs. The plan was approved unanimously.

The administrator in this instance did not climb the third slope merely because it was there but because once he rightly expected that once he reached the top the view would be vastly superior to that provided by either of the other two. The faculty, having been issued stocks in the enterprise, were committed to its welfare and proud of their contribution to it. Dozens were informed of conditions in one area of the university about which they had known little, and many gained knowledge about the complexities of administrating in a humane and sensitive manner.

Though some might argue that the mode of operation just described is both cumbersome and inefficient, ease and efficiency are frequently characteristics attached to actions only if one takes the short view. Most often when making decisions in an academic culture, one's only meaningful choice of style is to devote time in involving others, particularly faculty, before or after the deed. The administrator as teacher never begrudges the hours spent sharing knowledge with and listening to the suggestions of faculty before reaching decisions. He or she does so willingly not only because such is the only viable way to create a climate of shared purpose, not only because faculty are among the most intelligent and best-trained people in society who can make significant contributions to the leadership of an institution, but because the hours not spent educating and listening before acting are going to be spent nonetheless, with interest and penalties added, after acting. The explanations and justifications that follow a decision for which a faculty had never been prepared and to which it had never been asked to contribute will always ring hollow regardless of the acoustics.

Very specific occasions that afford administrators opportunities to encourage faculty leadership in many spheres of college/university life are those that appear as requests to support faculty initiatives. While the generous cheer on the worthy projects of others, nearly everyone reserves a special enthusiasm and affection for those ventures born of their own minds and hearts. Hence, administrators who are not inclined to censure that aspect of human nature are in a better position to work it to the benefit of their institution as well as to the benefit of the faculty who ask to launch new satellites.

Consider, for instance, the case of Professor A., a physicist of considerable talent who has the respect of both his colleagues and his students and who was suddenly awakened to the anorexic condition of the university's centralized academic advising system by the noise and confusion surrounding the implementation of computerized registration. The dean and the provost, both convinced that Professor A. did not mean to limit his concern to lamentations in the faculty dining room, met with him in order to seek his help in improving a system that they acknowledged to be weak. They granted him both a reduced teaching load and funds to attend national conferences that featured successful academic advising programs, in return for his leading the faculty of his college in the designing of a more effective student advising system. They made certain that the staff in the centralized Office of Advising supported his efforts and did not interprete them as interference, and an enthusiastic Professor A. now plans a study of the benefits of computer-assisted advising programs that are operative at Brigham Young University and elsewhere. The improvements made in his college will be studied in the other divisions of the university for possible implementation. A fine physicist and teacher was not transformed into an administrator; rather, a fine faculty member was given the opportunity to help lead a university toward excellence.

Genuine efforts on the part of administrators to share the governance of a college/university with the faculty will not relieve presidents, provosts, and deans from assuming the ultimate responsibility for decisions that define and direct an institution. Sincere attempts to develop faculty leadership will not guarantee consensus on all issues. Indeed, there will be times when an administrator will conclude that the majority voice, while the strongest, is not the purest. However, a faculty that is persuaded of the authenticity of an administration's desire to include others in its decision-making is a faculty that will generously respect, even support, conclusions that differ from their own.

In a 1936 letter to Elizabeth Ames, the Director of Yadoo, the novelist John Cheever wrote that an old lady in his D.C. boarding house claimed that all W.P.A. workers were lazy and generally good for nothing. Cheever was finding it harder and harder "to pass her the lima beans." Administrators who are sensitive to the complexities of leading colleges/universities through the eighties and nineties are finding it harder and harder to respond amicably to those in positions of power who seem unaware that the neglect of the development of faculty leadership is a fissure in an institution of higher education that might well signal the eventual disintegration of a united undertaking.

REFERENCES

Epstein, Joseph (Aristides). "The Bore Wars." *The American Scholar* (Winter, 1987), p. 24.

Handlin, Oscar. "Libraries and Learning." *The American Scholar* (Spring, 1987), p. 218.

5

Developing Faculty Leadership: A Faculty Perspective

ROSE-MARIE OSTER

The health and well-being of the more than four hundred thousand faculty members in the United States have surfaced once again as a national issue. Problems of faculty immobility, demoralization, and frustration, as well as issues relating to the impending waves of retirement and possible faculty shortages are once again part of the national dialogue.

The higher education community is equally, if not more, preoccupied with the subject of leadership. It is curious, however, that the national dialogue on leadership includes little if any discussion of faculty leadership. The underlying assumption is that leaders are synonymous with administrators. Yet it is obvious that all administrators are not leaders and that all leadership is not drawn from the administrative ranks. Good faculty leadership is the sign of a healthy campus, and the effective administrator understands its importance.

Thus, I am happy to find myself in agreement with the percep-

Rose-Marie Oster is professor of Germanic and Slavic Languages at the University of Maryland.

tions of faculty leadership expressed by Plante in the preceding chapter. Administrators play an important role in fostering faculty leadership, and shared governance is at the heart of the matter. Good intentions abound. Administrators talk about the importance of sharing information and decision-making with the faculty; the faculty is invariably discontented with the actual execution of these noble intentions. Faculty members talk about the obligation of administrators to make the hard decisions and are frequently resentful when they do. Both faculty and administrators insist that posturing and game-playing are counterproductive; both groups often engage in both behaviors.

The question that plagues, us, then, is how to make good intentions into a reality. Another look at the recent history of faculty-administrator relationships and the sources of current tensions is an important first step.

A Historical Perspective

The growth years of the 1960s brought plentiful opportunities for faculty. In short supply, faculty were courted by institutions, and promotion and tenure were relatively easy to come by. Opportunities existed outside the university in government and public service in a society whose possibilities seemed limitless. While some faculty members retreated from the social activism on campus stirred by the student movement, others rose to the occasion to take the lead in pressing for campus reform. Administrators, on the other hand, were more likely to take a defensive posture as campus security and stability were threatened.

As hard times came to higher education in the mid-1970s, opportunities for faculty mobility, career changes, and advancement diminished severely. The growth of campuses in the previous decade led to increased specialization of administrative jobs, and so a managerial class was born. Administration became a profession in itself, and administrators could move from campus to campus without the traditional ties to the local academic culture. The problem was severely compounded by diminished resources, and the prospect of slices from a smaller pie heightened tensions between faculty and administrators.

As a result, the campus climate and governance system began

to look different. Efficient management was a high priority for many administrators, and faculty felt increasingly alienated from the new value system and administrative procedures. Professional development programs proliferated to help administrators become more adept at their managerial tasks and run a tighter ship. Widening the gulf was the slow growth of faculty salaries, their loss of purchasing power during that decade, and the knowledge that administrative salaries were rising faster than those of the faculty.

Other traditional faculty rewards were also disappearing. Promotion and tenure were considerably more difficult to get. At research institutions especially, teaching and service were distant seconds to publications in the promotion process. Many nonresearch institutions began behaving like their research counterparts and the faculty who had been hired earlier were no longer valued. In short, the rules of the game had been abruptly changed, and faculty felt that they were the losers.

For many faculty then, the name of the new game was research and publications accompanied by loyalty to the discipline. For those not in that league, disposable time and energy were often focused outside the institution on consulting, outside pursuits, or leisure.

Hunkering Down in the Eighties

Plante appropriately points out the importance of including faculty in decisions that affect all aspects of institutional life and not simply those areas deemed to be the traditional purview of the faculty. In many institutions, this will take some doing, requiring a concerted effort to undo the faculty's retreat to their sacred provinces—such acknowledged faculty territory as the curriculum and the department, where disciplinary concerns reign supreme, as do ensuing turf battles. But even on the departmental level, much has changed in a decade. Today, the role of the department chair is changing on many campuses. More and more are appointed, and chairs are now commonly considered middle management. The increased power of the department chair as a manager has in some institutions increased the faculty's sense of disenfranchisement. In its most extreme form, a unionized faculty with the department chair outside the bargaining unit, or formally part of management, is a clear signal about the respective roles of faculty and chair.

Turning the Tide: Toward a New Model of Shared Governance

Given the legacy of faculty-administrative tension and the current state of faculty alienation, how can faculty leadership be developed? Again, Plante has gone right to the heart of the matter by citing shared governance as central to faculty leadership. Her observation that some faculty are simply not interested in leadership and have no particular aptitude for it is quite accurate. The healthy campus and the wise administrator will let faculty make those decisions for themselves, and leadership will bubble up of its own force.

Higher education and its environment have changed dramatically in the last quarter-century. Similarly, the model of shared leadership must change; it can no longer reflect a nostalgic view of the mythical community of scholars. We need some new definitions. Accordingly, this volume has proposed several new definitions: leadership now means envisioning teams as opposed to heroic individuals, dispersing of leadership to empower deans and department chairs as well as the top few decision-makers, diversifying the cadre of leaders to be more representative of our population, and finally, paying systematic attention to human resource development as an integral part of institutional development. Full partnership of the faculty yet reasonable division of labor is another key element of a new definition of leadership.

As Plante notes, administrators must be genuinely committed to fostering faculty leadership; insincere or superficial efforts will be ineffective and damaging. There is a prior commitment that she does not mention. The development of faculty leadership requires that *all* leadership development be taken seriously by senior administrators. The careful identification and cultivation of leadership throughout the institution will ultimately benefit the entire institution; to this end, it must be a part of overall institutional planning of human and financial resources. Leadership development should not simply hone the skills of individuals but engage disparate groups in joint planning and problem-solving.

It is important to reinforce Plante's point here that leadership development for faculty does not necessarily mean providing opportunities for them to become administrators, though this may be one of many paths. A broader and more helpful definition of leadership development is enabling faculty to have substantial responsibilities in the directing life of the institution. This may range from directing a self-study to developing an institutional plan for assessment or increasing faculty involvement in community outreach. The development of meaningful faculty leadership requires exposing faculty to all aspects of the institution and having them as full partners.

Getting from Here to There: Obstacles to Overcome

As an administrator, Plante chides her colleagues to avoid certain pitfalls if they are to foster faculty leadership. They must avoid the mere appearance of sharing power and make their efforts meaningful and sincere. Giving faculty clerical duties, she says, is a dead giveaway and a misuse of faculty time. Among the sins of time-wasting and insincerity is the "touching base" ritual with no further intentions. Plante exhorts administrators to include faculty in all aspects of institutional decision-making but to recognize at the same time that some faculty members prefer not to be leaders. On the positive side, she advises administrators to keep faculty informed, to solicit their advice on all matters, and to incorporate their initiatives into strategic planning. Administrators are fundamentally teachers, and knowledge sharing should be central to their profession. So much for administrative responsibilities.

Surely, faculty also bear responsibility for leadership. Leadership is to be claimed as much as it is to be bestowed. Yet faculty are often ill prepared for shared leadership by their training and disposition. In many disciplines, they have been trained to work in isolation. They value the professional autonomy that attracted them to the academic life in the first place. Many have little understanding of or experience with the satisfaction of being a member of a well-functioning team. In addition, when choosing among commitments, they will most likely turn to the discipline or department rather than to the institution. Disagreement within the faculty ranks on many central educational and curricular issues further exacerbates the problem of team development among the faculty. A divided faculty with uncertain loyalties makes leadership development for institutional benefit a difficult task.

Faculty share the blame with administrators of thinking the worst of the other group. In other words, they contribute to the "we-they" mentality. This behavior is more surprising when exhibited by academic administrators; after all, most were faculty members in an earlier incarnation. Some appear to have forgotten their origins. While most faculty have never been administrators, many are unwilling to relinguish the stereotypes that distance the two groups. Faculty often expect administrators to be uncollegial, power-hungry, and insensitive to the faculty. Such stereotypes often create self-fulfilling prophecies; thus, administrators may look upon faculty as hothouse flowers, too delicate to be exposed to the rough and tumble of administration or too unearthly to grasp the intricacies of subjects as terrestrial as financial management. Since stereotyping leads people to look for and reinforce the behaviors they expect to see, listening then becomes superfluous, for each group knows what it will hear. The problems of stereotyping and noncommunication feed each other.

Recommendations for Developing Faculty Leadership

Developing faculty leadership requires a commitment from both faculty and administrators; it is not the sole responsibility of administrators. Each group must examine and inevitably relinquish the stereotypes that have historically distanced them. Improved communications, mutual respect, and a willingness to share power are amply honored in academic rhetoric but too rarely translated into realities. Administrators inevitably describe their leadership style as consultative and collegial. Faculty typically intone that administrators are paid to make decisions; that's their job. Yet high-handed administrators and faculty unwilling to accept administrative decision-making abound. The challenge is to make the rhetoric and the verbiage match. The following recommendations provide specific suggestions for taking action to develop faculty leadership:

Create a Positive Climate

A positive climate is essential to shared leadership. Primary responsibility for creating this climate lies with the administration; without positive signals and rewards for faculty leadership, leadership simply will not develop (or it will develop as an adversarial phenomenon). Such a climate is created by abundant communication, meaningful consultation with the faculty, and inclusion of faculty in decision-making throughout the institution.

Administrators who can do this need certain qualities and skills. They must know how to build consensus, how to solicit genuine input into decisions, and how to articulate and interpret institutional mission to the faculty. They must have good skills in conflict resolution and be accomplished and serious listeners. As Plante notes, an administrator hoping to promote shared leadership must also value faculty contributions to all phases of institutional life. For example, faculty can play a useful role as institutional representative to state boards, governing boards, and even the legislature. Many administrators are unnecessarily paranoid about faculty representing the institution externally. If they are genuinely part of the decision-making process, they will be able institutional spokespersons. Faculty members who see themselves as part of the institutional team will not threaten it with unpredictable, "loose-cannon" behavior. A joint proposal or faculty input into board deliberations is far preferable to faculty groups lobbying independently or worse yet, adversarily, at the state legislature. Admittedly, not all faculty will be such cooperative allies, but efforts to make them genuinely so are preferable to a disenfranchised faculty with no avenues for meaningful participation.

Developing faculty leadership requires that faculty change as well. They must transcend narrow departmental or professional lines to take a broad and long-term view. Faculty need to understand and appreciate the institution beyond the department in order to respond to concerns in a larger context, to tie into the political process at all levels, and to represent the institution to its many constituencies. They must also understand the necessity of compromise, which need not be at odds with integrity. Compromise means neither selling out nor succumbing to unnecessary posturing in order to join forces with administrators to pursue the greater good of the institution.

All of this involves a long and rather cumbersome educational process, particularly at large institutions with complicated steering systems. The slowness of decision-making is the price we pay for participation in academe, and faculty must be willing to curtail the process when circumstances so dictate.

Understand How the Other Half Lives

Administrators interested in fostering faculty leadership must learn about the campus and the faculty culture as an important first step. It is particularly important for new administrators to learn who the faculty leaders are, how they are chosen, and how faculty leadership operates. The wise administrator will also recognize that these well-intentioned efforts to understand faculty may be met with suspicion.

In addition to learning about the culture, administrators should find out talents the faculty can offer to the institution: what expertise exists that could be useful for institutional development? Who is knowledgeable about assessment? Who knows about computers? Who could do a feasibility study for a day-care center? Faculty members are also often knowledgeable in areas outside their academic disciplines. They are frequently members of national boards, sit on panels and boards of trustees, are on city councils and school boards. Many are nationally known in this "other life," yet the campus community may fail to make the connection between these talents and the institution's needs. Some institutions have developed directories of expertise in research and other areas; but it is the rare one that uses them for its own benefit.

Faculty, too, must learn about the institution's operations and administrative culture. Committee work and faculty governance are traditional routes to such learning. But other opportunities can be created that benefit faculty as well as the institution. Internships in administrative offices can give faculty a valuable window on a different world, not necessarily as a prelude to moving into administration. Significant assignments to manage projects both within the academic area and outside can be powerful learning experiences. Seminars and workshops, as well as faculty exchanges or visits to other institutions can help broaden faculty perspectives.

Keep All Groups Talking

Open communications are central to shared leadership. On some campuses information trickles down from the top; administrators are often shielded from the faculty by overzealous staff who have little understanding of the laborious ways of faculty or who distrust open communication. Creating strong personal relationships will also contribute to campus climate conducive to shared leadership. Programs or structures to promote bonding between groups or among individuals are a helpful mode of communication and agent of change. A rather ordinary but enduringly successful communications-building activity is one or more meetings to explore issues or plan the future. The mere fact that the meetings are convened may be more important than their actual outcomes. Such meetings should enable faculty and administrators to bring up concerns in a nonthreatening environment, building trust and relationships that often continue. A retreat setting facilitates easy communication outside the formal sessions, and the conversations at meals and during free time are often the most productive.

Use the Self-Study Process

The self-study process has historically been an important vehicle for involving faculty in institutional tasks that foster shared introspection. Rather than serving simply as a bureaucratic requirement connected with accreditation, a self-study can involve the faculty throughout the process. Institutional assessment and introspection draw on the classic strengths of most faculty. While they may be slow to come to a decision even when time presses, they can be invaluable in long-term planning. The self-study can serve as a basis for a discussion of institutional expectations of the faculty leaders as well as provide an opportunity for faculty members to gain leadership skills.

Assign Responsibility

Given the complexities of relationships among the various campus groups, many institutions have individuals who are responsible for system relations or relations between campus and external bodies such as legislatures, coordinating boards, or alumni. While the job of serving as spokesperson for the faculty to the administration frequently falls to the chair or president of the faculty senate, this is not always the case. Few campuses have a faculty or staff member responsible for faculty-administration relations. Such an appointment might assist in creating a positive climate for institutional improvement and change, shepherd leadership development efforts, and improve communications on a long-term basis.

Select Administrators Carefully

A campus seriously interested in creating a shared leadership environment must pay close attention to the selection and composition of its institutional leadership team.

Democratizing a campus requires rethinking what we value in our leaders. Institutions need to identify persons who understand the changing roles of leaders and changing leadership styles. This, of course, involves a more lucid diagnosis of institutional problems and leadership needs than is often currently the case. Also, it is difficult for search committees to get beyond the usual rhetoric about shared governance espoused by most candidates. They will need to probe carefully into the person's behaviors and working relationships rather than rely on the individual's campaign speech. Also, the search committee must give candidates a clear view of the type of leader the campus is looking for. The search process can play an important role in effecting institutional change by ensuring that the administrators who are hired share in deed as well as in word and understand fully the value of shared leadership.

Reward Faculty Leadership

No discussion of faculty leadership is complete without considering the institutional reward structure. While teaching, research, and service are the sacred foundations of merit salary increases, promotion, and tenure decisions, the three often do not carry equal weight. In research institutions especially, service is a very distant third. In some institutions, the culture dictates that service is best left to those unable to compete in the research arena; in short, the "deadwood." As long as this attitude and its resulting practices prevail, it will be difficult to attract able faculty to leadership positions.

An important form of faculty reward is the knowledge that their contributions are real and valued. Even the willing faculty will get cynical. An administration with a history of putting faculty reports safely on the shelf cannot expect the game to continue. Faculty will soon get wise and refuse to play.

Conclusion

Changing institutional attitudes is no easy task. We have ample evidence in academe that it is sometimes more appealing to curse the darkness than to light the proverbial candle.

The academy abounds in masters of discourse who can extol the virtues of collegiality and shared leadership. The task for faculty and administrators is to get beyond the rhetoric and to adapt the structures and the academy's ways of doing business to the requirements of a new era.

If institutions are to flourish or even to survive, they have to develop mechanisms to support leadership development throughout the academic community. Administrators are responsible for beginning the process of changing campus atmosphere, for sending the right signals to faculty about the desirability of exerting leadership and its importance to institutional development. Administrators need to articulate the role of the faculty in the institution's future; they have to acknowledge faculty leadership both externally and internally and to reward it by making it a meaningful part of institutional decision-making.

Leadership development is also a responsibility of the faculty itself. Faculty members must be willing to commit themselves to the greater good of the institution and at the same time let administrators lead and forge the coalitions necessary for institutional progress.

Above all, faculty need to show the courage to take the leadership role, beginning with the areas of their own undisputed expertise. The nation's faculty are charged by some with having abdicated their responsibility in setting academic standards. It is incumbent upon the faculty to reclaim not only that institutional territory, but other ones as well. If faculty members truly believe that they *are* the institution, they must act accordingly.

6

Women as Leaders

DONNA L. SHAVLIK
JUDITH G. TOUCHTON

In the last decade women in American society have made dramatic gains as leaders. Two major political races in the 1986 elections were between women—the gubernatorial campaign in Nebraska and the U.S. Senate race in Maryland. By 1985 women had assumed 14.7 percent of the seats in state legislatures (Mandel, 1986). Two hundred women became CEOs of corporations whose assets exceed $5 million. Women also began to achieve prominence in public life. Some obvious examples are: Geraldine Ferraro, candidate for vice president of the United States; Sandra Day O'Connor, Supreme Court justice; Sally Ride, the first woman in space; Patricia Roberts Harris, the first black woman to hold a U.S. Cabinet post; and Katharine Graham, the head of a Fortune 500 company. Women in higher education are no exception to this pattern. Over 300 women now serve as chief executive officers of colleges and universities in the United States.

These indeed are impressive gains, but they do not begin to tell all the exciting, painful, and heroic stories of all the other firsts and seconds among women leaders over the last decade. They also do not tell the stories of the countless women leaders who have not been given an opportunity to serve when they were clearly ready and more than able.

Donna L. Shavlik is director of the Office of Women in Higher Education at the American Council on Education; Judith G. Touchton is deputy director.

This chapter examines the forces that have encouraged women leaders and the acceptance of women's leadership, discusses the perceptions and realities of the special leadership needs of women, and suggests ways in which institutions can be more responsive to women leaders and encourage their advancement.

Setting the Context: Forces Shaping Women's Leadership

There are a number of forces that have influenced and shaped women's leadership in higher education in recent history. Some of the major ones—federal legislation, leadership training programs, and public and private philanthropy—merit special attention here as a prelude to an examination of women's leadership on campus.

Social Forces and Legislative Interventions

The force of the law was powerful in setting the stage for women to assume a greater proportion of the leadership roles in higher education. Since 1972 a number of laws, regulations, and executive orders have been promulgated to advance the cause of equality for women in education. Some of the major ones include: Executive Order 11246 (as amended by Executive Order 11375), mandating the use of affirmative action; Title VII of the Civil Rights Act of 1964 (as amended), prohibiting discrimination in employment on the basis of race, color, religion, sex, or national origin; Title IX of the Elementary/Secondary Act of 1972, the first law prohibiting discrimination against students on the basis of sex, and also including some aspects of employment; Title VI of the Civil Rights Act of 1964 (minority women included in 1964), prohibiting discrimination on the basis of race, color, and national origin; Section 503 of the Rehabilitation Act of 1973, prohibiting discrimination on the basis of handicap; the Age Discrimination in Employment Act of 1967 (as amended), prohibiting discrimination on the basis of age; the Equal Pay Act of 1963 (as amended), prohibiting differential pay rates for women and men doing the same work; and the Pregnancy Discrimination Act of 1978, amending Title VII and asserting that pregnant women shall be treated the same for all employment-related purposes, as other persons not so affected but similar in their ability or inability to work.

These legal mandates have been a powerful force in getting institutions to establish new policies and procedures, to open access to women students, faculty, and administrators, to assess the climate for all women, to undertake studies to remedy inequities, and to examine other impediments to the full and equitable participation of women in the academy. The results have included more open searches, elimination of quotas on admissions, establishment of special recruiting programs for disciplines not usually chosen by women, salary equity studies and remedies, affirmative action procedures, more resources for women's programs, especially athletics, and recognition of special problems, such as sexual harassment. All these changes do not necessarily affect the promotion of women leaders directly, but they are influential in creating a better climate for the acceptance of women as leaders and in increasing the demand for them.

Several federal agencies were also instrumental in fostering an improved climate for women and in encouraging, directly or indirectly, women leaders. The Fund for the Improvement of Post-Secondary Education (FIPSE), the Women's Educational Equity Act Program (WEEAP), the National Institute of Education (NIE), the National Endowment for the Humanities (NEH), the National Institutes of Health (NIH) and the National Institute of Mental Health (NIMH) were chief among them. These agencies funded projects and programs that supplied data on the status of women, provided model training programs, helped initiate networks designed to promote women's advancement, created materials to help people recognize and deal with stereotyping and discrimination, and identified areas of differential impact on minority and handicapped women.

These interventions placed women squarely on the national agenda, not an insignificant part of the advancement experienced by women over the last decade. Women's advocacy groups and organizations, national studies on the status of women, special task forces and commissions, federal enforcement of equal opportunity laws, and increased visibility of women at national meetings and in the print and electronic media, all contributed to an increased awareness of women as a vital force in society.

Private foundations also played an important role in promoting women leaders in higher education. The Carnegie Corporation of New York and the Ford Foundation were primary, giving support to many of the leadership development programs established for women in the early 1970s.

Public policy, philanthropy, and training did not, however, fundamentally change the prevailing perception—that women who wished to be leaders needed to be *extremely well qualified*, have proven records of accomplishment, and be overprepared for their positions. While these extra demands on women have somewhat dissipated over the years, strong vestiges remain today. These expectations have caused many women to overprepare, doubt themselves, and limit their aspirations. This appears doubly true for minority women. Stephanie Marshall, writing about women leaders in elementary/secondary education, calls this complex set of events "role prejudice." According to Marshall, "Perhaps the most far-reaching barrier is role prejudice. Role prejudice is a preconceived preference for a specific behavior on the part of the visibly identifiable group. Society views the superintendency as a predominately male job. Consequently, women are not supposed to seek the superintendency." (Marshall, 1986, p. 11). This statement applies readily to higher education and partially accounts for women's behavior in striving to attain leadership positions and society's struggle to accept them. Therefore, it is not surprising that persons seeking leaders often cling to old stereotypes of leaders, demanding that women behave just like their male counterparts rather than enhancing their roles with the new and varied talents and fresh perspectives they might bring.

Leadership Programs for Women in Higher Education

In the early 1970s, the first leadership development programs designed specifically for women were created to address the problem of insufficient numbers of women in senior leadership roles. These programs responded to different perceptions of the special needs of women leaders—the expansion in size of the pool, the identification of potential new leaders, and the development of specific administrative skills. Some have endured to the present, and others lasted only a few years. (For a discussion of some of these issues, see Touchton and Shavlik, 1978.) Among the most notable programs are those listed below.

Institute for Administrative Advancement. The Institute for Administrative Advancement (IAA) was established at the University of Michigan in 1973 to enlarge the pool of "qualified women leaders" by encouraging and training women for administration. Its primary goal was to provide women with specific knowledge in the areas of budgeting, legal issues, funding, leadership styles, and institutional planning, information that was considered essential to their effectiveness as administrators in colleges and universities. IAA, which evolved into a coeducational program, conducted its last institute near the end of the decade.

HERS. The Higher Education Resource Service (HERS) was initiated by a group of high-level administrative women in New England who came together to share ideas, concerns, perceptions, and problems. They formed a group called New England Concerns. Eventually they, too, became interested in training as a method of access and created HERS-New England and a number of training programs to encourage and promote women leaders. Over the years the HERS network has grown to encompass HERS-MidAtlantic (now HERS-MidAmerica), which founded and runs the only comprehensive management training institute for women administrators in the country, and HERS-West. The Summer Institute for Women in Higher Education Administration, jointly sponsored by HERS-MidAmerica and Bryn Mawr College, has been operating since 1976. HERS-West developed a program for women in higher education in the western states focusing on institutional change and networking among women. HERS-New England currently operates an administrative skills training program.

Leaders for the '80s Project. In 1973 women in the American Association of Community and Junior Colleges established the American Association of Women in Community and Junior Colleges (AAWCJC). Subsequently leaders from AAWCJC and the League for Innovation in the Community Colleges created the Leaders for the '80's Project, now known as the National Institute for Leadership Development. This program has concentrated specifically on the advancement of women in the community colleges since 1981.

ACE's National Identification Program. Also in 1973, the American Council on Education created its Office of Women in Higher Education. Its mandate was to develop a program to increase the pool of women leaders throughout higher education. Thus, in 1977, the office established the National Identification Program for the Advancement of Women in Higher Education Administration (ACE/NIP), designed to build a series of interlocking networks of men and women leaders who were committed to women's leadership and who would participate in their identification, advancement, and support. Among the most visible and successful components of ACE/NIP are the ACE National Forums, small invitational meetings of "emerging and established leaders," which have been held since the inception of ACE/NIP. Over 700 senior women administrators have participated in the forums to date, along with over 150 presidents. Sixty of these women have subsequently moved into college and university presidencies. Many others have assumed positions of greater responsibility, becoming provosts, vice presidents, and deans.

The advancement of minority women was made a special focus of the ACE/NIP in 1980 to ensure that every effort was made to identify and promote minority women. This program was referred to as the Focus on Minority Women's Advancement (FMWA). Four of the sixty presidents emerging from the ACE National Forums are black women. Our work with the ACE/NIP and with hundreds of women and men administrators throughout the country have informed this chapter. (Taylor and Shavlik, 1977; Shavlik and Touchton, 1984).

All these programs share two underlying assumptions: that women's talent for leadership, as leadership is generally defined by the dominant male culture, must be recognized and encouraged; and that the unique insights and abilities of women that have not been considered valuable until recently—authenticity, caring, intuition, connectedness, and holistic thinking—must be celebrated.

Have these programs been a success? The difficulty of measuring outcomes of leadership development programs makes an unequivocal answer to this question difficult. There is little research on the effects of professional development programs, and, as Schuster and Perlman note in Chapters 11 and 12 of this volume, a direct relationship between program participation and career movement cannot be shown. Nonetheless, the perception of this relationship, as well as the data on career movement of program participants, suggests that these programs are effecting their desired outcomes. And there are some significant indicators that do point to success. The number of senior women administrators (presidents, vice presidents, and deans) has doubled over the last decade (Touchton and Shavlik, 1984). Twenty percent (N = 60) of current women presidents, numbering more than three hundred, have emerged from the ACE/NIP National Forums. There are many success stories among the more than eight hundred participants in the Bryn Mawr/HERS Summer Institute: many have been promoted, many have expanded the scope of their positions, and many have added significantly to their credentials following their involvement in the institute. Some of the Leaders of the '80s administrators have been promoted more than once, and almost all have advanced at least once since their participation in the first year of the program; and advancements for successive years are also dramatic. Every one of the programs mentioned has made special efforts to include minority women in each aspect of their programs. All of these programs work together to form an important set of networks that have encouraged and promoted women leaders, and will continue to do so.

The Inclusion of Women in Established Leadership Programs

ACE Fellows Program. The American Council on Education Fellows Program was established in 1964 to provide a means for identifying talented faculty and junior administrators and giving them an opportunity to be mentored by an experienced president or vice president for a year. This program has continued to serve as a major training ground for prospective college and university presidents over the years. This program primarily served men in its first decade, but in the mid-seventies women began to be included in significant numbers. Currently women Fellows constitute nearly half of each class and 29 percent of all Fellows. For the first time in its history, the 1986–1987 class was more than half women. With respect to advancement, women and men Fellows are attaining leadership positions roughly proportional to their participation in the program. Eleven percent of the women Fellows who participated in the first 18 classes have become CEOs, compared to 14 percent of the men; 13 percent of the women have become vice presidents, as have 20 percent of the men (Green and Chibucos, 1987).

I.E.M. The Institute for Educational Management, begun in 1970, is an intensive, comprehensive professional development program for senior-level administrators in colleges and universities. Its participants have included men and women since its inception, but the proportion of women has grown substantially over the years. Women comprised between 10 percent and 11 percent of the participants in the early 1970s, about 20 percent of all participants in the late 1970s, and in the last three years have constituted almost a third of all those attending the institute (McDade, 1986).

Most of the programs designed to provide skills and services for college and university administrators are now not only open to women but are also actively recruiting them. However, the curricula of these programs have changed little with respect to women's issues. While there is a beginning recognition that women's issues—such as the rising numbers of women in the work force, interpersonal dynamics between men and women in the workplace, work-home conflicts, equitable policies and practices in recruitment and selection, sex-role stereotyping in evaluation, promotion, and hiring—are very important to the environment and are concerns shared by many men, they have not become fully a part of these general leadership programs.

Perceptions and Realities of Leadership Development for Women

Initially, the special programs for women, as well as women's caucuses or small groups within established leadership programs, existed because of a commonly held belief that the way to promote women was to provide additional training opportunities for them. These training opportunities were designed to help them catch up with their male colleagues by substituting training for experiences they were not in positions to obtain. As these programs became more sophisticated planners realized that the same system that would hire men (primarily white) for their potential still would not necessarily hire women without track records, even with their newly acquired skills. This realization produced new activities to help women negotiate the system. These activities were designed to encourage women in the development of strategies to be included on important committees, learn their legal rights, gain experience in finance and administration, invent ways to help one another succeed, and create networks to promote and encourage women in administration.

Many of these special efforts adopted on behalf of women have improved the system for everyone. Searches are more open, salaries are less secretly determined and less discrepant, and people are beginning to recognize that changing student bodies demand diversity in leadership. Still, we have a long way to go before institutions show fundamental change in their encouragement, recognition, acceptance, and support of women. Women must still deal with the ways in which institutions discriminate against them both overtly and covertly. As long as this is true, women will have special needs and concerns. Perceptions about what women need will change only when institutional practices, not the women themselves, are viewed as the problem.

Judith Sturnick (1986, p. 22), president of the University of Maine at Farmington, speaks eloquently to this point. When talking about the ambiguity of functioning as women leaders in a male system, she said:

> [It] is a phantasm of cultural stereotypes, and multiple confusions about what is "appropriate" and what is "inappropriate" for a female in terms of the use of power, decision-making authority and permissible manifestations of our spiritual/physical/mental strengths. Our culture is a long way from having worked out these ambiguities; consequently, our lives are awash in these waves of confusion, identity crises and overt hostility from both men and women—forces which are intensified for the woman in a public, visible role.

Leadership Development: Women and Men

Women's needs are similar to men's in those areas generally regarded as "competency areas" for administrators and managers. Both must be able to work effectively with people, handle budgets and personnel, set policy and make decisions, know the significant issues, cultivate their ability to provide vision for their institutions, enhance their good personal characteristics and diminish their weaknesses, and develop their political acumen. They need to have training and advancement opportunities throughout their careers to prepare for new challenges and a changing world. They need to be viewed and respected as persons with varied strengths and weaknesses. And they deserve to be given opportunities commensurate with their talents and interest. Indeed, this entire book is devoted to leadership and its development, irrespective of sex.

Leadership Development: Focus on Women

Women do have some special needs, relating principally to the ways in which they are viewed and treated as members of a class, rather than as separate persons judged on their individual merits. These judgments often affect how women feel about their competencies. However, a warning is in order here about the dangers of overgeneralization. Just as women bring diversity into the workplace, so are women diverse among themselves. Nevertheless, women do share many views and experiences and some generalizations are warranted. It is also increasingly clear that men, too, experience many of the same problems as women. They are human problems, not unique to women, but experienced with more intensity by them because of the pervasive sexism in our society. When institutions are able to involve women as fully as men on the basis of individual merit, they will be more humane places for everyone. Until then, the ideas and concerns such as those below warrant our attention. An appreciation of these concepts is key to developing women's leadership abilities and potential.

Women have special strengths. Women will find it helpful to recognize in themselves their "traditional" abilities and talents, which recently have been rediscovered and celebrated as the "new directions or discoveries" of management gurus. The concepts of quality circles (work groups that promote effectiveness through interaction and cooperation), attention to each person's unique contribution to the whole, recognition of diversity as a way to increase productivity, intuition as a trusted tool for leaders/managers, and caring and nurturance as essential characteristics of successful leaders have recently received a great deal of attention in the management literature (see Cleveland, 1985, Drucker, 1981, Gardner, 1986, Kanter, 1977, 1985, Naisbitt, 1982, and Peters and Waterman, 1982).

Several examples from this literature illustrate the point. Naisbitt in *Megatrends* (1982) talks of the powerful aspects of networking in "smashing the pyramid" (in other words, dismantling the hierarchy) when he refers to the necessity of coping with such hierarchies if we are to deliver on the complex needs of today's society. Drucker (1981), when explaining the success of the Japanese, cites the use of what have been viewed as "female-oriented strategies"—for example, cultivation of relationships to establish common interest, loyalty, trust, and pride in the accomplishment of the whole. In describing excellent companies, Peters and Waterman (1982) say that they "seem to take all sorts of special trouble to foster, nourish, and care for what we call 'product champions' " (pp. xvii–xviii). Gardner (1986) notes that "young potential leaders who have been schooled to believe that all elements of a problem are rational and technical, reducible to words and numbers, and solvable by computers, are ill-equipped to move into an area where intuition and empathy are powerful aids to problem solving" (p. 13). Cleveland (1985) sums up the argument very well: "It is not accident or coincidence that women are breaking into the executive market just when the key to success in executive work is working-with-other-people skills" (p. 80). Clearly, emerging themes and buzz-words—fostering, nourishing, caring, relationships, intuition, and empathy—are very much at home in female value systems. All these strengths and skills make a powerful case for women to claim them as their own, enhance them in themselves, and impart them to their male colleagues. The kind of caring described so eloquently by Carol Gilligan in *A Different Voice* (1982) must be allowed to flourish in women leaders and to be unmasked in male leaders.

If women had not been so busy trying to emulate their male colleagues, would they not have contributed these ideas coming out of their own experiences in the workplace and at home? Kantor, recognized for her contributions to management literature and theory, has made contributions of this very kind; she has been able to identify and articulate many of these ideas and use them to inform her study of corporations. Most women, however, have been concerned with trying to change themselves rather than their places of work. Fortunately, that has begun to change over the last few years. Selected headlines from two articles in the November 1986 issue of *Working Woman* magazine (Hellwig, pp. 130,138,146; Friedan, p. 153) illustrate the point:

> Most career women with children keep working. Their new needs create whole new businesses.
>
> Nine out of ten Americans agree that it's important for dads to spend as much time with the kids as moms do.
>
> Women's decisions are influencing marketing as both buyers and sellers.
>
> Career, marriage, and children: Today women feel entitled to the same complex lives as men.

Sex discrimination is a reality. Women and men need to realize that sex discrimination in higher education is a reality, that it is pervasive, and that it exists in some form in all institutions. Sexism may be overt or covert, blatant or subtle, or all of these. But it is essential to recognize that it exists, and not minimize it as some people are prone to do. (For a discussion of sex discrimination on campus, see Sandler and Hall, 1986). Women today should be especially attuned to two important factors. First, while everything that happens to them is not gender-related, much that happens to them *is,* and in most situations both factors are operating. Second, women need to be alert to all possibilities, need to try to recognize what factors are operating and why, and need to be able to handle situations in all their complexity.

There are a number of ways in which sex discrimination is experienced. Some forms of discrimination are quite direct and easy to identify, particularly if the analysis is quantifiable (for example, salary inequity). Other forms are considerably less direct and may not even be recognized as discrimination. Women must understand and cope with the fact that some people will treat them not as individuals but as members of a class. For example, given the stereotypes that "women are not good in math" and "can't handle budgets," a particular woman's competencies in financial management may be doubted without even checking into her experience and reputation in her current or previous jobs. Another example involves the assumption, also a stereotype, that "women are not willing to move." In reality, geographical mobility is a matter of concern to men as well as women today, given the increasing number of dual-career families. It is a complex issue about which assumptions simply can no longer be made.

It is frequently hard for women to earn the recognition and distinction they deserve. For women and for minorities, there is a paradox operating: if they do well, they are regarded as exceptional, that is, nonrepresentative of their class; but if they fail, they are often regarded as representative of their class. Hence one is much more likely to hear "I hired a woman once, and it was a mistake—next time I'll get a man for the job" than "I hired a man once and he really did not work out well—next time I'll hire a woman."

Once women perceive sex discrimination, they may need to develop a support network to check out their perceptions. If they believe they have been discriminated against, they need to be the ones to address it either personally or by seeking changes in the institutional environment. If they do not act, it is unlikely that anyone else will.

Understanding how the system operates is necessary but not sufficient. Women must learn how to do more than work with men—they need to learn how to help their male colleagues adapt to having women as colleagues. Generally, men see the need for women to change rather than for themselves or the environment to change. Leadership development programs of the future must involve women and men together, exploring and perceiving areas of similarity and difference among them, appreciating and respecting differences as well as what they share.

Informal networks are very useful. On the face of it, both women and men must work within existing informal networks. The difference is that women still are excluded from many of these networks and outnumbered in many others. This has changed to some extent over the years, but not dramatically. One has only to look at the membership and the leadership of various organizations and associations to assess women's access, or lack thereof, to the power structure. Only 10 percent of higher education institutions are headed by women, only two or three of the higher education associations have women chief executive officers, few disciplinary associations or refereed journals have women heads, and only a few of the many outstanding women college presidents were named by their colleagues as "effective presidents" in a recent study on the college presidency (McMillen, 1986). Finally, and significantly, none of the studies on higher education of the past couple of years was written by a woman.

There are multiple approaches to being effective in the system. Women need to know how to be effective in "the system" and to recognize that there is no single way that works. There are enough women at senior levels now that a number of distinct types and attitudes are discernable. Some women are eager to blend in, to become part of the established order. Some believe it is important to understand the current structures as they operate, to master them, and then perhaps try to change them. Others wish to make their own mark but operate from a premise that institutional change is necessary to make that happen. Still others feel that it is their obligation to insure the recognition and advancement of women, and these consider their leadership role a forum for that purpose. And still others see the need to transform institutions and society in some major ways, recognizing women's contributions, values, and perspectives and seeking ways to instill them.

These "types" of women administrators are neither unique nor mutually exclusive, and there may well be others. What they all have in common, both with each other and with male leaders, is that they want to be influential. What they have in common with other women is that they feel marginal in some way, although their marginality varies considerably in degree. What is important for women is that they recognize their own styles, trust what they do, recognize that other effective ways exist, and give other women room to develop or exercise their own styles. There are many ways to be influential, and women need to respect the diversity among themselves as well as the diversity among male administrators.

Women have special needs with respect to family roles. Women must feel empowered to respect the needs they have that are associated with their family roles, such as dual career challenges, child care, and lack of a support system at home. The workplace as we know it was built on other assumptions, principally that men who could concentrate largely, if not solely, on the job would predominate. Although workers have changed dramatically in the last several decades, the workplace has not. Women need to put less energy into changing themselves and more into making institutions more hospitable to women and facilitative of their lives, whatever their family pattern or constellation. Women should not be apologetic or defensive because their multiple roles prevent them from being totally job-oriented. Men, too, need to be aware of the whole of their lives and of ways in which the institutional environment can support them in their family as well as institutional responsibilities. As men and women share domestic responsibilities more equitably, institutions will find ways to facilitate the new arrangements. Increasing everyone's conscious awareness of both the need to change and the ability to change will hasten the process.

Institutional and Individual Responsibilities for Developing Women Leaders

Until now this chapter has suggested how women can be successful in institutions as currently structured or slightly adapted to their needs. This last section calls for more fundamental change and presents recommendations to effect change.

Institutions must recognize that accommodating women is worth the price; higher education requires the kind of creativity and diversity that women can bring. What, then, are some of the responsibilities that institutions bear for the development of women leaders?

Respect diversity. All of us need to learn to respect diversity, not an easy task. The momentum to perpetuate the prevailing norms is very strong in most institutional settings, so developing a new mind set to appreciate what diversity means takes commitment and perseverance. The struggle to comprehend diversity is in the best tradition of the liberal arts and the scientific method of inquiry, combining what we know from past experience and tradition with a quest to understand what we do not know or understand. To appreciate diversity is to know its richness and to realize that it does not mean second class, decrease in excellence, or change for the sake of change. Diversity holds the potential for discovery, innovation, and enlightenment. Just as every major shift in values has wrought dramatic change, so, too, would the true celebration of diversity bring new vigor to our institutions.

In a speech given before the American Council on Education's 1986 Annual Meeting, Elizabeth Minnich gives prophetic voice to the idea of a learning environment that celebrates diversity:

> Imagine a culture, predicated on equality, in which no kinds of people, no kinds of art, no kinds of public participation, no kinds of music, no kinds of religion are judged *a priori* insignificant, of poor quality, uninteresting. Imagine, finally, a citizenry educated to think and make judgements about what is significant, interesting, good and useful that do not replicate the old false judgements made and built into our very modes of thinking when only the few were considered really human, let alone important.

Make leadership development a priority. Institutions must make a commitment to identify, encourage, and develop women and men, minority and majority, who have the potential for making a difference, in order to invest in all human resources. This suggestion sounds so simple that one might miss its vital significance and fail to create a plan for implementation. Despite extensive discussion on the topic of leadership in recent years, not much has changed. The Commission on Strengthening Presidential Leadership (1984) discusses the importance to higher education of cultivating its own leaders. Now, more than ever, the commission says, these leaders must be sensitive to the feelings, thoughts, and cultures of new and continually emerging constituencies. Planning for the development of talent at every level of the institution should be a major priority.

Make a commitment to women's leadership. Institutional leaders must make a commitment to the specific identification, encouragement, and development of women leaders as well as male leaders. Existing programs to identify and develop new leaders (notably the ACE Fellows Program and ACE/NIP) have shown that there are talented women ready and able to become major forces in higher education. What is needed is a commitment to them and the assurance that institutions are ready to consider and hire them.

Review existing policies. Institutional policies, procedures, and programs should be examined for unintended detrimental effects on women's advancement. The call for this review has been issued in many different forms over the last decade. Articles have been written calling for the study of specific issues such as salary equity. Many self-study guides have been prepared to give institutions some guidance both on the issues and the process. Institutions have established commissions or committees to identify and deal with the overall problems or targeted concerns. And, as a result, much has been accomplished for women at all levels on campus. Still, many institutions are plagued with continuing problems affecting the equitable participation of women in the institution: tenure and promotion policies that disadvantage women, reliance on informal networks to impart important information needed to succeed at the institution, absence of a sexual harassment policy, poor search and selection procedures resulting in the attraction of fewer women to the institution, rules that block women's progress (for example, restrictions on who can be a principal investigator on grant applications), lack of in-service training programs, and lack of attention to the campus climate for women. Resource materials are available to institutions that have a commitment to building a program fully responsive to the needs and talents of women. Some are listed at the end of the article. (See Pearson, Shavlik, and Touchton, forthcoming; Sandler and Hall, 1986; Bogart, 1981; and Tinsley, Secor, and Kaplan, 1984.) The important points here are making the effort and assigning sufficient campus resources to accomplish the tasks.

Relate leadership and "campus climate" to scholarship and curriculum. Institutions need to think about the ways in which scholarship and curriculum affect how women are viewed and view themselves as leaders. The new scholarship on women presents strong and compelling evidence that women's self-image and the ways in which women are perceived by men are greatly enhanced by a greater knowledge of the capabilities and qualities of women. Such knowledge cannot help but create a more favorable climate for women leaders on the campus and give vision to what the institution could be like if freed from the negative stereotypes of women. (See Pearson, Shavlik, and Touchton, forthcoming.)

Prepare an annual status report. Institutions should prepare an annual status report on women that would include efforts made to attract and support women leaders. This report should be comprehensive and include issues of importance to all women on campus—data on women administrators, faculty, students, and support staff. Minimally, this report should cover recruiting at all levels, salaries reported by position and compared with men, promotion and tenure decisions by gender (and race, ethnicity, age, and handicap), impact studies of new policies on women, continuing problem areas (for example, salaries), and numbers at every level. There are many models for such reporting (see Bogart, 1981; Sandler and Hall, 1986). Time and effort are required to develop such a report, so sufficient resources should be allocated to insure its quality and accuracy. The report should be presented to the entire community, and every group from trustees through students should have an opportunity to participate in an open discussion about the issues raised and to develop action plans for eliminating problems.

Construct more creative curricula for leadership development. A major contribution of women's studies and other special studies has been to promote new and different thinking about previously held beliefs, values, and knowledge. Because leaders need the benefit of new thinking to help them solve the many problems faced by higher education, we challenge all the leadership development programs to build a new curriculum. This curriculum would be predicated on the principles articulated in this chapter—learning to appreciate diversity, understanding that we do, but need not, live in a racist and sexist society, recognizing the potential social value of listening to "the marginal voice," and learning to recognize when the structures of the organization are likely to judge people on the basis of their class rather than their individual talents and thereby impede their progress.

Support women's involvement in women's networks. Women executives need to be in groups together where they can discuss common issues and concerns. These networks help women assess their performance accurately and judge whether their concerns are related to gender or to the normal conduct of the job. Of course, women also need the opportunity to be with male colleagues and talk about these same issues, but since the professional culture is so powerfully male, it is only possible for them to sift and sort what is happening to them by having female colleagues with whom to share perceptions and garner support.

Be creative and imaginative in seeking positive social change. A final challenge of this chapter is for institutions and individuals to invent additional recommendations to contribute to the process of developing and managing change. As a stimulus to beginning that process we offer two additional problems to think about. It often seems that the more one thinks about promoting social change, the more likely it is to occur. One problem area warranting attention, for example, is the socialization process of graduate training and the complex ways in which it perpetuates traditional values and behavior that often result in differential treatment and expectations of men and women. Another area, recently explored in a research study conducted at the Center for Creative Leadership concerns the "narrow band of appropriate behavior" allowed for women executives compared to the wider band accorded their male colleagues. (See Morrison, White, and Van Belsor, 1987.) What are the related issues in each area? What are the implications for women's and men's development? Are changes needed? What goals are suggested? How can these goals be addressed?

These recommendations and the creative process of developing additional ones, if taken seriously, should not only pave the way for greater participation of women leaders, but also improve institutional quality for students, faculty, administrators, and staff. More effective, efficient, intellectually alive communities can result from creating an atmosphere where women as well as men can help to determine the futures of our institutions.

None of the changes discussed in this article will result in the full recognition of women for their leadership potential unless we are willing to continue to question all values, all beliefs, all assumptions, and all actions that have led us to create societal structures disallowing women their full place in society. There are many different visions that can take us to the future—we can be dragged kicking and screaming into a changed world; we can tinker with some of the structures, policies, and values that prevent people from having an opportunity to be all that they can be; or we can learn to consider new values, new ideas, new structures, and new pathways in our quest to live in our pluralistic society. Some have the potential for great enlightenment, some the power of destruction. Clearly, our survival well may depend upon our ability to develop the fullness of the human spirit, male and female, whether we are talking about the leadership of higher education or of the world.

REFERENCES

BOGART, KAREN L. *The Institutional Self-Study Guide.* Washington, D.C.: American Institutes for Research, 1981. Distributor: Project on the Status and Education of Women, 1818 R Street, N.W., Washington, D.C. 20036.

CLEVELAND, HARLAN. *The Knowledge Executive: Leadership in an Information Society.* New York: E.P. Dutton, 1985.

COMMISSION ON STRENGTHENING PRESIDENTIAL LEADERSHIP, CLARK KERR, DIR. *Presidents Make a Difference: Strengthening Leadership in Colleges and Universities.* Washington, D.C.: Association of Governing Boards of Universities and Colleges, 1984.

DRUCKER, PETER F. *Toward the Next Economics and Other Essays.* New York: Harper and Row, 1981.

FRIEDAN, BETTY. "Where Do We Go From Here? The Next Step for Today's Working Women—and Men." *Working Woman,* November, 1986.

GARDNER, JOHN W. *Leadership Papers,* 1–6, 1986 and 1987. A special series of papers on leadership prepared for and available from Independent Sector, 1828 L Street, N.W., Washington, D.C., 20036.

GILLIGAN, CAROL. *In a Different Voice: Psychological Theory and Women's Development.* Cambridge: Harvard University Press, 1982.

GREEN, MADELEINE, and CHIBUCOS, THOMAS. *The ACE Fellows Program: An Assessment of the First Eighteen Years.* Washington, D.C.: American Council on Education, 1987.

HELLWIG, BASIA. "How Working Women Have Changed America." *Working Woman,* November, 1986.

KANTER, ROSABETH MOSS. *Men and Women of the Corporation.* New York: Basic Books, 1977.

KANTER, ROSABETH MOSS. *The Change Masters: Innovation and Entrepreneurship in the American Corporation.* New York: Simon and Schuster, 1985.

MANDEL, RUTH. Report of data from the National Information Bank on Women in Public Office, a project of the Center for the American Woman in Politics at Rutgers University (Ruth Mandel, dir.), 1986.

MARSHALL, STEPHANIE A. "Women Reach for the Top Spot." *The School Administrator,* November, 1986, pp. 10–13.

MCDADE, SHARON (director, Institute for Educational Management, Harvard University). Personal conversation, December 5, 1986.

MCMILLEN, LIZ. "Most Effective College Presidents Are 'Risk Takers' Who Rely on Respect, Not Popularity, Study Finds." *The Chronicle of Higher Education,* November 5, 1986, pp. 12–13.

MINNICH, ELIZABETH M. "Higher Education in a Radically New World." Speech given at the ACE Annual Meeting in San Francisco, October 6, 1986, unpublished.

MORRISON, ANN M.; WHITE, RANDALL P.; and VAN BELSOR, ELLEN. *Breaking the Glass Ceiling: Can Women Make It to the Top of America's Largest Corporations?* Boston: Addison-Wesley, (in press).

NAISBITT, JOHN. *Megatrends: Ten New Directions Transforming Our Lives.* New York: Warner Books, 1982.

PEARSON, CAROL S.; SHAVLIK, DONNA L.; and TOUCHTON, JUDITH G., EDS. *Educating the Majority: Women Challenge Tradition in Higher Education.* New York: Macmillan, forthcoming.

PETERS, THOMAS J., and WATERMAN, ROBERT H., JR. *In Search of Excellence: Lessons from America's Best-Run Companies.* New York: Harper and Row, 1982.

SANDLER, BERNICE R., and HALL, ROBERTA M. *The Campus Climate Revisited: Chilly for Women Faculty, Administrators, and Graduate Students.*

Washington D.C.: Association of American Colleges, Project on the Status and Education of Women, 1986.

SHAVLIK, DONNA, and TOUCHTON, JUDY. "Toward a New Era of Leadership: The National Identification Program." In Adrian Tinsley, Cynthia Secor, and Sheila Kaplan, eds., *Women in Higher Education Administration.* New Directions for Higher Education Series. San Francisco: Jossey-Bass, 1984.

STURNICK, JUDITH (PRESIDENT, UNIVERSITY OF MAINE AT FARMINGTON). Speech given to a Vermont ACE/NIP Conference at Stowe, Vermont, October 31, 1986.

TAYLOR, EMILY, and SHAVLIK, DONNA. "To Advance Women: A National Identification Program." *Educational Record, 58,* no. 1 (1977).

TINSLEY, ADRIAN; SECOR, CYNTHIA; and KAPLAN, SHEILA, EDS. *Women in Higher Education Administration.* New Directions for Higher Education Series. San Francisco: Jossey-Bass, 1984.

TOUCHTON, JUDITH, and SHAVLIK, DONNA. "Challenging the Assumptions of Leadership: Women and Men of the Academy." In Fisher, Charles, ed. *Developing and Evaluating Administrative Leadership. New Directions for Higher Education, 22*. San Francisco: Jossey Bass, 1978.

TOUCHTON, JUDY, and SHAVLIK, DONNA. "Senior Women Administrators in Higher Education: A Decade of Change, 1975–1983." Preliminary Report, November, 1984. Office of Women in Higher Education, American Council on Education, One Dupont Circle, Washington, D.C. 20036.

7

Strategies for Developing Minority Leadership

REGINALD WILSON
SARAH E. MELENDEZ

Developing leaders for a new era will require addressing the issue of the dramatic growth in the numbers and percentage of the country's population that is nonwhite. Indeed, the composition of college campuses has also changed significantly. Minorities accounted for 17 percent of enrollments in 1984, and approximately 10 percent of both faculty and administration in 1983. Nevertheless, the rate of increase in minority participation has slowed in recent years for Hispanics and American Indians, and blacks have suffered declines in enrollments, stagnation in doctorates earned, and serious declines in faculty participation. This situation represents a serious setback since, except for Asians, minority groups have not yet achieved parity in higher education participation.

The demographic realities must be reckoned with. With the decline in the eighteen-to-twenty-four-year-old white student cohort, the rapidly growing numbers of minorities in that age group will increasingly become the "typical" student as we approach the year 2000 (Hodgkinson, 1985). In order to maintain institutional size and job security, majority educators will find it in their self-interest

Reginald Wilson is director of the Office of Minority Concerns at the American Council on Education; Sarah Melendez is associate director.

to encourage and develop measures to assure the access, retention, and success of minority students.

If higher education is to reflect the diversity of the current and future student body in its leaders, it will require commitment of the higher education community to the development of minority leadership. The success of such efforts will be inextricably tied to the overall situation of minorities in higher education and the very real crisis we now face of participation of minorities at all levels. The current crisis can only be understood in its historical context, for the history of minorities in majority institutions is quite different from that of both majority men and women. Development of leadership among minorities is likely to proceed ineffectively, as is true of most present efforts, if both the current crisis and its historical antecedents are not properly understood.

The Current Status of Minorities on Campus

The dearth of black leadership in higher education is painfully clear from the numbers: white males hold approximately 70 percent of collegiate faculty and administrative positions. This is not accidental or the consequence of talent rising to the top. Women and minorities have been systematically excluded from participation in mainstream higher education since colonial times—minorities even more drastically than white women. For example, as recently as 1941 there were only two black professors in mainstream universities (Belles, 1969).

Most college presidents and the overwhelming majority of academic leaders are drawn from the faculty. Faculty, in turn, are educated and identified as graduate students. That is the traditional pipeline and will undoubtedly remain so. Quite simply, the crisis of minority leadership in higher education is the drying up of the pipeline, beginning with the supply of undergraduates. Black participation in undergraduate education, as a proportion of high school graduates, declined from 1976 to 1982 by 11 percent. Hispanic participation during the same period declined by 16 percent (Lee, 1985). Only Asian participation increased and native Americans have reached a plateau. Since blacks and Hispanics make up over 85 percent of all minorities and have the highest birthrates of all ethnic groups their decline in participation has a devastating impact not only on them but on the American economy and on American education as well.

Two events following World War II dramatically increased minority access to mainstream higher education. The first "revolution" was the G.I. Bill, which provided free college education for returning military veterans. One of its important goals was the reduction of the number of veterans immediately demanding jobs and disrupting the workforce and the economy. Despite its utilitarian purpose, the first G.I. Bill was a true revolution in education. For the first time hundreds of thousands of persons gained access to higher education, regardless of their ability to pay or previous high educational attainment. Minorities were highly represented among veterans taking advantage of these new opportunities. Subsequent G.I. Bills during the Korean and Vietnam wars swelled the numbers of minorities, many of them first-generation college attendees, in mainstream colleges and universities. This new crop of minority college graduates formed the pool from which future faculty members and administrators were drawn and who were to make significant inroads in predominantly white institutions.

The second "revolution" in minority access was the civil rights movement of the 1960s. Lyndon Baines Johnson's statement at Howard University in 1964, "We shall overcome," electrified the nation and began a series of initiatives—such as the 1964 Civil Rights Act—that dramatically accelerated the minority presence in higher education. The other part of that revolution began with the 1954 *Brown v. Board of Education* Supreme Court decision declaring segregated public schools to be "inherently unequal." It was inevitable that by 1972 Federal Judge John H. Pratt, in the *Adams* case, would similarly order the dismantling of segregated systems of public higher education, ultimately affecting nineteen states (Haynes, 1978). Subsequently, the establishment of TRIO programs, Pell grants, Guaranteed Student Loans, and College Work Study enabled the next generation of minorities, based primarily on need, to attend college and, in many instances, go on to graduate school and prepare for faculty positions (Adolphus, 1984).

Before World War II, women were substantially in women's colleges, the few Hispanics were in institutions in the West and Southwest (mostly Catholic), and blacks were restricted overwhelmingly to the historically black colleges. These restrictions were accomplished by both *de facto* discrimination in the North and, especially for blacks, by *de jure* segregation in the South. Even when blacks were permitted to attain graduate degrees in northern universities, it was expected, and insisted upon in most cases, that they would return to teach in the black colleges in the South.

In spite of these restrictions, minorities have produced a number of outstanding educational leaders such as the late Benjamin E. Mays, once president of Morehouse College, and the late Tomas Rivera, former Chancellor of the University of California at Riverside. These leaders emerged from predominantly minority circumstances to become not only role models on their campuses but leaders of national stature in the majority community as well. These leaders enriched the academy by their very presence—demonstrating the cultural diversity, the multiple styles, and the plurality of intellectual discourse that can characterize higher education at its best. While those characteristics enhanced the success of these leaders in substantially minority settings, they often posed barriers to the development and mobility of minority leaders in predominantly white universities that persist to the present.

Today, minorities constitute approximately 10 percent of administrators and 7 percent of faculty members. Since these numbers also include the faculty and administrators at historically black colleges, their real representation is even more modest. While Asians are more highly represented as faculty members than in the general population, they are still underrepresented as administrators (Wilson and Melendez, 1984). The number of black faculty increased up to 1976 and has declined since then. Hispanic faculty numbers plateaued during the same period. In 1979 blacks comprised 7.4 percent of administrators but in 1981 only 6.8 percent. Hispanics again plateaued during the same period at 1.4 percent and 1.7 percent respectively.

Numbers tell only part of the tale; it is important to understand where this small population of minorities actually is. Given the systematic exclusion of minorities from majority institutions, it is not surprising that a substantial number of minority faculty are found in ethnic studies, remedial and compensatory programs, and bilingual education, or as counselors and affirmative action officers. Similarly, many minority administrators head TRIO programs, Equal Opportunity programs, or other minority programs dependent on "soft money." The positions commonly held by minorities rarely lead to mainstream leadership positions. Therefore, most minorities on campuses are extremely vulnerable to cutbacks due to tight money or to conservative political swings away from commitment to equity and justice issues, cutbacks that are currently being experienced. Further, many minority administrators are trapped in dead-end positions with little hope of attaining real influence through a leadership position.

Another important feature of minority participation in post-secondary education is its concentration in community colleges. The explosion of access still did not permit widespread participation of minorities in four-year colleges and universities. When they were represented as faculty or administrators in these institutions, it was largely as administrators of minority programs, shepherding the flow of federal dollars.

Obstacles to Minority Advancement on Majority Campuses

What, then, are the causes of higher education's historic and continuing inability to incorporate minorities into the mainstream of its campuses? Ironically, university faculties are to some extent more liberal than the general population. For example, Oberlin College opened its doors to blacks before the Civil War. And many white faculty and students were active participants in the civil rights movement of the 1960s in the South. But these liberal political positions were not necessarily any threat to the status quo on campus or to the self-interest of individual activists. Their own positions and the racial composition of their own institutions were largely untouched. Undoubtedly, the perception by majority (that is, nonminority) persons in mainstream institutions that minority participation as faculty and administrators is a threat to job preservation is a tremendous obstacle. A second obstacle is the resistance of majority persons to confronting cultural differences and the efforts required to overcome their systematically exclusionist practices of the past. When pressed by the federal government and the courts to increase diversity, white institutions were more comfortable with increasing opportunities for white women who were perceived as being more compatible with the norms and values of the academy. As a further irony, the initial civil rights laws, promulgated originally to assist minorities, ended by benefiting majority women more than the minorities who were the initial target group.

Perceived threat and intolerance of diversity by majority leaders have spawned an array of problems that now seriously hinder the advancement of minorities on campus.

Faculty Shortages

Faculty, like other organisms, reproduce themselves to insure continuity. They accomplish this by seeking out and nurturing graduate students who are usually most like themselves. A survey by Nettles (1985) of faculty at majority institutions revealed that they did not advise or spend as much time with their minority students as with their majority students. Without significant numbers of minority faculty in mainstream disciplines, minority graduate students are deprived of role models and mentors who can groom them for future leadership positions. Since many minorities in faculty positions are in peripheral disciplines or programs, few are regularly able to identify promising minority scholars, get them into Ph.D. programs, and chair their dissertation committees. Majorities must consequently, in their own self-interest, become more involved both in increasing minority faculty and in nurturing potential minority scholars.

Cultural Barriers

Cronin (1984) lists among desirable leadership qualities self-confidence, energy and tenacity, risk-taking, and a sense of humor. These same attributes exhibited in minorities are often misread as arrogance, aggressiveness, non-conformism and lack of seriousness. Cronin further states that "the leader is very much a product of the group, and very much shaped by its aspirations, values and human resources." Barriers to developing minority leaders in majority institutions often include negative interpretations of the same behavior in minorities that is encouraged in majorities. Barriers are also sometimes created by different values about fundamental matters. For example, surveys regularly document widely divergent perceptions between majorities and minorities on the degree of racism in American life or the oppressive nature of the political establishment (Campbell, 1971). Although DeVries (Business-Higher Education Forum, 1986) optimistically opines that "leadership positions are being filled more and more by people who resemble less and less those they've succeeded," nevertheless, cultural and value differences still represent substantial barriers to both the development and the empowerment of minority leaders (Gardner, 1986).

Minority Scholarship

Most minorities still obtain their doctorates in education and the social and behavioral sciences—fields that are most sensitive to individual and philosophical differences in assessing scholarly research. Often scholarship in minority subjects or from a minority perspective is viewed as less than first-rate work (Melendez and Petrovich, 1986), while more traditional, though much more exotic areas, are viewed favorably. The tendency to devalue minority-focused scholarship, then, can become an impediment to objective evaluation for tenure and promotion decisions. Even in the biological sciences, exploring such topics as sickle-cell anemia (a predominantly minority disability) can be viewed as "exotic" work that is not in the mainstream of scientific endeavor (Keohane, 1986).

The "Old Boy Network"

The recommendation of candidates for faculty and administrative positions is usually enhanced by references and nominations from people in the field that one knows and respects. Minorities whose undergraduate work was in historically black colleges or whose research has been published in minority journals (even though refereed) are often given lower ratings in the selection and promotion process. Minorities generally know who the recognized white experts are in their field as well as who are the minority experts. Much less often do white scholars know the competent minority scholars, even when they are widely published and active in professional associations. References not emanating from the majority "old boy network" are often handicaps or, at best, unimpressive in making minority hiring decisions or giving consideration for upward mobility.

Strategies for Mainstreaming Minorities

If higher education is serious about the desirability of diversity in the country's campuses, it must make a commitment to mainstreaming minorities so that they will be able to move up into positions of leadership. Since leaders in higher education traditionally come out of faculty ranks, the development of minority leadership must begin with efforts to increase participation at all points in the pipeline, from undergraduates to faculty and administration. It is especially important for current leaders to watch for demonstrations of leadership abilities in their faculty and junior administrators and provide them with the necessary support, mentoring, and opportunities to learn the skills they need to assume higher positions and exercise greater leadership.

In order to develop minority leaders, current majority leaders need to look beyond their traditional networks, understand that management and leadership skills are transferable from minority projects to mainstream duties, and that the academy can benefit from diversity in its leadership. Such diversity in leadership can enable leaders to understand the existence and benefit of multiple world visions and different conceptual and analytical frameworks. For higher education to prepare its students for an interdependent world, where peoples with those different perspectives will insist on greater equality and partnership in the decisions that affect their well-being, it must demonstrate that diversity itself. And to achieve that diversity, colleges and universities will have to develop strategies to deal with the current and next generation of minority leaders.

The Present Generation

Developing the present generation of minority educators for leadership requires increasing the number of minorities with terminal degrees in a variety of fields as well as drawing more heavily on the existing pool of appropriately credentialed minorities for leadership positions. Many believe that the pool of doctorate-holding minorities has been exhausted, and we often hear, "I would love to hire a minority person, but I can't find one with the appropriate credentials." The statistics on faculty, tenure status, and administration until 1979 (the last year for which the U.S. Equal Employment Opportunity Commission has issued complete data) did not bear out the contention that the pool of qualified minorities had been exhausted. The 1981 statistics for new hires demonstrate clearly that the pool of minority doctorate holders has not been any more exhausted than the white pool (see Table 7.1). Whites continue to be hired at a rate disproportionately higher than their share of doctorates in tenured, tenure-track, executive, administrative, and managerial positions. This should dispel the myth that qualified white candidates are losing opportunities to less-qualified

TABLE 7.1. ***Percentage of doctorates and of tenured, tenure-track, and administrative positions by ethnicity for new hires, 1981.***

	Doctorates	Tenured	Tenure-Track	Executive Administrative Managerial
White	78.9	88.8	87.3	87.5
Black	3.9	4.9	5.4	8.5
Hispanic	1.4	2.1	1.6	2.1
American Indian	0.4	0.2	1.2	0.4
Asian/Pacific	2.7	4.0	4.5	1.4

Source: Equal Opportunity Commission, "EEO-6 Higher Education Staff" surveys, 1981 (unpublished tabulations).

minority candidates. As Table 7.1 illustrates, while whites held 78.9 percent of the doctorates among newly hired college personnel in 1981, they occupied 88.8% of the tenured faculty positions, 87.3% of the tenure-track positions, and 87.5% of the administrative positions. While minorities were also hired in these positions at a level beyond their representation in the doctorate pool, they were not as overrepresented as whites.

The figures indicate that blacks are significantly better represented in administrative positions than in the faculty, but many of these positions, as has been noted earlier, are in staff and minority programs, such as EEOC, Upward Bound, and student services—positions that do not require a doctorate nor are likely to result in promotions to leadership positions. A breakdown of the types of positions in administration held by minorities will probably confirm that they continue to be seriously underrepresented relative to their share of doctoral degrees, even in new hires, in the traditional line positions requiring a doctoral degree and from which administrators are usually promoted to leadership opositions. Because many of the minority administrators hold positions that do not require the doctorate, the figures of utilization of minority doctorates in administrator positions (8.5% for blacks and 2.1 for Hispanics) are actually inflated by the inclusion of those positions in the numbers.

Even though the pool of minority doctorates has not been exhausted, the production of minority doctorate holders must be increased significantly, for the percentage of doctorates among minorities is still unacceptably low. Increasing minority doctorate holders will bring the pool closer to proportional participation and help dissipate the perceived obstacle of "not enough qualified minority candidates."

Faculty and administrators already pursuing doctoral degrees constitute a special target group for consideration in efforts to increase the pool of minority doctorate holders. It is commonly accepted that minority faculty and administrators have many more demands on their time than their white colleagues, which makes it more difficult for them to complete their dissertations. Minority faculty, in addition to teaching a full load, often find that they are called upon to be unofficial faculty advisors to minority student groups and counselors to minority students. Furthermore, when there are only a few minority faculty or administrators on a campus, they are often called upon to serve on every committee. Those working on soft money must spend a considerable amount of time on fund-raising and writing proposals, an activity that often is not rewarded by increased responsibility or visibility. To compound the problem, the minority community near the campus often expects them to be active in that community. In such cases, the dissertation is placed on the back burner.

Institutions can play an important role in assisting minority faculty and administrators to acquire the doctoral degree. A formal mentoring system can provide junior faculty and administrators with mentors to guide them as to which assignments to undertake and which to reject, and how to set priorities and achieve a balance between career needs and all the demands made on them. The perspective of someone who has experienced the same types of pressures and demands can be very useful. Departmental scheduling can take into account time spent on counseling and committee assignments and on proposal writing. Minority faculty and administrators should not be expected to undertake any more committee assignments than their white colleagues. Financial aid, of course, is an essential factor in completion of the terminal degree, since many doctoral students must have external support to supplement their own resources.

A program that can serve as a model in assisting faculty to complete their degrees is the National Consortium for Educational Access, a partnership between historically black colleges and universities (HBCUs) and majority doctorate-granting institutions. The consortium works to increase the number of minorities holding doctorates in the sciences and technology. This three-year pilot program began operating in 1985 with the following objectives: ten HBCU faculty members will complete course work in a scientific/technological discipline; ten graduate students will complete at least one year toward their doctorate; three professionals will complete research on a postdoctoral grant; and six joint research ventures between HBCUs and majority institutions will be completed.

The program will provide faculty research workshops, training on computer systems, faculty exchanges, and joint research projects. This innovative, collaborative approach between HBCUs and majority institutions promises benefits to both types of institutions. It bears watching for possible expansion and emulation.

Yet another obstacle for minorities seeking to move up in administration is their lack of teaching experience, a requirement for a position in academic administration. Even when their academic preparation qualifies them for teaching, they are frequently hired as full-time administrators and their schedules do not permit them to teach. In some institutions, administrators are permitted to teach but are not granted release time or extra compensation. Institutions can do a better job of enabling minorities to acquire teaching experience: appointments can be made with faculty rank, and flexible scheduling would allow them to teach at least part-time. The benefits accrue to both the minority faculty member and the institutions with few minority faculty.

Minorities are also excluded from significant administrative positions by virtue of their exclusion from the "old boy network," which appears to be alive and well. While many white women have been able to penetrate these ranks in recent years, minority professionals generally have not. When majority leaders are asked to recommend individuals for positions, they naturally look to those in their network. It is important for these leaders to expand their networks to include minority men and women and to recommend them for mainstream positions. Getting into the mainstream of campus life is an important first step. Leaders should assign minority faculty and administrators to mainstream projects whenever possible. This will permit high-level administrators to observe the skills and style of their minority subordinates in nonminority activities.

The traditional networks also play a role in identifying potential leaders for participation in several prestigious leadership programs, which have become a valuable additional credentialing experience. The ACE Fellows Program, discussed fully elsewhere, is one such example. Minority Fellows within this program have, in fact, advanced at a slightly greater rate to senior administrative positions than their white colleagues, except to the position of president.

As of 1987, one hundred ten ACE Fellows Program alumni have become college presidents, and many more have moved up to positions of deans and vice presidents. Talented and ambitious minority faculty and administrators are often not nominated to this program because they have not been noticed by their president or other high-level administrator. Approximately 19 percent of the 812 fellows who have gone through the program through the 1986 class were minorities. The last six classes of fellows (1981–1986) included 26 percent minorities.

The Harvard Institute for Educational Management (IEM) has averaged 21 percent minority participation in its classes since 1982. Financial aid, provided by foundation and corporate donations, is available based on need, with priority given to women, minorities, and presidents of small institutions. A new program for middle-level managers was begun by IEM in 1986, focusing on skills development. Eighteen percent of the first year's class were minorities. Since minorities are most underrepresented at the dean level and above, this program for middle-level managers is likely to provide more opportunities for minorities as the program's existence becomes more widely known.

Both the ACE Fellows Program and IEM program often are hard-pressed to enroll Hispanics and American Indians. Exclusion from the traditional institutional networks that lead to being identified and supported for such programs is a continuing obstacle to minority advancement that can be overcome only by assiduous efforts of majority leaders to incorporate minorities.

Another different leadership development effort, targeted specifically at Hispanics, is the now defunct Hispanic Leadership Fellows Program, developed by the New Jersey Department of Higher Education and cosponsored by the American Council on Education and the Woodrow Wilson Foundation. Participants were faculty and junior to mid-level administrators in higher education. Fellows spent a minimum of two weeks at a host institution where they worked with a mentor on a project of mutual interest. In addition, during three seminars, in workshops, lectures, and panels, participants dealt with topics such as leadership style, communication skills, decision-making, budgeting, strategic planning, and other management and leadership skills. This program addressed the issues of culture and management and the particular concerns of Hispanics as managers, peers, and subordinates in mainstream institutions. Sixty-four fellows completed the program in three classes (1984–1986), and six of them were promoted or moved up to a higher position within two years of their fellowship experience. The program was discontinued when funding from the Fund for the Improvement of Postsecondary Education expired.

A good example of an institutional effort to ensure that women and minorities have opportunities to participate in leadership development programs is operational at Ohio State University. The Administrative Development Program was designed to increase opportunities for women and minorities to develop leadership skills and experience. A campus-based identification and screening process, conducted by a committee of peers, actively seeks women and minority candidates. They screen the candidates and select those who will be nominated for programs like the Harvard IEM and the HERS Bryn Mawr Institute. The university's commitment is clear—it pays the full costs of participation in those programs. Each year's participants return to the campus and serve on the campus-based committee the following year. Furthermore, in order to increase the pool of eligible women and minorities for such programs, they have instituted a small, campus-based leadership program. This program identifies junior and middle-level administrators and assigns them to an internship position with a mentor, placing them in a department other than their own for a three- to six-month period. The interns' own departments are paid for the interns' time to permit the hiring of replacements for the duration of the internship. Approximately one-third of the participants during the four years of operation of the program have been from minority backgrounds.

A number of participants have been promoted within the institution. Others have clarified their professional goals and affirmed their commitment to teaching and research. Most have enhanced their self-esteem and self-confidence and increased their job satisfaction. The success of such programs demonstrates that there is clearly a need for increased campus-based opportunities for minority faculty and administrators to acquire leadership experience and develop skills. Failure to provide these opportunities may result in many leaving the campus or staying in what they see as dead-end positions and losing energy and creativity. In either case, the entire higher education community loses.

The Next Generation

Efforts to identify and develop minority leaders for the immediate future must be accompanied by strategies to ensure that increasing numbers of minorities choose higher education careers. This will require increased efforts to attract talented minority students into doctoral programs and to provide them with support, mentors, and professional and leadership development opportunities.

Minority doctoral degree attainment increased for all groups between 1976 and 1981, but the increases for blacks, Hispanics, and American Indians were disappointing: from 3.6 percent of the total number of doctorates granted to 3.9, 1.2 to 1.4, and 0.1 to 0.3, respectively. It is clear that, at that rate, the attainment of a proportional share of the doctorates conferred will be in the distant future. Black doctoral attainment may well have suffered a setback that will not be evident for a few years: enrollment by blacks in graduate programs decreased 3 percent from 1978 levels (Lehner, 1980).

Programs to increase minority doctoral attainment have usually "skimmed" the best students. The Ford Foundation Fellowships for Minorities and the Danforth Foundation's Compton Fellowships, two of the best-known programs for minorities, are both examples of programs which select the "stars." Some contend that those students would probably obtain a doctorate even without the fellowships. There is another pool of candidates, however, who may have greater need for financial, academic, and other types of support yet who are not being identified by the existing fellowships.

There is a need to identify those candidates who have the requisite intelligence, commitment, and motivation, but whose test scores or GPA, or both, may be lower than the stars'. With sufficient financial aid to enable them to pursue full-time graduate studies, and with academic support services, mentoring, and counseling, these students can complete a doctoral program. Reaching out to these candidates will have the effect of enlarging the pool of minority doctorates, which the "skimming" types of programs often do not do. Many of these students often also have demonstrated leadership skills but need the appropriate credentials to assume leadership positions in higher education.

The McKnight Black Doctoral Fellowship Program in Florida is unique both in its funding base and in its focus. It is funded by a match of McKnight Foundation monies with monies from the state of Florida. The yield from these invested funds supports the doctoral study of twenty-five students each year. Thus, this program is funded *in perpetuity* rather than for a specified period of years. Moreover, the program focuses on the identification of good black scholars from state universities rather than the superstars from the prestige universities for whom everyone else is bidding. As a result, this program aims to widen the total pool of black scholars and ultimately will result in increasing their presence significantly in all kinds of institutions.

Graduate Education for Minorities (GEM) in Engineering encourages and supports minorities for graduate study. This is a particularly arduous task since few minority undergraduates choose engineering and science programs, and those who do are strenuously wooed to accept lucrative offers from private industry immediately after completing their undergraduate work. The lure is understandably powerful in light of the modest economic origins of most minorities and the attraction of immediate financial payoff for their years of difficult study. Thus, the genius of the GEM program is its ability to persuade minorities that it is in their long-term interest to delay such immediate rewards in order to pursue graduate study which ultimately yields greater rewards in upward mobility and recognition in their fields. Efforts are needed to increase the number of minority undergraduates choosing mathematics, science, and engineering majors in order to increase the potential pool of graduate students in these fields.

The Ford Foundation funds both a doctoral program and a postdoctoral program for minority scholars. These programs seek first-rate scholars who are primarily interested in research and *teaching* rather than in private industry. Consequently, these programs can, over the next five years, increase the number of minority scholars and faculty in major research universities.

The State of New Jersey Minority Doctorate Program was initiated specifically to increase minority faculty in New Jersey state colleges. This is done through a state-funded program of loans to minority doctoral students who are then forgiven these loans after completion of their degrees. The loan is forgiven by one-fourth for each year they teach in a state college or university. Thus, the state is assured of the teaching services of these scholars for at least four years even in technical and scientific fields. Scholars opting to leave teaching before the end of that period are required to repay the balance of the loan, a disincentive to leaving teaching at least before the loan is forgiven.

A number of institutions, such as Northwestern University, the University of California at Berkeley, and Washington University have established comprehensive retention programs that have been comparatively successful in graduating above-average numbers of minority students at the baccalaureate, masters, and doctorate levels, respectively.

Even after achieving the doctorate and securing a faculty appointment, minority educators continue to experience hurdles beyond those faced by all faculty. Moving up the academic ladder to positions of leadership in academic affairs requires a solid scholarly record. Minorities who are interested in research on issues of concern to minorities are often at a disadvantage because their interests are seen as too narrow or their discipline as too soft, or because they may develop new hypotheses and research models and question orthodox methodologies as they seek to expand the knowledge of their field while using a culturally relevant conceptual framework. Often, they cannot get their work published in mainstream journals. One consequence of this has been the emergence of several minority scholarly journals such as the *Hispanic Journal of Behavioral Sciences* and the *Journal of the National Association for Bilingual Education*. However, publication in these journals, notwithstanding the quality, is judged to be not as acceptable as publication in the mainstream journals.

The existing leadership development programs, such as those discussed previously, cannot meet the increasing need for minority leaders. This need will continue to increase as the minority population grows and the white population ages. A two-pronged approach to increasing credentialing opportunities is required. First, existing programs should develop "affirmative action" plans that would include goals for increasing the number of minority participants in each cohort. These goals will need to be set at a level higher than proportional representation if progress is to be made in solving the problem. This may require external funding from foundations and corporations, as one of the impediments to minority participation is often the cost. Second, leadership development programs targeted exclusively to developing minority leadership could be designed. State departments of higher education would be logical agencies for housing this type of program, as would some of the national higher education associations.

In establishing programs to create the next generation of minority scholars and potential leaders, the academy need not reinvent the wheel. Successful models exist in sufficient numbers with a variety of state and institutional configurations to fit most circumstances in public and private higher education. The problem is that they are scattered around the country and relatively unknown, or, worse, it is likely that many states and institutions lack the will or desire to emulate them. Consequently, there is certainly a role for the national higher education associations like the American Council on Education or the American Association of State Colleges and Universities as well as for individual leaders, especially those who command the respect of their colleagues, to exercise leadership; the role of both is catalyze their member institutions and state systems to individual and collective action in initiating similar programs to address this critical national issue, as well as to convince them that it is in their interest and the nation's interest to do so.

Summary and Conclusions

The history of higher education in its relationship to minorities unfortunately mirrors the history of the United States itself. Despite its claims to a liberal intellectual tradition and egalitarian values, the academy legally and systematically excluded minorities from mainstream participation just as did the larger society for much of its history. Indeed, academic scholars usually supplied the intellectual underpinnings to scurrilous racial theories that have plagued this society up to the very present. However, almost exclusively since World War II and especially during the last twenty-five years, court decisions, legislation, and some innovative programs have begun to redress the absence of minorities in higher education student bodies, faculties, and administrative positions. It is important to remember that most of the initiative for these changes did not come from academe, but were forced on it by the courts and the federal government.

Although these initiatives never resulted in proportional representation of minorities in the academy, they had results. However, the gains were tenuous and mostly peripheral to mainstream leadership positions in the academy. With a decline both in federal funding and institutional commitment, the numbers, while never great, began to decline for some minority groups and plateau for others. Ironically, the groups most affected are the largest, and as their numbers in the population grow, their proportional absence from the academy becomes increasingly conspicuous.

Increased minority participation is no longer only a matter of social justice or egalitarian principles, although these continue to be important. As minorities approach one-third of the population by the year 2000, their improvement in educational attainment becomes a matter of national concern, their economic viability affects that of every other group either positively or negatively, and their meaningful participation in the workforce is central to the nation's productivity.

Minorities cannot just be the foot soldiers in this country's continued struggle for leadership in the international economic order; they must be among the high command as well, which decides the direction of that leadership. Higher education, as the traditional supplier of the intellectuals and technicians who make up that leadership, is key to the meaningful development of minority leaders. The academy has a unique opportunity now not only to redress its previous dereliction of responsibility to its own values, but to be on the cutting edge of creating new leaders and leadership for the future.

REFERENCES

ADOLPHUS, STEPHEN H. *Equality Postponed: Continuing Barriers to Higher Education in the 1980s,* New York: College Entrance Examination Board, 1984.

BELLES, A. GILBERT. "The College Faculty, The Negro Scholar, and the Julius Rosenwald Fund." *Journal of Negro History, 54* (1969), 383–392.

BUSINESS-HIGHER EDUCATION FORUM. *Highlights of the Winter 1986 Meeting.* Washington, D.C.: American Council on Education, 1986.

CAMPBELL, ANGUS. *White Attitudes toward Black People* Ann Arbor: Institute for Social Research, 1971.

CRONIN, THOMAS E. "Thinking and Learning About Leadership." *Presidential Studies Quarterly, 14,* no. 1 (1984).

GARDNER, JOHN W. *The Heart of the Matter: Leadership-Constituent Interaction.* Washington, D.C.: Independent Sector, Leadership Papers/3, 1986.

HAYNES, LEONARD L. III. *A Critical Examination of the Adams Case: A Source Book.* Washington, D.C.: Institute for Services to Education, 1978.

HODGKINSON, HAROLD L. *All One System: Demographics of Education, Kindergarten through Graduate School* Washington, D.C.: Institute for Educational Leadership, 1985.

KEOHANE, NANNERL O. "Our Mission Should Not Be Merely to 'Reclaim' a Legacy of Scholarship—We Must Expand on It." *The Chronicle of Higher Education,* April 2, 1986.

Lee, John. *Student Aid and Minority Enrollment in Higher Education.* Washington, D.C.: American Association of State Colleges and Universities, 1985.

Lehner, Christopher, J. *A Losing Battle: The Decline in Black Participation in Graduate and Professional Education.* Washington, D.C.: The National Advisory Committee on Black Higher Education and Black Colleges and Universities, 1980.

Melendez, Sarah E., and Petrovich, Janice. "Hispanic Women in Higher Education: Overcoming Barriers to Success." Unpublished, 1986.

Nettles, Michael T.; Gosman, Erica J.; Dandridge, Betty; and Theony, A. Robert. "The Desegregation of Higher Education: An Analysis of the Influence of Race on Student Progress and Attrition." Unpublished, 1982.

Wilson, Reginald, and Melendez, Sarah E. *Third Annual Status Report on Minorities in Higher Education.* Washington, D.C.: American Council on Education, Office of Minority Concerns, 1984.

8

Building Leadership Teams

JOHN J. GARDINER

> Don't think you can do very much all by yourself. There are too many of them and only one of you. Leadership may appear to be a man on a white horse leading the multitude, but you'll do a lot better if you get off the horse and entice the best of the multitude to join you up front.

This statement by Rev. Theodore Hesburgh, attributed to Father John Cavanaugh (cited in Kerr and Gade, 1986, pp. 208–9) captures a central theme of this book—the need for a reformulation of the "man on the white horse" concept of leadership. The change involves sharing power and dispersing leadership throughout the organization. It is important to emphasize that the emerging model does not exclude the man or woman of vision and charisma; rather, it makes organizational leadership the responsibility of many able people, not a single omnipotent one.

As Green points out in Chapter 2, hard times and difficult circumstances often bring out the wish to find some wise and powerful leader who can lead an institution out of adversity. Fisher (1984) and the Commission on Strengthening Presidential Leadership (1984) are among those who would strengthen the president's hand, reemphasizing the traditional perception of strong leaders as confident, accountable, and wishing to maximize their power. The structure of academic institutions and the current climate, however, do not operate to strengthen the power of individuals. Multiple

John J. Gardiner is professor of higher education at Oklahoma State University.

constituencies, a segmented departmental structure, and the historic supremacy of faculty in decision-making on many fronts are but a few of the constraints placed on academic administrators.

The information age has further complicated matters with regard to leadership. Indeed, American higher education is not organized to function optimally in the emerging information age. Institutions have the capacity to generate a wealth of data, but their capacity to integrate and apply that information remains limited. Problems are interdisciplinary; solutions must be interdepartmental. Yet, colleges and universities reward disciplinary specialization, not interdepartmental synthesis. In an information society, emphasis changes from data gathering to knowledge processing. Transforming information gathered into useful, integrated, decision-making knowledge requires the use of interdisciplinary teams. But the structure and reward system of higher education are based on disciplinary specialization, and academic departments reinforce the segmentation of knowledge, thereby discouraging interdisciplinary collaboration.

Cleveland (1985b, p. 26) notes that while fewer than 10 percent of American workers were doing information work in 1920, today more than fifty percent of the labor force, as defined by the Census Bureau's employment categories, is doing information work. More and more of the labor force is engaged in services, and most of the service work force is involved in information processing. As Cleveland (1985b, pp. 29–33) observes, information, our "crucial resource," has several inherent characteristics: (1) information expands as it is used; (2) information is compressible—it can be integrated/summarized for easy handling; (3) information can and increasingly does replace land, labor, and capital; (4) information is transportable at great speed; (5) information is diffusive—the more it leaks, the more we have; and (6) information is shareable. Information differs from other resources in these ways. Most significantly, information as resource requires a sharing environment for optimal utilization.

Thus, new organizational forms that encourage collaboration will be required to adapt to the information-processing era. They will require an environment that fosters sharing ideas as well as encouraging risk-taking and creativity. While in some ways the structure of institutions promotes segmentation of knowledge and specialization rather than integration of information and collaboration, in another sense, higher education's characteristic organizational looseness and ambiguity are an advantage. Higher education's diversity, ambiguity, and slack allow for the creation of new structures within an institution (albeit generally slowly) and for the development of new informational networks and organizational models. While the interdisciplinary networks that are necessary to solve the complex problems of the information society are, as yet, largely unborn, models for the development of these networks do exist within and around America's leading research universities (Gardiner, 1985).

The creation of interdisciplinary problem-solving teams as the building blocks of the information-processing society will require changing our attitudes toward leadership and problem-solving. They will also require changes in our systems of selection, evaluation, and promotion of faculty and administrators. If faculty are to be recruited, as Riesman advises, as "members of collaborative teams" (1984, p. 234), higher education will need to rethink the definitions of scholarship and the reward system as it is currently structured. Similarly, the recruiting of administrators will need to take into account their role as team members as much as their individual skills and talents.

Leavitt (1975, p. 67) suggests that we would all be better off if groups rather than individuals made up the basic building blocks of organizations. Groups increase commitment, improve decision-making, and encourage innovation. An interpersonal environment that encourages broad participation, mutual respect, and the use of influence rather than authority may be established within groups. Group members thus experience a heightened sense of ownership and pride. The National Aeronautics and Space Administration's work clearly demonstrates the power of a coordinated team approach to the solution of complex, scientific problems. Today, the interdisciplinary team is widely accepted as a sound organizational approach to problem-solving. Teamwork helps group members to frame the problems and to see the texture of issues with greater insight and understanding. The information-processing university requires the use of interdisciplinary teams building bridges between the disciplines and encouraging collaboration across society as a whole (Gardiner, 1986). As Cleveland (1985a, p. 16) notes, "An information-rich environment is a sharing environment."

Teams and Leadership Teams

If team efforts characterize the information society, then a reworking of our thinking on leadership is in order. Should society's central concern be with the development of great leaders or with the development of great organizations? Should leadership be viewed as the province of individuals or of groups? In assessing the relationship between leaders and followers, John W. Gardner (1986b, p. 5) notes that "influence and pressure flow both ways." Followers are often in charge; leaders frequently follow. Both leaders and followers are shaped by each other and by their environments. Leadership evolves more from group interaction than from individual initiative. As Gardner observes, "Most of the leadership that can be called effective involves a number of individuals acting in a team relationship" (1986a, p. 15). Leadership, it would appear, is more the province of groups than individuals. As Green notes in her introductory essay, we are limited in our understanding of leadership development. We know even less about the development of great organizations and the kind of leadership that seems to encourage their emergence.

In an information society, leadership involves communication and interaction. It is not an act; it is a dialogue. The tasks belong to the group, and leadership roles are shared by group members. Cooperation is central to the accomplishment of group tasks. In the traditional bureaucratic model, information flows downward, with goals and objectives established at the top of the organization. In an information society, communication occurs in all directions, making use of the expertise of many people. Hierarchical structures do not work well in an information society. Therefore, there is a growing movement away from them toward networks and/or teams where small groups of people manage themselves. As Barnard (1938, p. 123) notes, "Informal organizations are necessary to the operation of formal organizations as a means of communication, of cohesion, and of protecting the integrity of the individual." When human commitment replaces bureaucratic authority as the driving force of society, informal organizations are taking charge. Leavitt (1975, pp. 69–70) observes that group membership fosters a sense of belonging and community that prevent isolation and improve communication. Put another way, "the pyramidal structure weakens informal links, dries up channels of honest reaction and feedback, and creates limiting chief-subordinate relationships which, at the top, can seriously penalize the whole organization" (Greenleaf, 1977, p. 63). With the centrality of communication and cooperation in the emerging information society, collegial structures become an organizational necessity, and leadership by example and persuasion, rather than by control, becomes the operational model.

Presidential Teams

"Groups can serve as hierarchical leaders of other groups" (Leavitt, 1975, p. 75). Leadership tasks can be shared by several individuals who are part of a group or team, or they may be handled by a single person. How these tasks are accomplished is less important than how effectively they are performed. This point is especially important for presidents, whose incredibly wide span of responsibilities and diverse constituencies make reliance on team members crucial. College presidents are the quintessential "knowledge executives" (Cleveland, 1985b) whose typical day might include politics, money, and football, as well as scholarship. In response to a survey (described below) conducted by the author, Reverend Theodore Hesburgh notes, "The simple fact is that the president can't lead as large and complicated an institution as a university all by himself." The knowledge executive must be an accomplished generalist with a broad understanding of many issues and an in-depth technical knowledge of very few. Thus, the president must rely on others.

There can be no doubt that teamwork is essential to successful leadership. Survey respondent Robert H. McCabe observes, "Shared concerns, common goals, and supportive interrelationships are basic to progress." Without an effective team approach, organizational vitality is not possible. C. Peter Magrath emphasizes, "Effective leadership without an effective team approach is a contradiction in terms." Robert B. Kamm adds, "There is no clearer manifestation of presidential leadership than to surround oneself with a team of able colleagues with whom the many diverse and complex responsibilities of the Office of the President can be shared." It is essential that the president be able to build and lead an effective team.

In an effort to learn more about the presidential team, a college or university's central leadership group, the author surveyed some of American higher education's leading chief executive officers. Reverend Hesburgh (cited by Fisher, 1984, p. 121) once observed that "anyone who isn't heard outside the campus isn't worth being heard inside." Using a similar rationale for sample selection, the author chose thirty individuals who have led and/or studied presidential teams. There was no attempt to make the sample a scientifically drawn cross section of American college presidents. Most of the people selected had been interviewed as part of the study conducted by the Commission on Strengthening Presidential Leadership (1984, pp. 119–41). A questionnaire was sent to two dozen college presidents representing a wide range of institutional types and to a half-dozen people who were not college presidents but who were perceptive students of higher education. All people selected were worth being heard "outside their campuses" on the basis of past and current associations and publications.

The questions asked of each were:

1. To what extent do you think it is important for a college or university president to be a good team builder/leader?
2. What is required to be a good team builder/leader?
3. Who are the critical members of the presidential team?
4. What are the characteristics of an *effective* presidential team?
5. What do you see as the major obstacles to effective team functioning?
6. What team-building ideas/strategies might you suggest to an incoming college or university president?

Over 75 percent of those surveyed responded; the thoughts of these individuals are incorporated with their permission throughout this chapter, and the entire group of respondents is listed in an appendix at the chapter's end.

While the number of persons serving on a presidential team may vary depending on the size and complexity of the institution, it was generally concluded by survey respondents that the team should include line officers who report directly to the president. The team working with Theodore M. Hesburgh consists of the individuals heading academic affairs, graduate studies and research, student affairs, university relations, and financial affairs. In his comprehensive study of management teams, Belbin (1981, p. 116) of Cambridge University observes that six team members is optimum.

The survey respondents agreed substantially about traits and behaviors of effective team leaders. Having a vision for the institution and being able to excite others with the articulation of this vision were important to many of those queried. Hesburgh notes that a "common vision" must be frequently emphasized by the leader and the team as they shape the course of their own particular activities. In other words, the vision guides the general direction and permeates specific activities. A group without a clear and compelling vision will not emerge as a united team. Arthur Levine recommends, "Begin with a dream."

That dream gets woven into the fabric and the history of the institution and becomes a part of what Riesman and Fuller (1985) call the "saga" of an institution. That saga is "an ethos or moral penumbra that helps shape the outlook of their graduates, quite apart from the academic or other skills accumulated during the course of their education" (1985, p. 63). In their study of two presidents who made a difference, namely, Virginia Lester and Robert Edwards (former presidents of Mary Baldwin and Carleton Colleges), the authors assess the degree to which a president can influence the development of a small liberal arts college by building on its saga. They conclude that presidents can make a difference; they can clarify purposes, work cooperatively, and exercise moral and intellectual leadership. Thus, as instruments of the saga, presidents serve as implementors of the shared dream.

Effective communication is essential in order to enable others to share this vision. Nason cites "the quality of infectious enthusiasm" as a central requirement for being a good team builder. "An educational philosophy, vision, integrity, commitment are all important, but the capacity to excite others with one's philosophy, vision, commitment must also be there," Nason adds. Communicating is not a one-way process; the leader must work toward shared organizational values by demonstrating a genuine willingness to listen, interact, and be responsive. Nannerl O. Keohane identifies "sensitivity, persistence, sense of purpose, and ability to *listen* to other people" as important. Michael Maccoby sees a requirement of effective team leadership as an "ability to develop participatively a vision and organizational values; ability to lead a strategic dialogue; willingness to share power and ability to create power for others; interest in responsiveness to people." The leader creates an atmosphere of participation and shared ownership of the vision through persuasion rather than force, as Lewis B. Mayhew observes. And persuasion involves dialogue, compromise, excellent listening, and willingness to share the credit as well as the work.

All of this takes time, which is generally in short supply in most organizations and institutions. McCabe notes that "expressing conflicting views requires considerable interactive time." Maccoby agrees, citing the inability to invest the necessary time as a major obstacle to effective team building. Cooperation and communication take time, but the returns in an information-processing age make them a good investment.

Trust is also critical in the development of effective teams. Richard M. Cyert describes the effective presidential team as "a group that trusts each other and can work together and has the welfare of the total institution as its major objective." The leader sets the stage for an atmosphere of trust by operating openly and creating an atmosphere in which all participants are winners. Alfred M. Philips describes the ideal team as "positive people who have confidence in themselves and who truly understand that when everyone wins they win." Trust also involves the license to disagree openly. John W. Nason notes the importance of "free and open argument without having to be diplomatic." While disagreement may be frequent and open in a team, ultimately each member must be loyal to the group and "have a united stand before the public once decisions have been made," Nason emphasizes.

Trust is the basis of information sharing that is central to the information society. It is the president's responsibility, notes Peter Mcgrath, to "set the standard of trust, which is a two way street, [and to] provide the leadership to make sure that all team members have access to the same information and discuss it openly among themselves and with the president." Honesty and the free flow of information are critical to effective team functioning.

For some, a sense of humor is a valued characteristic of team members. Humor can serve many purposes in an organization. It can provide relief from the tension that inevitably results from conflict, from difficult circumstances, or the pressures of time. Humor is sometime a socially acceptable expression of hostility, and individuals can make fun of themselves or of situations in a permissible manner. Humor can also create a bond among individuals, the sense of sharing that comes from a good laugh or a series of "in-jokes." Or it can be one of many forms of personal expression. As Magrath puts it, "A good team can both cry and laugh together." Humor, as a form of communication, sometimes affectionate, at other times biting, can help teams coalesce.

Teamwork is predicated on the willingness of individual team members to submerge their needs for dominance and individual visibility. One president identified the "ability to subsume ego for the greater good of all" as the primary characteristic of effective team members. Not surprisingly, several of the individuals surveyed identified "big egos" as the major obstacle to effective team functioning. "Turf building and inferiority complexes" are added as central concerns by Nannerl Keohane. Overweening ambition and end runs to trustees were cited as evidence of pathology among team members.

Manageable egos are a requirement not only of the team members but also of the president or team leader. Cyert points out that it is highly unproductive for a president to keep subordinates divided in order to increase his or her own personal power. And indeed, it takes a secure individual to delegate and to share power and recognition.

The selection of individuals who will be good team members requires some special efforts. Higher education's attempt to make the search and selection process objective have caused many committees to place too much emphasis on credentials and accomplishments and not enough on style and fit. It is easier to determine what responsibilities an individual has held and what he or she has published than to determine what kind of colleague that person will be. As Green points out in Chapter 10, only careful reference checks and extended conversations with supervisors, colleagues, and subordinates can yield a picture of day-to-day life with this person. What is his or her frustration tolerance? need to dominate? ability to give and receive feedback? None of these characteristics is evident on a curriculum vitae, but they are vital to effective teams.

Nathan M. Pusey cautions presidents to use "great care in choosing congenial associates whose understanding of the purposes of the institution are similar to his own." There are dangers inherent in seeking such congenial associates, of course, or in overemphasizing fit. Good fit may come at the expense of diversity and controversy. It is natural for people to want to surround themselves with individuals with whom they feel comfortable more than with those who will bring different perspective and different personal values. In selecting their team members, presidents must balance and trade off between creating a synergetic group and a comfortable team of like-minded individuals.

Strategies for Developing Team Leaders

Effective team-building depends on communication, human relations, and consensus-building skills of chief executive officers. Once again we face the question head-on of how these skills and abilities can be developed. Hackman (1983, p. 13), citing M. Beer, outlines four approaches to team development: (1) goal-setting and problem-solving consultations, (2) assistance in improving interpersonal relationships among members, (3) role definition and negotiation, and (4) integrated consultative approaches such as the managerial grid.

Hackman (1983) notes that a supportive organizational context can nurture team development. He observes that effective reward systems have the following three features: "challenging, specific performance objectives . . . positive consequences for excellent performance . . . and rewards and objectives that focus on group, not individual, behavior" (pp. 26–28). These features suggest parameters for formal team-building programs. These programs have often included the development of challenging goals and objectives, exercises in human relations, listening, consensus-building, role clarification, and problem-solving, as well as consideration of alternative reward strategies based on group productivity.

One technique of improving the presidential team functioning, proposed by the traditional organizational development literature, is process consultation. Using this technique, developed by Schein of M.I.T., a team takes a good look at how it is functioning today in order to learn ways to function more effectively in the future. Data gathering and diagnosis activities by group members and/or outside consultants typically precede the development of action plans.

Merry and Allerhand (1977, pp. 251–52) observe that if a team has the concepts and criteria to analyze its effectiveness, it will find ways to improve itself. Dinsmore (1984, p. 71) advocates formal team-building programs as the most effective way to heighten project synergy. The programs for team-building described by Dinsmore range from an intensive one-day workshop to a longer course conducted over several months. Team-building consultations seem most useful during periods of growth, crisis, and/or change. Consultants tend to emphasize the recognition and acceptance of differences among team members as a central activity used to build trust and pull the group together into a working unit.

Some of the symptoms that might be observed in a group needing team development include the lack of a shared vision, unnecessary duplication of effort, competition, low morale, and poor communication. These symptoms signal the need to regroup, to refocus attention on the fundamentals of team development.

A lack of shared vision, for example, suggests that individual or unit goals have not been successfully related to institutional goals. Goal-setting interventions might be needed to encourage vice presidents to feel personally invested in the corporate mission and better establish their own connections to specific institutional priorities. The process of clarifying and focusing goals is a valuable group exercise and is recommended as a useful ongoing activity for the presidential team. Webster (1979, p. 242) notes that "work groups become teams as they develop and share group objectives, relate them to institutional goals, and support one another in accomplishing job responsibilities." By helping presidential team members to define institutional goals, to clarify roles and responsibilities, and to establish plans and strategies, the president is able to help guide the growth and development of the institution toward its loftiest goals and objectives.

Another important strategy for team-building that was identified by a number of survey respondents is the presidential retreat. David G. Brown suggests a three-day retreat using an agenda generated earlier by participants. Robert McCabe advises that such retreats "incorporate discussion of institutional values and regular interactive sessions." Adds Arthur Levine, "Embrace collegial governance with senior officers."

Peter Magrath emphasizes the importance of administrative routine in developing a presidential team. He advocates regularly scheduled meetings frequent and long enough (two to three hours) to cover all critical issues.

Task forces that cut across institutional lines represent an alternative approach for organizing teams. These interdisciplinary groups offer opportunities to focus the insights and resources of many people toward the resolution of campuswide concerns. William F. Miller suggests that these task forces have "specific goals . . . such as new curriculum, new research objectives, new faculty policies" dealing with current issues that lead to "fulfillment of a vision." Miller further recommends that presidents be active participants so that they can lead by example.

Delegation is a time-honored management technique, considered by most to be indispensable to presidential success. It is also critical to the success of the team members, who as senior executives will function best under conditions of reasonable autonomy. Howard R. Bowen maintains that the president should delegate everything possible, leaving himself or herself "no defined residual responsibility." The chief executive officer's role is to do whatever needs to be done that is not covered by others, and that, he notes, still leaves the president "with a heavy agenda."

The President as Servant

In this chapter, a model of team-building is described in which the leader nurtures the development of others and where individual ego needs are often submerged for the greater good. It is the antithesis of the knight on the white horse, of the leader described by Fisher (1984) who consciously cultivates distance in order to enhance power.

In fact, according to the model of team leadership, the president as team leader might be viewed as servant first. He or she strives for service above self, trying to develop an environment that supports individual growth and mutual support. The president, like the department chair that Bennett describes, is a leader among peers, *primus inter pares.*

Hesse describes this model of leadership in *Journey to the East,* in which we see a band of men on a mythical journey. Greenleaf (1977, p. 7) describes the role of the servant Leo as the sustaining spirit of the group. When Leo disappears, the group falls into disarray, and its members abandon the journey. Leo, it turns out, is the indispensable leader. Thus, the great leader of Hesse's tale is servant first. Greenleaf (p. 10) notes, "A new moral principle is emerging which holds that the only authority deserving one's allegiance is that which is freely and knowingly granted by the led to the leader in response to, and in proportion to, the clearly evident servant stature of the leader."

How does one reconcile the leadership concept of first among equals with the human and organizational need for forceful leadership? First, one must consider the fact that the role of being first among equals does not necessarily prevent one from exercising forceful leadership on behalf of the corporate will. In fact, it might be supposed that with the support of one's colleagues that forcefulness might be more focused and inspired, drawing its strength and sustenance from the will and conviction of the group. But what of situations in which consensus does not exist among group members and forceful leadership is required? What of situations in which the president's vision is opposed by members of the leadership team?

The Chinese philosopher Lao-Tse describes the most effective leaders as nearly invisible. When a successful leader has accomplished his other goal, followers believe that they did it themselves. Put another way, leadership is a series of transactions between leader and associates that results in a shared vision and consensus and from which the leader draws strength.

The president's major role, then, emerges as the institution's chief consensus builder—the embodiment of the corporate will. It must be emphasized here that group consensus does *not* imply group unanimity. The support of *all* members of the presidential team is never required; the emergence of group consensus on issues of campuswide concern is. Ultimately, the sharing of power and responsibility among team members will be called for as this leadership model is more fully accepted.

Greenleaf (1977, p. 63) notes that "to be a lone chief atop a pyramid is *abnormal and corrupting*. None of us is perfect by ourselves, and all of us need the help and correcting influence of close colleagues." Leadership teams offer institutions better information integration, more useful interaction, and more responsive decision-making. If teams are the foundation of the information society, then the president as servant is the emerging leadership model.

Concluding Thoughts

Leadership by example sustains trust. The sublimation of ego and the goal of service often elude us, but it is possible to strive to reach beyond oneself. As Riesman (1983, p. 275) notes in presenting his idea of academic citizenship: "We are not moral isolates, each a polar bear on a separate ice-floe." Team leadership requires listening, patience, and accepting rather than fearing criticism. It empowers leaders to nurture the development of others, to see that leadership is dispersed, and that there is new talent in the making. As Maccoby (1981, p. xvi) puts it, "If I had to choose one quality to distinguish the best new leaders, it is openness to criticism, the passion for continual self development, which teaches the leader to value the development of others."

As Hodgkinson (1981, p. 728) notes, higher education administrators must be teachers. Teaching may take many forms. It includes the development of others, as well as the communication of important concepts. One of these concepts is the institution's mission, which must be communicated to the various publics. Burns (1978, pp. 425–26) goes beyond communicating ideas in his concept of transformational leadership. Leaders teach values and goals and are able to unite leader and associates in the pursuit of shared "higher" goals. Real leadership is ennobling.

Commitment, not authority, will produce the best results in an information society. Leadership by example and persuasion will point the way, as Gardner (1986a, p. 23) writes:

> Perhaps the most promising trend in our thinking about leadership is the growing conviction that the purposes of the group are best served

> when the leader helps followers to develop their own initiative, strengthens them in the use of their own judgment, enables them to grow and to become better contributors.

The leadership team offers just such an opportunity to the college or university president—"a system or framework within which continuous innovation, renewal and rebirth can occur" (Gardner, 1964, p. 5).

The interdisciplinary group is emerging as the workplace for the modern information-processing society. Using the disciplines as tools, the modern academic team challenges the complex problems of society through focused interaction. Teamwork helps group members to frame the problems and to see the texture of issues with greater insight and understanding. The power of the group to meet the challenges of the information society needs to be unleashed in the processes of forming leadership teams, building bridges, and encouraging collaboration across the college and university. The presidential team offers an opportunity to begin the change process at the top. The president as servant can personify the ideals of team leadership. The challenges will be great, but the rewards will be greater.

Appendix: Individuals Who Responded to the Author's Questionnaire

Howard R. Bowen
President, University of Iowa (1964–69)
President, Claremont Graduate School (1970–75)

David G. Brown
Chancellor, University of North Carolina-Ashville (1984–)

Richard M. Cyert
President, Carnegie-Mellon University (1972–)

James L. Fisher
President, Towson State University (1969–78)

David D. Henry
President, University of Illinois (1955–71)

Theodore M. Hesburgh
President, University of Notre Dame (1952–87)

Ira Michael Heyman
President, University of California, Berkeley (1980–)

Robert B. Kamm
President, Oklahoma State University (1966–77)

Nannerl O. Keohane
President, Wellesley College (1981–)

Arthur Levine
President, Bradford College (1982–)

Robert H. McCabe
President, Miami-Dade Community College (1979–)

Michael Maccoby
Director, Project on Technology, Work, and Character and Director, Harvard Program on Technology, Public Policy and Human Development, Harvard University

C. Peter Magrath
President, University of Minnesota (1974–85)
President, University of Missouri (1985–)

Lewis B. Mayhew
Professor, Stanford University (1962–)

William F. Miller
Provost, Stanford University (1970–79)
President, SRI International (1979–)

John D. Millett
President, Miami University (1953–64)
Chancellor, Ohio Board of Regents (1964–72)

John W. Nason
President, Swarthmore College (1940–53)
President, Carleton College (1962–70)

Rosemary Park
President, Connecticut College (1947–62)
President, Barnard College (1962–67)

Alfred M. Philips
President, Tulsa Junior College (1969–)

Henry Ponder
President, Fisk University (1984–)

Nathan M. Pusey
President, Harvard University (1953–71)

Paul F. Sharp
President, University of Oklahoma (1971–78)

Barbara S. Uehling
Chancellor, University of Missouri (1978–87)
Chancellor, University of California, Santa Barbara (1987–)

REFERENCES

BARNARD, C. *Functions of the Executive.* Cambridge: Harvard University Press, 1938.

BELBIN, R.M. *Management Teams: Why They Succeed or Fail.* London: Heinemann, 1981.

BURNS, J.M. *Leadership.* New York: Harper and Row, 1978.

CLEVELAND, H. "Educating for the Information Society." *Change, 17* (July/August, 1985a), 13–21.

CLEVELAND, H. *The Knowledge Executive: Leadership in an Information Society.* New York: E.P. Dutton, 1985b.

COMMISSION ON STRENGTHENING PRESIDENTIAL LEADERSHIP, CLARK KERR, DIR. *Presidents Make a Difference: Strengthening Leadership In Colleges and Universities.* Washington, D.C.: Association of Governing Boards of Universities and Colleges, 1984.

DINSMORE, P.C. *Human Factors in Project Management.* New York: American Management Association, 1984.

FISHER, J.L. *Power of the Presidency.* New York: ACE Macmillan, 1984.

GARDINER, J.J. "Excellence in Research: Creative Organizational Responses at Berkeley, Harvard, M.I.T., and Stanford." Paper presented at the Annual Meeting of the Association for the Study of Higher Education, Chicago, March 17, 1985 (ED 259 624).

GARDINER, J.J. "Building Bridges between the Disciplines: Collaboration in an Information-Processing University." Paper presented at the Twelfth International Conference on Improving University Teaching, Heidelberg, Germany, July 16, 1986 (*Proceedings,* II: 363–372).

GARDNER, J.W. *Self-Renewal: The Individual and the Innovative Society.* New York: Harper and Row, 1964.

GARDNER, J.W. "The Heart of the Matter: Leader-Constituent Interaction." Independent Sector Leadership Paper 3, Washington, D.C., June, 1986a.

GARDNER, J.W. "The nature of Leadership: Introductory Considerations." Independent Sector Leadership Paper 1, Washington, D.C., January, 1986b.

GREENLEAF, R.K. *Servant Leadership.* New York: Paulist Press, 1977.

HACKMAN, J.R. "A Normative Model of Work Team Effectiveness." Technical Report No. 2, Research Program on Group Effectiveness, Yale School of Organizational Management, November, 1983.

HODGKINSON, H.L. "Administrative Development." In *The Modern American College,* A.W. Chickering, ed. San Francisco: Jossey-Bass, 1981, 721–729.

HOMANS, G.C. *Coming to My Senses: The Autobiography of a Sociologist.* New Brunswick, N.J.: Transaction Books, 1984.

KERR, C., and GADE, M.L. *The Many Lives of Academic Presidents: Time, Place, and Character.* Washington, D.C.: Association of Governing Boards of Universities and Colleges, 1986.

LEAVITT, H.J. "Suppose We Took Groups Seriously . . ." In *Man and Work in Society.* New York: Van Nostrand Reinhold, 1975, 67–77.

MACCOBY, M. *The Leader: A New Face for American Management.* New York: Simon and Schuster, 1981.

MERRY, U., and ALLERHAND, M.E. *Developing Teams and Organizations.* Reading, Mass.: Addison-Wesley, 1977.

RIESMAN, D. "Some Personal Thoughts on the Academic Ethic." *Minerva, 21,* nos. 2–3 (Summer/Autumn, 1983) 265–284.

RIESMAN, D. "Afterword." In *Liberating Education,* Z.F. Gamson, ed. San Francisco: Jossey-Bass, 1984, 217–242.

RIESMAN, D., and FULLER, S.E. "Leaders: Presidents Who Make a Difference." In *Opportunity in Adversity: How Colleges Can Succeed in Hard Times,* J.S. Green and A. Levine, eds. San Francisco: Jossey-Bass, 1985, 62–104.

WEBSTER, R.S. "A Management Team Approach to Institutional Renewal." *Educational Record, 60,* no. 3 (Summer, 1979), 241–252.

PART THREE

Strategies and Resources

This final section deals with various approaches to identifying, developing, and selecting administrative leaders. Administration does not have a tradition as a profession in higher education. As Green asserts in Chapter 1, colleges and universities have traditionally been resistant to leadership and management development for a number of reasons. Most academic administrators "fall" into administration and learn on the job. Administration is often considered unworthy of study, and the conventional wisdom insists that any halfway intelligent person can figure out how to discharge these responsibilities. Since the academic culture places a high value on collegiality, it is somehow unseemly to aspire to leadership positions or to prepare oneself consciously for them. National leadership and management development programs have only a twenty-year history; on-campus programs are sporadic and subject to the vagaries of institutional funding. It is no exaggeration to claim that higher education has barely begun the job of developing its human resources.

Part 3 begins with an examination of administrative careers. Understanding these patterns and analyzing them as Kathryn W. Moore does in Chapter 9 enable us to formulate a leadership development agenda that is responsive to the following questions: What skills and abilities do administrators bring from their previous positions? Which ones are lacking and which ones require further development? How do conventional career patterns enhance or obstruct the development of generalist leaders who have a holistic appreciation for institutional functioning? What are the career routes of women and minorities? Are they different from those of majority men? The answer to these questions and to other similar ones can provide a solid grounding for leadership development efforts, which can be targeted to address the shortcomings of the system as it has evolved and to dispel some of the myths that have prevented the opening up of leadership opportunities.

Moore's research does indeed dispel some myths, among them the "belief that there are greater coherence and cogency in administrative careers than actually exist." Indeed, there are *no* clear career routes into such functional areas as admissions, development, or administrative affairs. While one predictably would enter academic administration from the faculty, the progression is not clear-cut. Further, there is often little crossover among the various nonacademic areas, and even less between them and academic affairs. Leadership development efforts should consider these patterns as they identify needs for skill development as well as broaden the horizons of participants to prepare them for the complexities of institutions. Moore also points out that the search process selects individuals whose work experience is in similar institutions—administrators who move within the orbit of community colleges, state colleges, or historically black colleges, for example—and thus is failing to encourage breadth. Also, the lack of opportunities to move across functional lines suggests that institutions are failing to groom internal talent. The numbers also corroborate impressionistic conclusions about underrepresentation of women and minorities in "mainline" administrative positions: women constitute only 13.8 percent of all deans or directors in the four-year sample and, like minorities, are most frequently found in the positions of head librarian, registrar, and director of financial aid. There is indeed an untapped pool of potential leaders.

In the Chapter 10, Madeleine F. Green looks at the selection of administrative leaders. It is worth repeating that administrative responsibility does not guarantee leadership, nor are campus leaders necessarily to be found in ranks of administrators. But to the extent that administrators are the designated leaders on campus, their selection deserves as much attention as their development. As Green states, "No matter how effective colleges and universities are in identifying and developing new talent, a weak selection process will render these efforts practically useless." The selection process is crucial to ensuring that institutions find administrators who are capable of responding to the new higher education environment. It is also key to ensuring diversity among leaders and to opening up leadership positions to women, minorities, and individuals with nontraditional backgrounds. While the search process as it has evolved over the last ten to fifteen years has become more open and more consultative, it has also become more cumbersome and, some would argue, more conservative and less risk-taking. Search committees may agree on the candidate who is most palatable to all, but not necessarily on the one who is best for the institution. By imposing restrictive definitions of required experience, credentials, or institutional background, hiring officials or search committees are certainly contributing to the rigidities of career mobility that Moore describes, if not actually causing them. The selection of administrative leaders represents a major opportunity for the higher education community to deliver on its rhetoric and to select the kind of leaders who will truly lead colleges and universities into the future. Green outlines the common pitfalls of the search process, and provides recommendations for conducting more effective searches.

Chapters 11 and 12 examine formal training programs as a method of leadership development. Clearly, formal programs are only one form of professional development, but they are probably the most conspicuous nationally and the most systematically developed efforts. In Chapter 11, Jack Shuster describes the twenty-year history of nationally sponsored programs, examining the impetus for their development and, for some, the reason for their demise. He also examines the objectives, the participant characteristics, the curriculum, and the outcomes of three long-running "management institutes": Harvard's Institute for Educational

Management, the Summer Institute for Women in Higher Education sponsored by HERS/Bryn Mawr, and the College Management Program of Carnegie Mellon University, which are all intensive programs of two-week duration and longer.

A more personal approach is taken by Daniel Perlman in Chapter 12, as he reviews his own developmental experiences leading to a college presidency and his experiences as a participant in some half-dozen well-known leadership development programs. He describes the varied motivations of individuals to participate in leadership development programs and reflects both on the tasks of institutional leaders and on which ones can be taught. And finally, Perlman considers the relationship of individual development to institutional development.

Part 3 examines the practices and programs of higher education that bear directly on our efforts to identify, select, and train leaders. The chapters are descriptive and practical and the book culminates with a conclusion of concrete suggestions that boards and campus leaders should consider as they chart the institution's course. The conclusion synthesizes many of the recommendations by the contributing authors and, like the whole of this volume, strives to put leadership and its development high on the agenda of decision-makers.

9

Administrative Careers: Multiple Pathways to Leadership Positions

KATHRYN M. MOORE

Leadership is a critical need of all organizations, and all must have the means of ensuring the flow of new talent. Recruitment, training, promotion, and job motivation are important tasks of organizations for developing leadership. Additionally, work positions must be organized into career lines, paths, ladders, or job clusters. These career structures serve to facilitate recruitment, socialization, and motivation, and to reduce the costs of turnover. In short, career lines are one of the means used by organizations to allocate and educate for leadership roles. However, in contrast to business and industrial organizations, where there has been much attention to career mobility in relation to organizational functioning, relatively little scholarly attention has been devoted to these factors in the development of administrative leaders in colleges and universities.[1]

Each institution tends to view its personnel needs as specific to its history and mission. And administrators tend to approach their careers with a similar sense of individuality. Part of this attitude derives from the deeply embedded notion that academic administrators, unlike managers in businesses or even in the public

Kathryn W. Moore is professor and director of the Center for the Study of Higher Education at the Pennsylvania State University.

schools, have essentially temporary careers built on top of their permanent careers as faculty members. This notion appears to persist despite the hundreds of administrators who have devoted ten, twenty, even thirty years to their work as administrators and many of whom have also prepared formally for it. Moreover, although most institutions are quite serious in seeking to hire administrators who have much more in the way of preparation and experience than simply having worked for the college, still the belief persists that academic administration is not a full-fledged career and that a labor market does not operate.

Elements of Careers in Administration

A college or university administrative career can be defined as a series of jobs involving tasks of governance and management that over time tend to have increasing responsibility, reward, and recognition. While this is only a working definition, it makes explicit a number of important elements.

First, any discussion of careers as structures of organization must take into account the unique characteristics of colleges and universities as distinct from other types of organizations. Colleges and universities are generally characterized by flat hierarchies (Scott, 1978; Estler & Miner, 1981; Holmes, 1982), and thus there may be few clearly defined steps upward. Because of the relative lack of traditional upward mobility, a variety of other forms of administrative career mobility may occur, including increased job responsibility (Estler & Miner, 1981); change in titles to reflect excellent work (Scott, 1978); job mobility by leaving one institution for another, and lateral mobility (Scott, 1978). Lacking a clear, formal administrative hierarchy, "progress may be actually determined by more subtle, intangible, and culturally specific criteria" (Holmes, 1982, p. 31). Thus, any interpretation of administrative careers and career mobility in postsecondary organizations must be approached with considerable caution.

Time is a key element of administrative careers, but it is used in a variety of ways. Organizations commonly use time to set limits on careers; such as job entry after college at age twenty or older, and final exit or retirement at age seventy or earlier. Another measure of time is time in position. In some occupations, such as faculty, time accrued in position may result in a specific set of contractual conditions called tenure or seniority.

Time in position can also be thought of as "speed." Using this notion we distinguish individuals whose careers are fast-track from those that are slow or stuck. That is, some individuals rise through the positions in a hierarchy at a rapid clip and achieve a top position at a relatively young age. Other individuals rise through the same hierarchy at a slower pace. Many never reach the top. Some business organizations, such as those studied by Kanter (1977), develop and use fast-track career routes to train and test promising young executives. Although there appears to be little deliberate career structuring in academe, some individuals still find ways of reaching top positions in a short time.

Finally, time is often used to measure the length of an entire career, and frequently it is combined with years of service to a particular college or university. Organizations tend to reward long careers at least in a token way.

Still another element of careers is the position or job itself. As White (1970) and others have demonstrated, positions often have histories. This is notably true of the college or university presidency, but it is true of other administrative positions as well. New occupants often learn that they have inherited a legacy of debts and credits from past holders of their positions (Kauffman, 1980). The new occupant may quickly learn that he or she is expected to defend particular interests because the predecessor "always did it." Or the new occupant may find that he or she was chosen specifically to shore up perceived weaknesses their predecessor had.

It is sometimes assumed that the ladder to top positions includes a finite set of positions through which an individual must move; for example, assistant dean to associate dean to dean. But, as most observers of academe know, the hierarchies in higher education are seldom as rigid as they are in other organizations such as the military or the civil service. Administrators not only change positions, but the positions that they occupy may evolve. For example, the position of dean can retain the same title for many years while during the same time it alters dramatically in scope or organizational location (Estler & Miner, 1981). Some people are skilled at extending the positions that they occupy, and some institutional environments are hospitable to such job evolution. Other people prefer or are obliged to change positions when they outgrow them.

Administrative *positions* are highly dependent on the organization in which they are located. Even the position of president, which we have studied most extensively, receives its essential dimensions from the college or university in which it is found. No presidency is exactly like another, primarily because of its organizational context. In contrast, administrative *careers* in higher education, while shaped by the organizations that compose the marketplace, are not necessarily bound by any one college or university. Careers in administration can and do extend beyond single organizations. As Gross and McCann (1981) and others have shown, academic administration appears to be unusual in that it is common to bring in someone from outside when top positions, especially the presidency, need to be filled. Other administrative positions tend to rely on loyal insiders, even alumni, but these positions are often in support areas, such as dean of student affairs or director of alumni affairs (Marlier, 1982). These facts are relevant to our discussion of career lines. It is important to distinguish the career lines that rely most heavily on insiders from those that rely on outsiders, especially for top leadership posts.

This subject leads to the matter of functional areas of administration such as student personnel services, business affairs, alumni affairs, or academic affairs (Van Alstyne and Withers, 1977). For each top position in the various functional areas a series of more or less standard positions may precede it. It is commonly believed that, once launched in a given functional area, individuals do not move easily to another. Job requirements and credentials can be so distinctive within a track that lateral mobility is difficult. While our research shows that there is considerable truth to this, especially in some areas, there is still a great deal of cross-functional movement (Twombly, 1985).

This brief discussion of some of the basic elements of administrative careers would not be complete without attention to the three Rs: responsibility, recognition, and reward. Implicit in the notion of career lines is the idea that successive positions involve increasing responsibility, demand greater skill, and confer greater rewards and status. These elements are not perfectly linked. We can all think of positions in which rewards are out of line with their scope of responsibility or visibility. But, in the ideal career, these elements align with the rank that the position occupies in the organization. Increasingly, organizations need to be mindful of these elements in their career structures.

An Administrator Career Profile

In light of these elements of administrative careers as shaped by postsecondary education organizations, let me review and summarize the ongoing research of the Leaders in Transition project

(Moore, 1983). It is a useful way to understand career progression in postsecondary education. This research has examined over five thousand careers involving line administrators (deans and up) in four-year and two-year institutions. We began the project in 1981 as an attempt to gather benchmark data on administrators' careers in 1,400 four-year colleges and universities. Then in 1984, we administered a second mail survey to a national sample of administrators in 1,200 two-year colleges. These data permit us to develop a profile of administrators nationwide and to examine their career histories in some depth.[2]

Diversity by Race and Sex

Since the 1970s equal opportunity has come to mean more than providing access to students; it has meant improving employment and advancement opportunities for faculty and staff within colleges and universities themselves. When we established the sample sizes for the Leaders in Transition surveys, we did not know the percentages of women and minorities in administration. We therefore chose sample sizes that we hoped would capture a sufficient number to make further analysis possible. In this way we would also have the first nationwide indicator of administrative diversity.

When the four-year and two-year samples were analyzed by sex, women constituted 20 and 25 percent respectively. The three administrative positions that employed the largest number of women in the four-year sample were head librarian, registrar, and director of financial aid. The same three positions also contained the largest number of minority administrators. For male respondents, the top positions were president or chancellor, chief business officer, and registrar. Women in the two-year colleges were the majority of head librarians, and also represented 40 percent or more of chiefs of student affairs and directors of learning resources. Minorities constituted more than 15 percent of only one category, directors of financial aid.

Of the 653 deans or directors in the four-year sample located in twenty-nine different academic fields or schools, 13.8 percent were women. The four common fields for more than half of the women deans were nursing, home economics, arts and sciences, or continuing education. There were no women deans of business, engineering, law, medicine, or physical education in the sample although we know there are a few. Minority deans or directors of academic units represented 5.5 percent of the total. The greatest concentration was in education.

It appears that women and minorities are able to build careers in some administrative areas more easily than in others. Some career areas, such as student personnel and financial aid, appear to be quite hospitable to women and minority group members, while others, such as academic affairs, have almost no representation from these groups. Hence, women and minorities may become pocketed in certain functional areas or positions, a circumstance that makes subsequent career mobility difficult.

First Person to Hold Position

To trace the rapid expansion of new jobs at many colleges and universities over the past few decades, we asked respondents to indicate whether they had been the first person to occupy any of their paid positions. The results showed that 18 percent were the first person to hold their current positions in four-year colleges and about 22 percent were similarly the first in two-year colleges. White males were more likely to hold new positions than were minorities or women in both two-year and four-year colleges. While we might expect this trend to have been reversed in recent years because affirmative action policies encourage the filling of new positions with women and minorities, these data as well as other research (Dingerson, Rodman, and Wade, 1980) suggest that it has not changed.

Doctoral Degrees

As another means of tracing the career paths of college administrators, we asked respondents to list their earned degrees. Over 50 percent held a doctorate, of which the Ph.D. was the most common type. Clearly individuals are becoming increasingly disadvantaged if they lack the doctorate, even when competing for the many entry-level administrative positions in today's administrative market. For example, women seeking top positions should realize that 80 percent of all presidents and provosts hold the doctorate and that 90 percent of the women in such positions have it.

It is interesting to note that a rather substantial 13 percent of both the four-year and two-year study respondents had degrees in higher education or educational administration. These degrees have sometimes been disparaged as not sufficiently academic, yet their numbers are growing. Overall, education doctorates are held predominately by women and minority group members and by those in the two-year college group. In fact, the two-year college sector is notable for having requested and designed doctoral programs to meet their growing need for administrators (Moore, Twombly, and Martorana, 1985).

Overall, one of the strengths in the backgrounds of administrators generally is their personal investment in education. When it is noted that most administrators' parents got no farther than a high school education, while over 50 percent of the administrators themselves hold the doctorate, it is clear that these are people who believe in the efficacy of education. Nor is it surprising that they have committed themselves to a type of organization that promises to assist others to achieve their educational aspirations. As leaders, perhaps these administrators need to make clear the personal roots of their commitments. This may be especially important today as new waves of first-generation students enter our colleges. These students need to know that their leaders share the same belief in education and, more than that, administrators are the living proof that education leads to social mobility.

Age

Administrators in both samples ranged in age from twenty-four to seventy-four. Nearly one-third were between forty-five and fifty years old. Age is a highly salient factor in career considerations. Despite legal and other impediments, organizations in general have tended to discriminate on the basis of age; colleges have been no different. On the one hand, the system is based on forms of seniority, such as tenure, but on the other hand, the system favors youth, especially in entry-level positions.

When the Leaders in Transition data on age distributions for the four-year group were plotted by sex, we discovered an interesting skewing in the proportions of males and females by age. At ages twenty to twenty-nine, the proportions of men and women were nearly equal. For ages thirty to thirty-nine, there were two males for every female; for ages forty to forty-nine, there were four males for every female; for ages fifty to fifty-nine, there were three males for every female; and for ages sixty to sixty-five, there were two males for every female. These data suggest several things about the career possibilities for men and women. For example, because there are so few women among the most populous ranks of forty and fifty-year-olds, any move by a woman will receive a lot of attention, and it is likely to be perceived as a gain for all women. Moreover, women in the ranks of the thirty-, forty-, or fifty-year-olds have to compete less with other women for any given position than they do with men, because in most cases there will be more male than female candidates. These cohort effects may have implications for how individuals view promotion chances and work environments. For instance, older men may be quite unused to working with women or having them as supervisors while younger men may view this as a norm.

Marital Status

The majority of administrators were married and living with their spouses. However, there were differences in marital status by sex in that twice as many male administrators were married. Also, far more women than men were single by virtue of membership in a religious order. No minority administrator was in a religious order. Particularly high percentages of presidents were married and their spouses tended to be homemakers. The spouses of married females tended to be employed either as college professors and administrators or in business and management. These are striking differences that may play a role in individuals' career behavior as well as their perceptions about careers and career mobility.

This brief examination of the personal and educational backgrounds of the administrators suggests that collegiate administrators are remarkably similar: most are white males between the ages of forty-two and fifty-nine, married, with some advanced education, many with doctorates. In other words, the leadership group at the top of the universities and colleges of this nation are similar to their faculty colleagues. Women and minorities are not as well represented in administration as they are in the faculty or as students. Although the Leaders in Transition data are samples and not a census, they strongly indicate the long way higher education has to go in achieving diversity among its leadership. The implications for this homogeneity within the administrative cohort will be discussed below. Before doing so, however, let us shift the focus somewhat to the workings of the administrator marketplace.

The Administration Marketplace

What are some of the factors that motivate administrators to change positions, and how do they go about finding out about and becoming a candidate for the position? Clearly, a variety of issues are important. Among them are the characteristics of the individual, of the position, and of the employer. Granovetter (1981) has pointed out that an often-overlooked but critical variable in career mobility is the matching process that brings an employer, a position, and an eligible individual together.

Information is crucial in the matching process. Supply-side economists argue that employees or job searchers engage in a rational job search process in which they gather complete information before making decisions. Granovetter (1981) has found, however, that employees prefer information from personal contacts, which is thought to be more reliable. From the demand side, employers engage in "signaling" in order to minimize the risk of hiring employees whose real productivity is unknown. Education credentials and recommendations are frequent signaling and screening techniques. In higher education, the type of institution of employment (for example, two-year college, research university) is thought to be a highly important signaling and screening device (Caplow and McGee, 1958; Brown, 1967).

From the individual's point of view, there are several factors involved in career or job change decisions. Spilerman (1977) labels them "push" factors, "retention" factors, and "pull" factors. Push factors are those considerations that make continuing in a line of work (or position) unattractive (for example, task alienation). Retention factors are attachments to the career line that cause an employee to stay despite dissatisfaction (for example, seniority, pensions, age), and pull factors are countervailing options open to an individual in other careers (for example, higher salary, prestige, duties).

Veiga (1983) also discusses barriers to moving to another company or geographic location in terms of those factors that are linked with the career path chosen and those associated with the motives for wanting to move. Barriers are such factors as age, fringe benefits, community ties, spouse's career. In careers where career paths are clearly specified, it is easier to choose to follow a "good" path. This, however, is not the case in higher education, where career paths have not been clearly identified. The main motives for moving, in Veiga's framework, are the fear of stagnation and career impatience.

In order to understand better the job search process from both the individual and organization perspective, Leaders in Transition respondents were asked a series of detailed questions concerning the search and information-gathering process leading to their current positions. If the respondents indicated that they were seeking a job change, they were asked about the type of options they were considering and also about how they were going about searching for a new position. We also were interested in learning about the "push" factors that may influence administrators to move and the "pull" factors that may influence administrators to stay where they are. Although there are certainly differences in the job search process between four-year and two-year institutions, it seems useful to discuss most of the information together, as there are many commonalities as well.

Job Search Factors

For the most part, the job market appears to function fairly straightforwardly and formally. That is, most people report learning about their current positions through formal job announcements from the hiring institution, and most report applying for the job formally. Personal contacts were important both as sources of information about jobs and in making nominations, but particular individuals closely tied to the administrator, such as a mentor, appear not to have as much importance in securing the job as in other forms of career enhancement.

A small, but important, percentage of administrators report the perceived presence of unfair hiring practices such as "wired searches" or "insider advantages," but, overall, the reported information attests to a labor market that is currently perceived to be reasonably open and fair. Perhaps this circumstance is so favorable because the market for administrators is still dynamic. If it were tightening down as much as the markets in other sectors, we might expect to hear more complaints. Moreover, it is useful to remember that the persons reporting in this survey are the successful candidates who doubtless have an investment in the appropriateness of the current hiring procedures.

Finally, although the data do not substantiate this comment directly, it seems clear that the introduction of affirmative action hiring practices in the mid-seventies, while not accomplishing the direct goal of greatly diversifying the administrative work force, did have the salutary effect of making employment practices more formal and perhaps more open. Women were no more likely than men to complain of unfair searches, but minority group members, especially Hispanics, expressed strong concerns with the process.

With respect to the factors that attract individuals to their positions and those that keep them there, we learned that they are not always the same. For example, respondents generally noted that salary was not a highly important factor in attracting them to their current jobs, but salary is rated highly as a factor in keeping them. Duties and responsibilities of the position are generally important as both a pull and a push factor, but personal status and prestige appear to have more potency in pushing people to consider moving on than in attracting them in the first place. Readiness for a change is also both an attractor of people to jobs and a motivator to leave present ones. Concerns about benefits for self or family members generally received low ratings on both sides of the job movement question, perhaps because the respondent groups were so overwhelmingly the male members of families in which the wife was listed as a homemaker. The women administrators in the sample did tend to value these benefits more highly.

When confronted directly with the question of whether they were actively seeking or considering a job change, the majority of administrators said "no." However, there were some differences among the types of administrators. Chief business officers and presidents were the most likely to say they were staying put. Directors of continuing education, campus executives, and chief academic officers were relatively more likely to be considering or actively seeking a job change. Most administrators were interested in a job change to a higher level or to a different institution, but did not express as strong an interest in changing functional areas.

When administrators were interested in making a job change, they reportedly did the same things that got them their current job: applying in response to job announcements and making personal contacts with colleagues. These fairly traditional techniques were chosen over the more intensely personal, such as using a mentor, or the more clearly impersonal, such as using an employment agency.

Mentors

While mentors did not appear to be used very actively by most administrators in seeking new jobs, nevertheless women, minorities, and younger administrators were exceptions (Moore, 1982). It is perhaps not surprising that age is a factor, because most respondents indicated that a mentor was important to them at the beginning of their careers. While mentors' active participation in day-to-day matters becomes less important as individuals mature, it may be important in landing the first job as an administrator. Generally, however, the mentor's role was viewed less as job-placement agent and more in other areas of career development.

At the same time, women and minorities may need the help a mentor can provide in landing jobs as well as in carrying out duties. For these individuals, the assistance of a powerful spokesperson in their behalf may make a difference not only in how they approach and win a new job but in how the employing institution through its agent search committees views the candidacy of such persons. (Moore et al., 1983).

Finally, it is important to note that over half of all the respondents said that they had a mentor, and further that mentorship is contagious. That is, if you have had a mentor you are much more likely to be one. This informal, but highly potent, source of administrator development needs further exploration.

Organizational Factors That Affect Career Mobility

College and universities provide the context in which people build administrative careers. Individual administrators are never entirely free to pick and choose among positions. Rather, each institution establishes positions and chooses individuals to occupy them in intricate ways. Institutions can do many things to create a pool of candidates for their positions. Policies and procedures can be designed to reduce, expand, enrich, or impoverish that pool. For example, a college decision to conduct an internal search or a decision to consider only individuals with five years of experience or those with a Ph.D. are decisions that will determine who will be a viable candidate for the position. Until affirmative action policies came into being, the matter of job searches seemed not to have been systematically organized. It is still not well understood.

Institutions can take actions that determine the kinds of people who can become candidates. Policies can be set that affect the distribution of opportunities for any and all groups. Affirmative action guidelines are designed to do this in a positive way. Other policies can have indirect but negative effects. For example, in the past, antinepotism rules often prevented spouses, who were usually female, from working on the same campus as their partners. Moreover, the prevailing belief that married men were the best candidates for a presidency worked to the disadvantage of women, but also of single men.

Dimensions of Career Mobility

Two important dimensions of career mobility are movement up an institutional hierarchy, the career ladder idea, and movement across institutions. The larger percentage of administrative movement is of the ladder type within one institution. With the exception of presidents, approximately 60 percent of four-year administrators made their most recent career move by changing jobs within their current institutions. In general, those moves are assumed to be upward. Downward mobility, while it occurs, is seldom so described, especially since the move from administration to faculty is viewed by many as a promotion! Within the category of internal job changes, there is also a substantial group of lateral moves across functional areas, as well as cases in which the job is enlarged around the individual (see Estler & Miner, 1981).

However, Birnbaum (1971), Kauffman (1980), and others have noted the tendency, or at least the belief, that in order to move up, an administrator may need to move on to another institution. When we used the Leaders in Transition data to examine interinstitutional mobility (Smolansky, 1984; Moore and Twombly, 1985), several things stood out. First, most movement among institutions is confined to type. That is, administrators tend to make job moves among institutions of the same type in which they already work. For our purposes, we used the Carnegie codes of institutional type embellished in some cases by more information on resource level, mission, and region of the country (Smolansky, 1984; Carnegie Council on Policy Studies in Higher Education, 1976). We found that institutional type is indeed a leading factor in limiting or channeling job movement. Community colleges tend to form one system for administrative careers, liberal arts colleges another, public doctoral universities yet another, and so on.

Functional Areas

Functional areas (academic affairs, business, physical plant and maintenance, student affairs, external affairs, administration, and finance) are the other major topographical feature in the career map. These functional areas form the home base of expertise and experience. Many are rather well differentiated internally, operate more or less autonomously with respect to selecting and training new recruits, and turn for guidance to external professional associations and even licensing agencies for leadership and standards. Business affairs is an example of a fairly self-contained operational area in which few persons from within the area migrate to other functional areas except at relatively early stages. Indeed, businesspeople are as likely to leave academe as to change areas.

Academic affairs is a rather more complex area. It can be broken down into undergraduate and graduate fields and disciplines, professional schools, and often continuing and extension education. But in addition to the discipline or field-specific core of this functional area, it has another differentiating characteristic: it is highly permeable to the entrance of faculty members into positions at all levels. The chief academic officer position is a principal steppingstone to the chief executive position, yet it is also frequently filled by persons who have held no prior administrative positions. For example, 47 percent of the provosts in the four-year Leaders in Transition sample came directly to their position without having ever having been a department chair or dean. In short, the ladder within academic affairs has many missing rungs. Deanships do not necessarily lead to the provost position nor do positions as head of department lead to deanships (Moore et al., 1983). Hence this most vital, functional area is both unladderlike and highly permeable to nonadministrators, that is, faculty members. This underscores the great strength of the faculty in our institutions. It also argues that a takeover by "professional administrators" is not likely in the near future.

Once having acknowledged the ease of access to administrative careers that is accorded faculty, however, we must hasten to say that prior administrative experience is increasingly part of the credentials of mobile administrators. In the community colleges, for example, a lateral move to the same functional position in another community college is quite common. For instance, over 19 percent of chief academic officers and 22 percent of chief business officers in the two-year college sample made lateral moves to attain their current positions (Salimbene, 1982; Moore, Twombly, and Martorana, 1985). Presidents at both two-year and four-year colleges also showed a tendency to make lateral moves.

Geographic Mobility

Smolansky (1984) has also noted the strength of geographic region as a features of administrator mobility. She found that mobility of four-year administrators often occurs within a fairly well defined geographic area. This is echoed in the respondents' own indication that geography was a factor in staying where they were or in considering a new position.

To summarize, some important organizational features affecting career mobility are institutional type, functional area, and geographic region. Movement among institutions tends to be confined primarily within the same type and often within the same national region. Moreover, individuals at the chief line-officer level, including the president, show a tendency to make lateral moves rather than leave their institutional networks. Is this the result of individual or institutional preferences? Probably both. But any cursory reading of job announcements will confirm the frequency with which a preference is expressed for individuals with experience in a similar type of institution.

In the face of large applicant pools within a given institutional group, such a practice is, if not laudable, at least understandable. But the price is a major reduction in the influx of individuals with differing institutional perspectives or even administrative expertise. Moreover, below the presidential level the narrowness of selection is even more pronounced with administrators from inside the same institution receiving the overwhelming preference; although the formula may vary by functional area, by institution, or by particular job. Whether this is wise administrative practice is another matter, but it is certainly widespread.

Implications for Policy and Practice

Today, both institutions and their administrative personnel are far more complex and sophisticated than they ever were before. It seems likely that many, if not most, institutions do not fully understand their own career structures. Movement among positions is often uneven, nonstandard, and noncomparable. Status, opportunity, and reward are not always effectively linked. Nevertheless, the administrative function continues to expand in colleges and universities. The demand placed on administrators to perform new and more intricate tasks increases, and the need for competent, committed individuals to perform these tasks will not diminish.

Administrators are clearly mobile, whether measured in terms of "distance" from their home state, or by length of time in positions, or by number and kinds of career moves. When it is understood that many administrators' careers are built on top of (or in addition to) lengthy preparation for and service in the faculty, the propensity for additional career mobility is worth noting.

A unique characteristic of this mobility is the tracking by institutional type. Looking at it from the point of view of the administrator marketplace, there appears to be a strong bias toward hiring administrators whose education and work experience have been in a similar—if not the identical—institution. From the point of view of the individual, it appears that an administrator's mobility is more bounded by the nature of the institutional context than by the work experience itself.

A Need for Staff Development

As the demand for more extensive and expert managerial skills increases, it is likely that socialization to an institution's mission and philosophy may not warrant the major emphasis it has held in the past. In its place greater emphasis on actual prior managerial experience may occur. Therefore, direct, specific preparation (training) for academic administrators may be a useful and necessary investment for both individuals and institutions.

Staff development is a sometime thing in most institutions, especially for the upper echelon of administrators. It is usually assumed that the senior administrators should know their business, otherwise why have them? But the soundness of this assumption is questionable, especially in view of the changing external environment most institutions are facing and in view of the signs of unrest, dissatisfaction, and high turnover among administrators (see Kerr and Gade, 1986).

There are discernible career tracks in some functional areas. Career advancement is increasingly linked to knowledge and experience in the stronger of these tracks. While career moves across functional areas are still common, in the nonacademic areas especially there is a growing awareness that a base level of administrative knowledge and understanding is needed, even required. As individuals identify internal mobility as the most likely career opportunity they also may expect a more "rationalized" career system in which opportunities for promotion are present and accessible. The wise institution may want to consider how best to link the "carrot" of promotion to the "stick" of increasing job effectiveness and efficiency. A sound and savvy staff development program may be the key. If institutions want to depend on their homegrown talent, perhaps they ought to cultivate it more.

Expanding Diversity

Examination of the career patterns of this sample of incumbents and comparison with the "ideal" career ladder presented in the literature have proven illuminating (Moore et al., 1983; Twombly, 1985). Clearly there is a belief that there are greater coherence and cogency in administrative careers than actually exist. Apart from faculty experience, many, many different kinds of experiences in higher education (and some outside) are substituted for any and all of the projected rungs on the ladder. This suggests either a recognition of the multiplicity of roles and experiences that may prepare an individual for academic leadership—or a persistent bias against direct, specific preparation for such posts in preference for unplanned "natural" selection processes. While the latter explanation, if true, may be satisfactory if it is perceived as benign, effective, and efficient in accomplishing institutional objectives, that sense of satisfaction must and should diminish if it can be proven that any or all of these conditions are not being met. That is, there are grounds in the Leaders in Transition survey to argue that the selection of administrators has not been entirely benign toward women and minorities. And there is some evidence to suggest that the preference for those who come from a similar type of institution may not be entirely effective or efficient when considering the total pool of those who have administrative skills or experience. In the face of growing demands for enhanced institutional effectiveness, this tendency is likely to change. Those who select chief line administrators need to draw more widely from the rather large pool of experienced administrators in institutions unlike their own.

This will mean, however, that search committees and those who charge them with their duties will need to have clear ideas of the kinds of knowledge, skills, and understanding they are seeking. They will need to know how to elicit the appropriate kinds of information about the candidates' experience, leadership styles, and career aspirations. This means search committees need to be more sophisticated about administrators' career patterns and also organizational needs in order to enable them to look beyond institutional kinship networks.

Improving the Search Process

This brings us to a comment about the search process. Generally, the Leaders in Transition data suggest that searches are perceived to be open and fair, at least by those who have made it in the system. But has that been more by accident than design? There is an enormous institutional investment in searches, but the payoff, if measured simply by job turnover, does not look good. Institutions need to devote more energy to examining the nature and kind of openings they have as well as the process for administrator searches that they are using. They also need to follow up after a search is completed to see what went well and what went wrong. If institutions persist in viewing the selection of administrators on a case-by-case basis without examining the organizational dynamics, they will likely continue to consume great quantities of resources, time, and good will without deliberately improving the quality or altering the characteristics of their administrative cohort.

Institutional self-analysis of the administrator work force should also include a look at the internal promotion histories of the staff for several years back. Institutions should know on an aggregate basis who received promotions, at what age, whether they crossed functional areas, who was in the pool, what happened to unsuccessful candidates later, and so forth. Just as there are pressures from external agencies to make selection processes more open and rational, so there are pressures inside the institutions for more open and rational career processes, for staff development, and for promotion opportunities. The career consciousness that is so observable among students is also a growing factor for administrators, especially among younger staff.

Tools for Institutional Improvement

These pressures for improved career advancement processes can be used constructively by any institution that seeks to improve its overall administrative effectiveness and efficiency. But it requires that there be more systematic and comprehensive attention given to administration and to those who perform it. How are administrative functions organized and who is expected to do them? What are the prevailing organizational beliefs; what is the culture? For example, are former faculty members normally asked to serve as administrators in all areas, or are some areas treated separately? Are there career tracks and do people move across them? What sorts of "outsiders" have been hired? How important is loyalty, alumni status, or long-term service? Does top leadership want to convey a new organizational ethos or preserve an old one? In either case, would cross-training between academic and nonacademic areas be useful? There are no right answers to these questions, but it would be helpful if institutions began to ask them of themselves.

With respect to diversity, the data indicate that more effort is needed if women and minorities are to have greater opportunities to participate in academic administration at the highest levels. Yet, lower-level administrative posts do not exhibit much greater diversity from which to draw future academic leaders. Moreover, since current female and minority incumbents do not appear to differ in most respects from the background qualifications of their male and white counterparts, there is room for more vigorous recruitment and career encouragement of women and minorities.

This raises the issue of mentors. The role of a mentor is usually viewed as someone who helps an individual to learn and to advance. But there is the possibility of viewing mentors as organizational talent scouts and leadership developers. It occasionally happens that an individual leader will play the role of mentor for others and may even acquire a reputation for doing so, but this is usually a voluntary and highly idiosyncratic activity. Yet some colleges and universities have found ways to harness the potency of mentoring for deliberate use in leadership development among their administrators and faculty. They may identify and encourage specific individuals to get special training or experience, or they may devise various high-level administrative internships so that senior administrators can work closely and constructively with younger colleagues. In the case of women and minorities, we know this is a particularly effective way to prepare them and to assist them to break into administrative positions. Some institutions appear to have recognized early what others may come to see; namely, that identifying and nurturing people with diverse backgrounds and experiences strengthens the institution just as it provides needed career opportunities for those individuals.

Vital, dynamic leadership is necessary for colleges and universities as it is for all other organizations. However, scholars of postsecondary education have paid relatively little attention to administrators' careers and what they mean for institutions. As noted earlier, one of the basic purposes of developing and sequencing positions is so that training or socialization in one position will introduce the incumbent to the tasks of the next position. Thus, awareness of how positions can serve as appropriate training ground and how they may vary depending on the demands of the higher positions is essential to developing viable career routes to leadership positions. Much depends on a thoughtful examination of the career structures of any given college or university.

The ultimate question is: will the career lines developed be able to provide the kinds of experiences necessary for preparing leaders for a new generation? The present research cannot answer this question, but it may still be helpful to individuals and institutions for whom the answer so greatly matters.

NOTES

1. There are many varieties of leadership. I do not assume that leadership does or should reside solely with administrators. Indeed, faculty and student leaders may be more vital within an institution than its administrators.
2. The Leaders in Transition project surveys were funded by the Pennsylvania State University, the Ford Foundation, and the Exxon Educational Foundation with support from TIAA-CREF. The survey questionnaires used in the project were developed at the Center for the Study of Higher Education at the Pennsylvania State University. The stratified random sample involved line administrators in accredited four-year and two-year degree-granting institutions. The sample was further stratified by position type according to HEGIS information. Thus, such generic titles as president, provost, vice president, registrar, and dean were included, but assistant and associate titles, except for assistant to the president, were excluded. The response rates for both surveys was 71 percent and 75 percent, respectively. It should be noted that the four-year sample included fifty-five positions including dean through president. The two-year sample included only nine titles: the chief administrative officer of the functional areas of business, student affairs, continuing education, head librarian, financial aid, and learning resources, as well as the chief academic officer, campus executives, and president. Hence, the two samples are not comparable in this important respect.

REFERENCES

BIRNBAUM, R.F. "Presidential Succession: An Interinstitutional Analysis." *Educational Record, 52* (Spring, 1971), 133–145.

BROWN, D.G. *The Mobile Professors.* Washington, D.C.: American Council on Education, 1967.

CAPLOW, T., and MCGEE, R. *The Academic Marketplace.* New York: Basic Books, 1958.

CARNEGIE COUNCIL ON POLICY STUDIES IN HIGHER EDUCATION. *A Classification of Institutions of Higher Education,* rev. ed. Berkeley, Calif.: The Carnegie Foundation for the Advancement of Teaching, 1976.

DINGERSON, M.R.; RODMAN, J.A.; and WADE, J.F. "The Hiring of Academic Administrators since the 1972 Higher Education Guidelines." *Research in Higher Education, 13* (1980), 9–22.

ESTLER, S.E., and MINER, A.S. *Towards a Model of Evolving Jobs: Professional Staff Mobility in the University.* Paper presented at the American Education Research Association Annual Conference, 1981.

GRANOVETTER, M. "Toward a Sociological Theory of Income Differences." In I. Berg, ed., *Sociological Perspectives on Labor Markets.* New York: Academic Press, 1981.

GROSS, E., and MCCANN, J. "Careers of Academic Administrators in the USA: An Approach to Elite Study." *Research in Sociology of Education and Socialization, 2* (1981), 127–167.

HOLMES, D.R. "Exploring Career Patterns in Student Affairs: Problems of Conception and Methodology." *NASPA Journal, 20,* no. 2(1982), 27–36.

KANTER, R.M. *Men and Women of the Corporation.* New York: Basic Books, 1977.

KAUFFMAN, J.F. *At the Pleasure of the Board: The Service of the College and University President.* Washington, D.C.: American Council on Education, 1980.

KERR, C., and GADE, M.L. *The Many Lives of Academic Presidents: Time, Place, and Character.* Washington, D.C.: Association of Governing Boards of Universities and Colleges, 1986.

MARLIER, J.D. *Factors Relating to the Extent of Inbreeding among College and University Administrators.* Unpublished doctoral dissertation, the Pennsylvania State University, 1982.

MOORE, K.M. *What-to-Do-until-the-Mentor-Arrives.* Vol. 1: The Professional Advancement Kit. Washington, D.C.: National Association of Women Deans, Administrators and Counselors, June, 1982.

MOORE, K.M. *Leaders in Transition: A National Study of Higher Education Administrators.* University Park, Pa.: Center for the Study of Higher Education, The Pennsylvania State University, 1983.

MOORE, K.M.; SALIMBENE, A.M.; MARLIER, J.D.; and BRAGG, S.M. "The Structure of Presidents' and Deans' Careers." *Journal of Higher Education, 54,* no. 5 (September, 1983), 501–515.

MOORE, K.M., and TWOMBLY, S.B. *Administrator Mobility: Crossing the Boundary between Two Year and Four Year Colleges and Universities.* University Park, Pa.: Center for the Study of Higher Education, the Pennsylvania State University, 1985.

MOORE, K.M.; TWOMBLY, S.B.; and MARTORANA, S.V. *Today's Academic Leaders: A National Study of Administrators in Two-Year Colleges.* University Park, Pa.: Center for the Study of Higher Education, the Pennsylvania State University, 1985.

SALIMBENE, A.M. *Pathways to the Presidency: An Examination of the Careers of Current College and University Chief Executives.* Unpublished doctoral dissertation, the Pennsylvania State University, 1982.

SCOTT, R.A. *Lords, Squires, and Yeomen: Collegiate Middle-Managers and Their Organizations.* Washington, D.C.: AAHE-ERIC Higher Education Research Report, No. 7. Washington D.C.: American Association for Higher Education, 1978.

SMOLANSKY, B.M. *Job-Transition Behavior in the Labor Market for Administrators in Higher Education.* Unpublished doctoral dissertation, the Pennsylvania State University, 1984.

SPILERMAN, S. "Careers, Labor Market Structure, and Socio-Economic Achievement." *American Journal of Sociology, 83* (1977), 551–593.

TWOMBLY, S. *The Structure of Careers of Top-Level Two-Year College Administrators: An Internal Labor Market Approach.* Unpublished doctoral dissertation, the Pennsylvania State University, 1985.

VAN ALSTYNE, C., and WITHERS, J.S. *Women and Minorities in Administration of Higher Education Institutions: Employment Patterns and Salary Comparisons.* Washington, D.C.: College and University Personnel Association, 1977.

VEIGA, J. "Mobility Influences during Managerial Career Stages." *Academy of Management Journal, 26* (1983), 64–85.

WHITE, H.C. *Chains of Opportunity: System Models of Mobility in Organizations.* Cambridge, Mass.: Harvard University Press, 1970.

10

Selecting Campus Leaders

MADELEINE F. GREEN

How well higher education selects leaders is crucial to the quality of institutional leadership at all levels. No matter how effective colleges and universities are in identifying and developing new talent, a weak selection process will render these efforts practically useless. What benefit will higher education derive from the existence of the pool of able administrators if it does not select wisely from among them? An informed and sophisticated search process will increase the probability of finding an individual with the most appropriate talents and skills for that institution, the so-called "best fit." And that will rarely happen by accident.

Hiring a new administrator is a real opportunity for an institution. It is an occasion to reassess institutional practices and goals and to bring together many members of the campus community to take stock of the present and to consider the future. While this is especially true of the appointment of a new chief executive officer, the selection of new administrators at every level presents the same opportunities for redefinition and self-examination.

But a search is also laborious, time-consuming, and expensive. Understandably, few institutions look forward to conducting a

The author is grateful to Donna L. Shavlik and Judith G. Touchton for their advice on this chapter. They are the principal authors of the first main section, which deals with problems of the search process.

search. Most search committee members serve infrequently and bring varying levels of experience to bear on the effort. No matter how experienced search committee members are, some collective reinvention of the wheel each time is inevitable.

Also, the search process is a human and highly subjective endeavor, no matter how fair and dispassionate a committee tries to be. The personalities and the values of individuals play an important role, and individual biases and agendas as well as the chemistry among the team members inevitably shape the course of this group activity. And all of this occurs in the context of institutional history, culture, and politics. While a search may seem to be procedurally straightforward, it is in reality highly complex and often unpredictable.

The search and screen committee as we commonly know it has been widely used for the past fifteen years. It was conceived as an antidote to the positions never advertised, privately filled, often through the old boy network. Affirmative action pressures led to national advertising, broadly representative search committees, and procedures designed to ensure the openness of the process. Today's searches are for the most part genuinely open, and although everyone has heard of the search where the outcome was known from the beginning, most do represent a sincere effort to cast the net widely and find the best person possible. But good intentions do not necessarily produce good results, and many searches go awry for easily preventible reasons.

No two searches are exactly alike. A search is actually a complex set of activities, not a single process. The variations in how these activities are handled reflect the great diversity of institutions in size, type, mission, tradition, and politics, as well as the individual differences among persons responsible for the search, selection, and negotiation. Every institution will want to conduct a search somewhat differently, and rightly so. But there are certain basic principles that underlie all effective searches—that they be humane, fair, flexible, efficient, and appropriate to the institution. Similarly, there are certain problems that are common trouble spots. Different committees will run into them in varying degrees and at various points in the search. To recognize these pitfalls and anticipate how they might impede the search constitute important preventive measures that may be the difference between a good selection and a poor one.

Problems Frequently Encountered in the Search Process

Emphasis on process, not results. Sound procedures are essential but insufficient. A good search requires creative energy and thought in every phase, and often that means not relying too heavily on procedure. An advertisement in the *Chronicle of Higher Education* is only a first step in identifying a candidate pool. It must be augmented by contacting colleagues around the country and seeking personal referrals. This process is especially important in recruiting women and minorities.

Similarly, in an effort to ensure adequate representation of all segments of the campus community, hiring officials often appoint too large a search committee. Again, the process may be correct, but an unwieldy search committee will at the very least have scheduling problems and, at worst, be able to agree only on the least objectionable candidate. The process may very well be better than the results.

The search is seen as a problem, not an opportunity. The search and selection process has come to be regarded as a problem to be resolved, rather than a opportunity for positive change. A preoccupation with process, or with getting the job finished, often precludes a careful review of the institution's needs at a particular point in time. The very first step in selecting a new administrator should be an analysis and definition of institutional needs and the kind of new leadership that can best meet those needs.

Committees reinvent the wheel. When searches occur infrequently and when committee members are inexperienced, they often discover the process as they go along. This problem is compounded by the lack of helpful information and guides to the search process below the presidential level. There are a number of resources to assist in presidential searches that can be adapted (see Nason, 1984; *ACE*, 1986), and there is a small body of literature on administrative searches, but a need exists for a concise, inexpensive handbook for search committees that will guide them through the process and alert them to potential problems. The American Association for Higher Education is in the process of developing such a handbook.

Consultants can also be helpful in the search process. They can be used in a variety of ways, from organizing the search, to guiding the committee, to checking references. Expert advice can improve the process, although it adds to the cost and it is often time-consuming to shop around for a knowledgeable consultant suitable to a particular institution.

Institutions don't profit from experience. A look at the recent past should be instructive in a search. Assuming that the search is seeking to replace an individual, it is useful to discuss the circumstances surrounding that individual's tenure in the position and his or her departure. There is some obvious risk involved in such a discussion, for it may become unnecessarily personalized or touchy, but the absence of such a discussion is risky, too. A discussion of the requirements of the position and the institution in light of past events, led by a skillful and tactful chair, should improve the result. Questions to address are: What were the successes of the person leaving? What skill, attributes should the next person have, not have? What is the legacy of the departing individual in terms of work done? Undone? Of the expectations created? Of damage to be repaired? Led with care, this discussion can help clarify the values and agendas of the search committee members, and make explicit certain issues that would otherwise be a troublesome undercurrent.

Searches take too long. Scheduling problems with large committees and slippage in the timeable, among other problems, can slow down a search maddeningly. The longer a search drags on, naturally, the more eager committees are to get it over with. A search for an administrative officer should take four or five months; longer searches run the risk of exhausting committee members and losing good candidates to other positions. A committee chair must be a good manager as well as a sensitive facilitator to keep the process moving. Also, adequate support staff and resources are essential to a fast-moving search.

There is a lack of confidentiality. Many searches suffer from excessive publicity and lack of confidentiality. Unfortunately, in some states sunshine laws make confidentiality impossible. But in searches where this is not the case, breaches of confidentiality will cause some potentially good leaders to be reluctant to become candidates and others to withdraw from the process prematurely.

Searches are passive, not active. Too much reliance has been placed on advertising, posting, and screening applications. Too little attention has been given to the role of tapping a wide variety of informal networks and of actively seeking names of qualified candidates who might be attracted to the job. That is not to say that the best people in higher education are sitting demurely in their offices waiting to be discovered. It is undoubtedly also the responsibility of talented individuals to step forward and to make their presence known. Yet openly aspiring to an administrative position is somehow unseemly in the academic culture. One waits to be called to leadership positions. And certainly, the game of the nomination letter reflects these values. The mores of the search process dictate that it is more respectable to be nominated than to apply. In light of these customs, a passive search is doubly defeating: it will not turn up the people who have not thought of themselves as appropriate candidates, and it gives the advantage to those who know how to play the search game.

Institutions suffer from the "walk on water syndrome." One has only to read a few position advertisements to recognize how the vision of a new administrator represents a campus wish list. An institution perceiving a need for strong academic leadership to reinvigorate a dispirited faculty may instinctively, for example, envision a new dean of scholarly accomplishment, who can manage with consummate ease, and who is sufficiently warm and caring to win the trust and affection of the faculty. Few mortals are equally strong in all areas, and the wise committee will discuss which are the indispensable qualifications and which are desirable but not essential. Thus a more realistic assessment might produce a new dean with a more modest scholarship record but with a keen interest in innovative programing, faculty development, and interdisciplinary teaching. There is no ideal or perfect chief academic officer or chief development officer out there, only the best match for the institution at a particular point in its history.

Institutions don't put their best foot forward. The task of dealing with large numbers of applications understandably puts committee members in the mode of *screening out* rather than *inviting in.* A search must start with the notion that the institution is recruiting the best candidates it can find, and that requires "selling" the institution to the candidates, just as it requires the candidate to convince the institution of his or her worth. Even the mechanics of the process are an important message to the many candidates, administrators, and referees all over the country about how courteous and well organized an institution is. Accurate and timely communications present a positive image about the institution. And when candidates are brought to campus, courteous attention to scheduling, to providing a cordial reception, and to attending to such amenities as meeting the candidate at the airport and allowing some private time to the person during the campus visit are all positive messages about the college community. Recruiting a new administrator is like a courtship—both candidate and institution must show themselves to be worthy and desirable partners for each other.

Institutions don't probe enough. Three letters of recommendation and two or three telephone calls do not constitute a thorough background check. Most people who have served on search committees agree that letters of recommendation are only minimally useful. If committees use them, they should only request letters after the first cut is made. Requiring letters at the beginning creates an immense paper load with little benefit at this stage. During the second phase, they may provide some additional information or insight about the candidates, but these advantages may be easily outweighed by the general level of hyperbole that provides little differentiation among candidates.

Committee members should thoroughly discuss their approach to the telephone checks beforehand. An agreed-upon list of questions is useful, though each interviewer should have maximum latitude to conduct the conversation in whatever way is most productive. Listening for pauses or evasions and vigorously following up on every clue is essential. Reading through a prepared list of questions or noting the responses will generally not yield the subtle information so necessary to a good background investigation. Consultants can be particularly useful in conducting reference checks. The best are highly skilled at telephone references and bring a consistency to the task that a committee cannot.

Interviews are overvalued, background checks are underused. Interviews provide essential information about candidates, but they do not tell all in a day or two. A good interview will yield a lot of information about how a candidate thinks and interacts with others. But it will not necessarily reveal what a person is really like on the job. A true and complete picture of a candidate can only emerge from talking extensively with others who have worked with that individual over an extended period of time. Insight about how a candidate weathers stress, about personality and temperament, and about strengths and weaknesses should be gathered from multiple sources. Here, the use of the telephone is crucial, and search committee members should get permission from candidates to go beyond the list of referees. A thorough background check covers a wide network of people, not simply the three or four individuals who are the candidate's strongest advocates.

Some searches are wired. Unfortunately, some states require that a search be conducted for every major position, even if a suitable candidate has been identified. Sometimes, hiring officials will go through the process to satisfy various constituent groups or because they believe that affirmative action laws require it. While the intent may be to keep the process open, the result is to waste time and institutional resources and to create cynicism on campus and outside when the word inevitably gets around that the search is wired. Whether the desired candidate be an insider, an outsider, or someone already in an "acting" position, there are occasions, especially when that person is a woman or minority, when a national search will be more harmful than helpful.

Insiders are not valued. Most major administrative posts are filled by individuals from outside the institution. Understandably, higher education values "new blood" and fresh perspectives. But the prevailing assumption that "outsiders" are better is worth careful examination. The identification and grooming of internal talent can provide an important source of leaders. And certainly, women and minorities can be brought along and prepared for leadership positions on their own campuses; the likelihood of diversifying campus leadership this way may produce far better results than casting about in a national search.

In each case, the costs and benefits of internal versus external candidates must be weighed. National searches are expensive and time-consuming, and the external candidate remains an unknown until he or she actually assumes the position. On the other hand, new people with different backgrounds and experiences can inject new life into a campus and infuse a campus or unit with enthusiasm and ideas that no insider could provide.

But the very essence of leadership development is tapping into leaders on campus and fostering their growth. Campuses that cannot envision "one of theirs" as a leader may harbor unrealistic expectations—possibly the wish to be saved from themselves.

Hiring officials relinquish control of the process. The chief executive officer should clearly be in charge of searches for senior administrative officers, and so on down the line. The hiring official must meet early in the process with the committee to discuss and define the position, write or rewrite the job description, and assess institutional needs. The committee must have a clear understanding of the hiring official's views concerning appropriate qualifications, the institution's needs, and the desirable fit, so that these important issues don't end up surfacing late in the process and getting resolved at the expense of the candidates. Committees must acknowledge the importance of personal chemistry between the president and senior administrators and be cognizant of it as they proceed. The chief executive officer or hiring official should also use the first meeting to agree upon timetable and process. How will the various cuts occur? How many will be interviewed? Will there be telephone interviews of the "semifinalists"? Are the resources there to support the desired process? If not, what adjustments are preferable? Regular communications between the committee and the hiring official are essential.

The final hiring decision should always be made by the administrator responsible for the search. To retain this authority, the hiring official should request an unranked list of three to five finalists. Before making an offer, the hiring official should call the candidate's referees as well as a variety of other persons who know the individual. Even if these calls have been made by a member of the search committee, the hiring official would be well advised to conduct a background check firsthand. These conversations can be especially productive if the person responsible knows the referee personally. This prior relationship will generally (but not always) result in a more candid conversation than one conducted with a stranger.

Similarly, affirmative action need not be left to chance. The hiring official can develop guidelines to ensure that the committee produces results, that is, identifies women and minority finalists. Unless there are extraordinary constraints presented by an inadequate national pool, it is perfectly appropriate for the hiring official to insist that the short list have a minimum number of women and/or minorities on it. In short, every appointment made represents an opportunity to shape the institution, and presidents and other administrators would be unwise to let these golden opportunities pass them by.

Academic mores dictate rigid career paths. Unfortunately, academic tradition limits the pool of good candidates by the unwritten code of career movement. There is very little mobility across institutional sector lines, upward in the pecking order of institutions, or across functional areas of institutions. Thus, "appropriate" candidates tend to be those from similar institutions (or "better"), and from the same functional area (as, for example, academic affairs, student affairs), persons who have performed a similar job in the past. It is understandable that such a profile may minimize the risk, but it unfortunately excludes people with nontraditional credentials who may perform extremely well in the position. Related to the constrictions on mobility is the notion that one has to have done the job already in order to get the job in the first place, that is, one has to be a dean before one can be a dean elsewhere. The catch-22 is obvious, but perhaps less glaring is the extreme disadvantage this presents to women and minorities, who are few and far between in line positions.

Academic culture also favors outsiders over insiders, supposing that only outsiders can bring new ideas. But experience in another institution is no guarantee of breadth of perspectives. Obviously, insiders have disadvantages—political alliances, enemies, being too much of a known quantity—yet in some instances the stability, awareness, and understanding they bring may be crucial. Vision and perspective are broadened in a number of ways, and knowledgeable and broad-based individuals may be right there on campus, ready to assume leadership.

Steps in the Search Process

While the pitfalls are many, a search can be structured and conducted so as to maximize chances for success. Certainly, there is no recipe for a foolproof search, for it is such a human and subjective undertaking. But a well-constructed process that tries to anticipate some of the difficulties just reviewed can go a long way in improving the outcome. The following sequence of events provides a guide to the process.

1. *Assess institutional needs.* Hiring a new administrator represents an opportunity to take stock of the institution and the kind of leadership required at that point in time. Early in the search the president or hiring official should consider these issues and engage a variety of individuals and constituent groups in the process of defining the present needs of the institution.

2. *Determine a process and timetable for conducting the search and making the final selection.* The hiring officer should decide how the search will be conducted. What is the most desirable timetable? Will a consultant be used? If so, how? All searches need not be conducted in the same way. Consider not using a search committee. A position that does not require widespread acceptance by the college community, such as a position in development or business, may not require a committee at all. Or the committee's mandate might be to screen the candidate to a specified number, such as to the top twenty-five candidates. Or a consultant might perform that function, and the committee might then narrow the group to five

and participate in the interviews. The possible combinations are numerous.

3. *Select committee members, clarify the mandate, and provide adequate resources.* When selecting search committee members, the hiring official should attempt to balance the objectives of keeping the committee reasonably small (five to eight members) and selecting strong individuals, while providing for adequate representation of various groups. If the political considerations outweigh those of quality and manageable size, the search is likely to get bogged down. The charge to the committee must be made clear (as specific as directing that, for example, the product of your deliberations should be a short list of three to five individuals, including at least one woman and one minority, to be brought to campus for interviews). Based on discussions of procedure with the committee at the early stages and at various points along the way, the hiring official may want to adjust the timetable and process developed in the previous step. Staff support for the committee must be designated, as well as a budget for administrative or interview expenses.

4. *Develop criteria for selection, and determine conditions of employment.* Early discussions of the hiring officer and the committee should center on the institution's needs, the job description, and the qualifications being sought. A clear picture developed early will minimize the floundering later on and prevent redefining the position midstream. Such a redefinition will generally require that the search be canceled and reopened; it will be a legal requirement if the new position requires a person with different qualifications or experience. The actual review of dossiers inevitably helps a committee or hiring official clarify what is wanted and needed in a candidate. The presence or absence of certain experiences and credentials on the résumés under review will make the discussion of ideas that were an abstraction in the early stage more real and concrete. For example, what constitutes evidence of "leadership" in a vita? Often, committee members will interpret candidates' accomplishments differently. For some, accomplishments in an administrative capacity demonstrate leadership; for others, steady career progression up the administrative ladder is important. By the same token, faculty leadership responsibilities or a high level of involvement and responsibility in one's own discipline may be considered important.

5. *Design a communications process with candidates and others to provide information in a timely and courteous manner.* As the

committee begins its work, it should lay out the various points at which decisions will be made and candidates notified. Sample letters should be discussed. For example, the first cut, based on the screening of dossiers, may generate the first round of refusal letters to candidates, with the rest receiving a letter informing them that they are still under consideration. Or, if the screening is more gradual and the initial group of 150 is cut in half and then in half again, a letter might go out after the second cut. Whatever the system used, all applications should be acknowledged and candidates should be kept informed as the search proceeds. Failure to do so is a sure sign of a poorly administered search and a negative reflection on the institution's image.

6. *Develop a pool of qualified candidates that includes men and women, majority and minority.* The hiring officer, search committee members, and members of the campus community should actively recruit candidates, tapping into networks of colleagues around the country and organizations in a position to help identify good people. An active search means letters and phone calls to colleagues and to potential candidates. It does *not* mean "dear occupant" letters to national or disciplinary associations or other organizations unfamiliar to the writer. This is not to say that people involved in a search cannot become familiar with individuals in organizations who are in a position to be helpful, but rather that it is best to research who can be helpful and how best to get to them before firing off an unguided letter requesting nominations. The best contacts are personal ones, to individuals who feel a personal obligation to respond to a request from a friend or colleague and who are in a position to identify suitable candidates. Everyone in higher education has a network of colleagues—in the institution, the discipline, or the professional society, among others. The task in an active search is to tap into as many of these networks as possible.

7. *Screen candidates to a "select list" of those most able to meet the needs of the institution.* Ideally, each curriculum vitae should be read by every member of the search committee, but time and the size of the pool may make this option highly impractical. Whatever the process, each vita should be rated according to agreed-upon criteria. This first cut should narrow the pool to those who meet the qualifications determined earlier. The committee might want to designate a target number (for example, twenty to forty) or may want to defer that decision until the members actually see the pool.

8. *Collect additional information on the "select list" to further*

row the field. Sometimes, an informal check may help narrow the pool. A call to a candidate to clarify his or her experience might be helpful. For example, an unusual organizational structure might confuse the committee about the person's actual level of experience: how much responsibility, for example, did the person bearing the title of dean actually have? What does that title mean in the particular institution? Or, a confidential call to a friend of a search committee member to understand why the person spent only one year in a particular job might elucidate matters. (Confidentiality is especially important at this stage, since many of these inquiries will be quite preliminary.) The more a committee knows, the better, and information gathered at this early stage will yield fewer surprises later. If letters of recommendation are to be used, they should be requested at this point, either by contacting the candidate or the referees listed by the candidate. Alternatively, the committee members may want to call the referees, dividing up the calls among them.

9. *Choose finalists and collect additional information on them.* The development of the shortlist should take into account the letters of recommendation and/or the telephone checks. As a clearer profile of the candidates' experiences, styles, strengths, and weaknesses emerges, the committee will be able to further discriminate among the candidates.

10. *Interview finalists and collect additional information on them.* As the finalists are brought to campus, committee members will want to continue their calls, approaching a wider array of people, including those not listed as references, in order to develop a detailed understanding of the candidate.

11. *Evaluate candidates by comparing the established criteria.* After all the finalists have been interviewed, and after reports from the various constituent groups involved in the process have been received, the committee should meet to reevaluate the candidates, being sure to compare them according to the criteria established early on. This analysis can be a useful balance to the dazzling candidate who interviews well but who in actuality may be less qualified, less appropriate, or simply less desirable. The evaluations should be shared with the hiring official, who makes the final decision.

12. *Offer job to top candidate.* After weighing the evidence, the hiring officer decides on the top candidate and offers him or her the job. The administrator in charge will generally wait to inform the other finalists about the outcome until the offer has been for-

mally accepted to provide a fallback plan in the event the first-choice candidate does not accept.

13. *Negotiate terms of employment.* Issues such as salary, benefits, housing, assistance to spouse in locating a position (if any), length of contract, tenure, evaluation, and termination are resolved at this point. Issues left unresolved often come back to haunt the newly appointed administrator and the president. "We'll work that out later" is usually an unwise course.

14. *Notify all persons involved in the process.* Finalists, as well as all those involved in the decision, should be informed first.

15. *Announce appointment.* Then the announcement can be made to the campus community and the public at large.

16. *Plan transition.* Too often the process ends with the announcement of the appointment. But assisting with a smooth transition is enormously helpful to the new administrator and to the community. Certainly, the president or hiring official will play a key role. But one or more members of the search committee might remain as a "transition committee" to take an active role in helping the new person adjust easily and become integrated in the campus community as quickly as possible. Help with the adjustment to the new campus is especially important to the woman or minority who is conspicuous by the absence of a peer group. Isolation can be a very real problem for the first, or near-first woman or minority, and a thoughtful support mechanism can ease that transition.

17. *Prepare final reports for historical and future use.* Since searches do reoccur, the committee that can document its work will give the next one a leg up on the process. Also, search committee records should be clear and well documented for legal purposes.

The following checklist provides a summary of the important steps to be taken at various stages of the search process:

A CHECKLIST FOR HIRING OFFICIALS AND SEARCH COMMITTEES

Checklist for the Hiring Official: Getting Started

1. Determine scope of search and selection process: inside or outside, search committee or not.
2. Draft position description; determine selection criteria.
3. Arrange for staff support for the search and selection process.
4. Determine budget; allocate funds for the search.
5. Determine composition of the search committee (if used); select chairperson.

6. Establish groundrules for committee—e.g., who makes final decision; define task of committee and expectations for communication among committee members and with campus constituents.
7. Review all of the above with the search committee; adjust as appropriate.
8. In consultation with the search committee, determine timetable for search, screening, and selection; establish procedure to conduct initial screening; determine approximate number of candidates to remain after first cut and number to be interviewed. Also, consult with search committee on organization of interview process, who will interview, and assignment of major responsibility for interview process.

Checklist for Search and Screen

1. Decide scope of search: national, regional, state, campus.
2. Develop procedures for communicating with candidates, nominators, and referees.
3. Announce the vacancy internally.
4. Assign to a person or the chair the responsibility of searching out women and minority candidates. Determine sources of advertising for women and minority candidates.
5. Advertise publicly.
6. Solicit nominations through networks, formal and informal, by mail and telephone. Make certain to include women and minorities among the contacts.
7. Establish screening criteria.
8. Compile and screen dossiers; select a group of finalists (approximate number predetermined by the committee.)
9. Document rejections with reasons.
10. Check that qualified minority and women candidates have survived the process.
11. Reopen the search if necessary.
12. Notify finalists to send references or contact referees. Use the telephone to check references.
13. Notify candidates who have been eliminated.
14. Determine other referees to contact; determine who will contact them.
15. Narrow list to small number of candidates to be interviewed.
16. Notify candidates who have been further eliminated.

Checklist for Interviewing

1. Send all candidates detailed information about the campus—including catalog, faculty handbook, academic plans, other relevant documents to help candidates understand as much as possible about the institution.
2. Decide how to handle interviews of internal candidates; do not assume everyone knows them.
3. Set interview schedule. Decide which individuals and groups shall participate.

4. Discuss committee interview techniques, strategies, and issues.
5. Designate primary hosts. See that candidate is met at the airport, has travel arrangements taken care of, and is generally assisted with the logistics.
6. Conduct campus visits and interviews.
7. Contact additional references as necessary by phone.
8. Notify finalists as to when they can expect to hear.

Process of Final Selection

1. Committee reconvenes to consider all persons interviewed and to review their candidacy against the established criteria.
2. Committee presents findings to hiring official. Ranked lists are not recommended.
3. Hiring official checks references personally, selects top choice, offers position.
4. Hiring official negotiates terms to be confirmed in writing. These terms should include agreement on the process and frequency of evaluation of the new administrator. If an agreement is reached, unsuccessful finalists are notified; if not, another offer is made or the search is reopened.
5. Committee notifies unsuccessful finalists.
6. Hiring official informs key persons on campus before public announcement is made, e.g. future staff.
7. Appointment is announced.
8. One or more persons on the search committee are designated to ease the transition of the new appointee.

Recommendations to Improve the Search Process

Keep your eye on the result, not the process. The most important outcome of a search is finding a person who will be effective in the position. While an orderly, well-organized process is indispensable, adherence to procedure will not necessarily ensure the best outcome. Search committees need to focus on institutional needs, on "fit" and the qualities and credentials truly required for the position, rather than on following the procedures that are supposed to yield the right results.

Examine all assumptions. All information is processed through a series of individual "screens" or biases. While many search committees and hiring officials have the best of intentions with regard to affirmative action, the low numbers of women and minorities in significant administrative positions give clear evidence that something is not happening. Overt discrimination is not the major problem today, for it is both socially unacceptable and illegal to openly declare "I wouldn't want to hire a woman or a minority person for this position." A more likely comment would be, "I would dearly love to see a woman or minority as vice president, but I am afraid that this campus community just isn't ready for one. He or she would be destined for failure." An open discussion of what might help or hinder affirmative action would provide a useful starting point for this important undertaking.

The chair has an important role to play here. He or she must watch for these biases and bring them to the attention of the group. Research involving the review of scholarly papers when the author's sex was identified and when it was not, revealed that the women's scholarship was judged more harshly (Sandler, 1986). Similarly, such subtle kinds of discrimination as revealed in the statement, "He has already published four papers," when contrasted with the statement, "She has only published four papers," need to be pointed out in as constructive a manner as possible. Letters of recommendation can also be subtly biased. Male referees will refer to a woman's physical appearance as "pleasant" or "attractive" but almost never do the same in describing a man. Similarly, a majority person recommending a minority candidate may define that person by his minority status ("One of the most promising minority persons I've met") rather than by his or her accomplishments.

Other kinds of assumptions or biases may also limit the search. In searches for academic administrators, individuals with degrees in education (for positions other than deanships of education, of course) are often ruled out as less well credentialed, carrying less credibility with the faculty. Again, a discussion of the committee's and the hiring official's values and attitudes with respect to academic credentials or specific job experience will illuminate their conscious and unconscious biases and may thus prevent them from interfering with the openness of the search. In short, the more assumptions about sex, race, credentials, career paths, and any other factors entering into the search process that can be made conscious and discussed, the more unlikely it is that unspoken or unconscious bias will contaminate the process.

Put yourself in the candidate's shoes. Search committees are notorious for inconsiderate treatment of candidates. They are often inconsiderate simply because they do not think through the effect of their actions (or lack thereof). Unacknowledged applications, late communications, clumsy form letters, and a host of other bureaucratic sins give the impression of a sloppily run institution and of an uncaring attitude about individuals. Similarly, at the interview, a grueling schedule, lack of attention to the candidate's personal well-being, or an atmosphere of "running the candidate through the gauntlet" contribute to a negative impression. The recruiting process is like a courtship, and unless the institution can create a positive atmosphere and put its best foot forward, it is unlikely to woo the candidate of choice.

Abandon all hope of the ideal candidate. Too many searches are conducted in the hope (rarely explicit) of finding a knight on a white horse to solve all the institution's problems. No candidate will have all the desired qualifications or be equally strong in all areas. It is crucial that a search committee, with the guidance of the hiring official, take stock of the institution and its current needs before the search starts. "Saviors" are usually doomed to failure when the institution has not sorted out what it really needs and what it can give up in a candidate.

Consider the use of consultants. There are now a large number of independent consultants who can be hired to do various tasks, at very varied prices, to assist institutions with a search. Consultants can help the committee save time, serve as an objective presence, and assist in some of the more time-consuming tasks. They can be used for all or part of the process, depending on the needs of the institution. For example, they may work with the hiring official and the committee on the institutional needs assessment and get the process rolling. Or they may be hired to help develop the candidate pool, especially in areas where institutional contacts are likely to be inadequate. Another area where experienced consultants can be very helpful is in checking references. There are advantages to having one individual take on this responsibility, since calls from many members of the search committee may make it difficult to draw any meaningful comparisons. Also, experienced reference checkers may be more accomplished in probing, cross-checking conversations, and otherwise ferreting out hard-to-find information about the candidate.

Caution should be exercised, however, in selecting consultants. The field is burgeoning, and clearly some consultants are better than others. Some are new to higher education and bring a corporate rather than collegiate perspective to the search process. Consultants must be both credible to those involved in the search and compatible with the institution's operating style. Thus, being a wise consumer of consultant services requires some time, and hiring officials should check with previous clients to determine their level of satisfaction with the work of the consultants. In the final analysis, the search must belong to the institution. The role of the consultant is to serve as catalyst and facilitator, rather than director.

Check references with greatest care. Horror stories abound about the information never uncovered by the search committee—the phony degree, the alcoholic candidate, the sexual harrassment case. As I mentioned earlier, most letters of references are of little use. At best they can raise a few red flags or provide information about the candidate's salient strengths. Rarely does a portrait of the individual emerge. Thus, extensive telephone checks are essential; They should go beyond the lists of referees and probe, probe, and probe some more. Too often, telephone interviews consist of a list of questions read by the interviewer, with little follow-up on particular points made. Open-ended questions such as, "How would you describe Ms. X's working style?" or, "What are some of his strengths and weaknesses?" or, "How would the faculty describe her?" or, "How would her staff describe her?" should yield insights that can be probed further and cross-checked with other people. Listen for hesitations. Find out why a referee has nothing but praise. Is the candidate really perfect? Or is there something else the referee might share? The reference net should be cast widely, and as many individuals as possible who might have useful insights should be contacted. Subordinates and colleagues are as useful as (if not more so than) superiors.

Consistency among telephone interviewers is also a problem that the committee should address. If the committee is going to divide the responsibility, it should develop a list of questions each member will use as guidelines but not follow slavishly. Each member should take on the task of checking one candidate to ensure good cross-referencing. Consultants can also perform this task or can assist the committee in planning to do their own reference checks. Finally, hiring officials would be well advised to check the references of the final candidate personally before making an offer. While this entails another round of phone calls to the same individuals, it is well worth the effort.

Conclusion

Searches start with the premise of weeding out or closing down, that is, getting the pile of one to two hundred vitae down to a manageable group. Admittedly, that is the mechanical task of the search committee, but it is also helpful to think in terms of "opening up."

A search is an opportunity to open up institutional issues as well as to open the institution to new ideas and people.

It is worth concluding with the observation that participation in a search should be a form of professional development for the committee members—a broadening experience that provides greater insight into the institution. It should enable the group members to focus on the broad picture, to discuss institutional issues and agendas, and depending on the position being filled, to get an education about the different functional areas of the college or university. A faculty member on a search committee for a development officer should gain a greater understanding not only of that individual's responsibilities but also of his or her entire operation and relationship with the rest of the institution.

Finally, searches should not be episodic "hit and run" endeavors. Unfortunately, we do not have a tradition in higher education of identifying and grooming new talent in a continuous cycle. Thus, administrative vacancies tend to take institutional leaders by surprise, or at least to make them start from ground zero in replacing individuals. But searches are really a part of an ongoing cycle of institutional assessment, identification, and development of new leaders, followed by renewed search and again assessment. Searches are an important step in the life of any institution. They represent an opportunity to identify administrative leaders who can make a real difference to the future of an institution.

REFERENCES

American Council on Education and Association of Governing Boards of Universities and Colleges. *Deciding Who Shall Lead.* Washington DC: Author, 1986.

Nason, J. *Presidential Search: A Guide to the Process of Selecting and Appointing College and University Presidents.* Washington, D.C.: Association of Governing Boards of Universities and Colleges, 1984.

Sandler, B., and Hall, R. *The Campus Climate Revisited: Chilly for Women Faculty, Administrators, and Graduate Students.* Washington, D.C.: Association of American Colleges, Project on the Status and Education of Women, 1986.

BIBLIOGRAPHY

There is a much greater body of literature on presidential searches than on administrative searches below the presidential level. See especially, Nason, John W. *Presidential Search: A Guide to the Process of Selecting and Appointing College and University Presidents.* Washington, D.C. Association of Governing Boards of Universities and Colleges, 1984. Also useful for its insights on the presidential search process is The Commission on Strengthening Presidential Leadership, Clark Kerr, dir. *President Make a Difference: Strengthening Leadership in Colleges and Universities.* Washington D.C.: Association of Governing Boards of Universities and Colleges, 1984. A useful set of guidelines for search committees is *Deciding Who Shall Lead.* Washington D.C., American Council on Education and Association of Governing Boards of Universities and Colleges, 1986.

On administrative searches, consult the following:

BIRNBAUM, ROBERT. "Searching for a Leader." *AAHE Bulletin, 35,* no. 9 (1983), 9–10.

BROMERT, J.D. "The Role and Effectiveness of Search Committees. *AAHE Bulletin, 36,* no. 8 (1984), 7–10.

FORTUNATO, RAY T., and WADDELL, D.G. *Personnel Administration in Higher Education: Handbook of Faculty and Staff Personnel Practices.* San Francisco: Jossey-Bass, 1981.

GEIS, F.L.; CARTER, M.R.; and BUTLER, D.J. *Seeing and Evaluating People: A Summary of Scientific Research on Perceptual Bias.* Delaware: University of Delaware Office of Women's Affairs, 1982.

KAPLOWITZ, R.A. *Selecting Academic Administrators: The Search Committee.* Washington D.C.: American Council on Education, 1973.

MOORE, K.M. Examining the Myths of Administrative Careers. *AAHE Bulletin, 35,* no. 9 (May, 1983), 3–6.

MURRELL, P.H. Finding the Best Person for the Job: The Search Committee and Affirmative Action. *Journal of Employment Counseling, 17,* no. 3 (1980), 167–72.

REID, J.Y., and ROGERS, S.J. Search for Academic Vice-Presidents and Provosts. *AAHE Bulletin, 33,* no. 9 (May, 1981), 4–6.

SCOTT, R.A. "Robots or Reinsmen: Job Opportunities and Professional Standing for Collegiate Administrators in the 1980's." *Current Issues in Higher Education,* no. 7 (1979), 17–22.

SOCOLOW, D.J. "How Administrators Get Their Jobs." *Change, 10,* no. 5 (May, 1978), 42–43, 54.

TAYLOR, E., and SHAVLIK, D. Selecting Professionals in Higher Education: A Title IX Perspective. Washington D.C.: Resource Center on Sex Roles in Education. National Foundation for the Improvement of Education, n.d.

11

Professional Development Programs: Options for Administrators

JACK H. SCHUSTER

We begin this exploration with a straightforward question for which a simple answer exists:

Q: How much is known about the characteristics and effectiveness of management training institutes designed to promote the professional development of college and university administrators?

A: About the characteristics, a fair amount is known; about program effectiveness, next to nothing.

Thus, while more is now known about career trajectories of colleges and university administrators,[1] very little has been published that examines one vitally important aspect of that phenomenon: the relationship between administrators' careers and the various modes for developing administrators' leadership and management skills. The exceptions for the most part are program descriptions prepared by one or another of the management institutes or other activities, but these descriptions are unencumbered by impartial,

Jack H. Schuster is professor of education and public policy at the Claremont Graduate School.

An earlier version of this chapter was first presented at a symposium on Mid-Level Administrators in Academe, 1986 Annual Meeting, Association for the Study of Higher Education, San Antonio, Texas, February 21, 1986.

detailed data about program effectiveness. This is particularly troublesome, because college and university administrators have been reminded repeatedly over the last two decades that as campus resources have grown ever scarcer, they must become especially adept in their leadership and management roles. Clearly, the development of administrators who are able to function effectively in the complex and distinctive organizational settings of higher education has been a priority for years. Yet there exists no systematic evidence to establish what are the most effective pathways for honing the appropriate skills or, even more fundamentally, to demonstrate what in fact are the most essential competencies for administrators to acquire (McDade, 1986).

Defining the Topic

At the outset, several preliminary issues must be addressed in order to delimit the scope of this examination, for there are myriad opportunities for college and university administrators, in all types and at all levels of responsibility, to improve their prowess.[2]

Sponsorship

Programs for the professional development of administrators are organized by an assortment of sponsors. They include, for example, single campuses as well as professional associations or organizations, some operating within and others outside higher education. Some campuses, particularly the larger ones, provide considerable in-house training activities, as do multicampus systems. Innumerable professional associations provide management training for higher education administrators. To suggest but a few among dozens: the National Association of College and University Business Officers (NACUBO), the Council for the Advancement and Support of Education (CASE), the College and University Personnel Association (CUPA), and the National Association of Student Personnel Administrators (NASPA). All have rallied to the cause of developing management training opportunities for their particular clientele. Still further, the American Association of University Administrators, an organization formed in the early 1970s specifically to address issues of relevance to middle-level administrators, has a keen interest in management training for its broadly defined constituency and, indeed, began in 1985 to publish its own *Journal for Higher Education Management*.

There are also an endless array of management-related activities proffered by organizations outside the higher education realm; these include, for example, the far-flung programs of the American Management Associations, the American Society for Training and Development, the National Training Laboratories, and University Associates, Inc. However, the extent to which higher education administrators actually participate in such programs is unclear, and their perceived usefulness is wholly unknown. Another variation on the theme: the Bush Leadership Fellows Program, which includes but is not restricted to educators and which serves a geographically restricted area (Minnesota, the Dakotas, and part of Wisconsin).

Internships constitute another mode for developing administrative skills. Among these, the best known by far is the American Council on Education's Fellows Program, a yearlong administrative internship designed to afford a more extensive taste of administrative life (described later in more detail). An example of an "in-house" internship program is the California State University's Administrative Fellows Program, which generally selects a dozen interns from among the system's nineteen campuses. Previous yearlong internship programs, no longer extant, include two designed for women, which were supported mainly by the Carnegie Corporation in the mid-1970s: the Sixteen College Administrative Intern Program (housed at various women's colleges) and the smaller Claremont Women Administrators Program (at the Claremont Colleges).

Still other modes include short, more narrowly focused workshops (ranging from a day to, say, five days in length); national- or state-level identification programs for aspiring women administrators; and annual conferences of national or regional professional organizations (most notably, perhaps, those of the American Association for Higher Education and the durable National Conference of Academic Deans, begun in 1941 and held annually at Oklahoma State University since 1948). Formal academic courses, perhaps pursued as part of a degree program in such fields as management or higher education certainly play a role, very possibly one of growing importance (Dill, 1978; Haynes, 1985).[3] In that regard, it is worth noting that some highly respected higher education leaders did their doctoral studies in (of all things!) higher education.

The presidents of two university systems—David Gardner, University of California, and Stanley Ikenberry, University of Illinois—come most readily to mind. One might even cite ad hoc lectures and "the literature" on higher education administration as management training tools.[4]

Defining a Management Institute

The next task is to define a management training institute. There are no guidelines in the literature to establish where an "institute" ends and some other form of professional development begins. For present purposes I shall define a management training institute as (1) a program of a week's duration or longer, (2) the content of which is directed at improving management/administrative skills, (3) offered to administrators at North American colleges and universities, (4) at which attendance is not reserved for personnel from a single campus or multicampus system. Others might insist that "an institute" must be of longer duration.[5] Such distinctions, however, are unimportant. The shorter residential programs, lasting, say, one to two weeks, tend essentially to be scaled-down versions of the longer, higher-priced models and appear, as suggested elsewhere, to serve useful purposes (Schuster, 1984).

We next must wade into a semantic swamp and decide whether "management training," for our purposes, should be understood as being limited specifically to the development of basic management-related skills (for example, planning, budgeting, evaluating, negotiating, marketing, and so forth). Or should management be defined more broadly to encompass, in traditional academic terms, training for "administration" and "leadership"?

The term "management," once an anathema in higher education circles, acquired a certain cachet in the early 1970s, or even a few years before, and leadership development activities began to adopt the management nomenclature. Thus were born various "management" institutes and training activities. However, their curricula and methods probably were more similar to than dissimilar from those of their predecessor activities, which had spurned the "management" terminology. Curricula have continued to shift over time, but they do not amount to a radical break with the traditional methods for training administrators. Accordingly, for the balance of this discussion, "management" will be used in its more generic meaning, in the broader sense in which Peter Drucker describes a manager's paramount responsibility as that of directing an organization's vision and resources toward the end of achieving the greatest results. Thus, "management," "administration" and "leadership," despite some contentions that they occupy different domains, are hereafter regarded as being too closely intertwined in practical usage to exclude any of them from the scope of this exploration.

The Opaque Box

As suggested at the outset, little is known about the effectiveness of management institutes. So far as this writer is aware, the absence of methodical information does not result from secretive institute administrators who are determined to hide "trade secrets." Competition among the various institutes for scarce "paying customers" certainly exists, but to my knowledge the absence of published systematic information is attributable to the paucity of research undertaken on the topic. The consequence is not so much a "black box," which completely masks from view the training processes and outcomes in question, as it is an opaque box, one which reveals at least some discernible rudimentary information. On the whole, however, very little is known about who takes advantage of what kinds of training opportunities and at what stages of their careers. Nor is information readily available on the finances of such activities, including the extent to which participation in training is subsidized by employers or is paid for by participants themselves. Even less is understood about the *effectiveness* of various types of programs, either from the vantage point of the "consumers" or their employing institutions; thus, almost nothing is known about the actual impact of such activities on administrative careers—although various programs do draw attention to the promotions their "graduates" subsequently earn. In all, the opaque box yields few fundamental insights, and, accordingly, this paper attempts a preliminary exploration of some aspects of the management training phenomenon. The emphasis in this chapter will be on the residential "higher education management institute," although other activities are discussed by way of background. In the sections that follow I seek, first, to describe, by way of background, several significant early efforts to establish management training opportunities for administrators; second, to provide a brief account of the three best established management training institutes for administrators; and, third, by way of summary, to suggest lessons derived from the available evidence regarding management training.

Background: Varied Responses to "the Management Crisis"

Higher education's "distant early warning" line began to pick up signals, even in the early 1960s, that boom times would not persist indefinitely. Growth had been rapid as the number of institutions, programs, students and faculty—and the corresponding budgets—mushroomed. Administrators, governing boards, and public officials were grappling with unprecedented sustained growth. Soon, advocates of streamlining the unwieldy higher education enterprise began to suggest that economies—possibly very significant savings—could be realized through the more efficient management of colleges and universities. One can debate whether the resulting "management revolution" is of relatively recent origin or has been around for some time. George Keller, for instance, in 1983 described the "unprecedented revolution" in the way colleges and universities are now being managed (Keller, 1983, p. 3). On the other hand, already two decades earlier Rourke and Brooks had written a study entitled *The Managerial Revolution in Higher Education* (1966). (This "revolution" may be longer-lasting than the American, French, or Russian varieties!) In any event, one early response was the Academy for Educational Development's establishment in 1970 of a Higher Education Management Division (supported by grants from the W.K. Kellogg Foundation and the Olin Corporation Charitable Trust). Calling for a "drastic improvement in the management of higher learning," the Academy, which since its inception in 1961 had championed long-range planning, suggested that achievable improvements in campus operating efficiency on the order of 10 percent would save higher education some $2 billion each year (Academy for Educational Development, 1970).

Other important events ensued. Three early developments, each a large-scale response to the perceived crisis of inefficient management in higher education, merit particular mention:

The National Center for Higher Education Management Systems

The National Center for Higher Education Management Systems (NCHEMS) was established in 1971 as an independent, nonprofit organization designed "to improve planning and management in postsecondary education." NCHEMS had been formed out of

WICHE's rib (the Western Interstate Commission for Higher Education, which encompassed the thirteen western states and had been pressured in the late 1960s by several states—most prominently, California and Oregon—to generate comparative higher education data to facilitate planning). This led in 1968 to the establishment of a project called WICHE Management Information Systems (WICHE-MIS), directed initially by W. John Minter. By 1970 this project evolved into a wider-ranging endeavor, WICHE Planning and Management Systems (WICHE-PMS), and all states, not just the Western ones, were invited to participate. New York and Illinois joined the project. Soon a "National Center"—NCHEMS—was created to respond to the swelling interest in more efficient management.

Support for NCHEMS has come from many sources over the past two decades. In its early years funding came primarily from the U.S. Office of Education's National Center for Educational Research and Development, supplemented by other federal funds and a generous Ford Foundation grant. The National Institute of Education was created in 1972, then became the major source of support for NCHEMS. Over the years NCHEMS has produced a prodigious number of materials and management training programs, including "direct assistance" activities for campuses. Its management seminars and workshops have been attended by close to thirty thousand individuals. However, the 1985 reorganization of federal support for laboratories and centers dealt NCHEMS a hard blow. Unsuccessful in the intense competition to retain major federal funding, some key staff have departed. NCHEMS' future is cloudy. At this writing NCHEMS has abandoned its program of organizational studies for lack of funding. (That was the closest NCHEMS had come to engaging in basic research.) However, NCHEMS continues an array of service activities, including consulting, sponsoring seminars (typically on planning, program review, and budgeting), and undertaking policy analyses for diverse clients.[6]

The Higher Education Management Institute

In 1976 the Exxon Education Foundation made a multimillion dollar commitment to launch the Higher Education Management Institute (HEMI) as a nonprofit public foundation. The challenge to institutions of higher education, HEMI declared, was enormous. In building a case for the elaborate program HEMI would attempt, it conducted a nationwide survey of campuses and concluded that no more than 2 percent of colleges and universities "have any semblance of management development and training." Furthermore, HEMI estimated that each year some ten thousand individuals moved into a first or significantly different higher education management position and, further, that among the 101,750 "middle and upper level managers," the estimated annual turnover was about 18,000 (Fisher, 1978).[7]

HEMI opened its headquarters in Coconut Grove, Florida, and proceeded to develop an elaborate array of program materials designed to engage individual campuses in complex needs assessment activities. HEMI also launched a number of regional program centers. In November 1979, HEMI relinquished its independent status in order to join forces with the American Council on Education. Having relocated most of its activities to Washington, D.C., HEMI, now armed with the ACE imprimatur, ambitiously expanded its reach. There it continued for another two years before its life at ACE, once filled with much hope, expired in January 1983. Conceptually overextended and undersubscribed by potential campuses, this bold experiment appears in retrospect to have constituted the higher education management movement's version of the Edsel.

American Council on Education

Meanwhile, the American Council on Education was expanding its involvement in management-related activities. For perhaps two decades ACE has occupied the premier role of facilitator of leadership development programs. In one sense, ACE had been interested in "leadership development," broadly defined, since its founding in 1918. Its more formal involvement, however, can be dated to 1965 when two significant events occurred. The Council initiated its Academic Administration Internship Program, as it was first called, with a hefty $4.75 million, three-year grant from the Ford Foundation. Such internships were not new. A similar, much more modestly funded Program of Internships in Academic Administration had been launched, funded, and operated from 1962 to 1966 by the Ellis L. Phillips Foundation. During that five-year period the New Hampshire-based foundation (which itself had received additional support for the intership project from the Hazen Foundation and the Ford Foundation's Fund for the Advancement of Education) supported forty-four administrative interns, mainly full-time faculty members flirting with administrative careers (Hefferlin and Phillips, 1971; Phillips, 1986).

ACE Fellows. The Phillips and ACE internship programs overlapped during academic year 1965–1966, and from that point on ACE had the field to itself. Along the way, the Lilly Endowment, Rockefeller Foundation, and the Andrew W. Mellon Foundation have each supported one aspect or another of the ACE Fellows Program.

In its first twenty-one years (1965–1966 through 1985–1986), the internship program has produced 845 fellows. Discounting the first year, class sizes have ranged from fifty-one to thirty-one, averaging forty-one. Until 1972–1973, male participants overwhelmed women by an eight-to-one ratio. Since then, women have held 40 percent of the internships (45 percent from 1980–1981 through 1985–1986), and the proportion of minority participants has risen sharply, as seen below:

Years	*Males*	*%*	*Females*	*%*	*Minorities*	*%*	*Total Fellows*
1965–66 to 1972–73 (8 yrs.)	279	(89)	34	(11)	32	(10)	313
1973–74 to 1985–86 (13 yrs.)	316	(60)	214	(40)	129	(24)	530

The Fellows come from all types of institutions. Most of them have been affiliated with public institutions (69 percent); relatively few come from two-year colleges (7 percent). At the time they were selected as Fellows, a third (32 percent) held "pure" faculty appointments while 66 percent occupied administrative posts (Pearson and Marmion, 1985, pp. 31–32).

Also during 1965, the *Institute for College and University Administrators* (ICUA), which had been created with much foresight in 1955 at the Harvard Business School, was relocated to ACE.[8] A decade later, in 1975, ACE established the Office of Leadership Development in Higher Education to coordinate activities of ICUA and the ACE Fellows Program. That office also produced several publications, the most relevant for present purposes being the *Guide to Professional Development Opportunities for College and University Administrators* (American Council on Education, 1979). The *Guide* had been initiated in 1971 by the Academy for Educational Development's Management Division, with support principally from the Kellogg Foundation, for the purpose of providing a comprehensive listing of "seminars, workshops, conferences and internships."[9] Produced solely by the AED for four years, the 1975 *Guide* was published jointly as a "cooperative service" of AED and ACE. Subsequent editions of the *Guide* were produced solely by ACE. The last edition (1979) had swelled to 195 program descriptions spread over 248 pages. However, the project soon became unwieldy; "the compilation task grew as the number of programs grew dramatically, and as ACE was unable to devote sufficient staff effort to the project, it was abandoned" (Green, unpublished).

In 1978 the ACE's Office of Leadership Development was expanded and redubbed the *Center* for Leadership Development. Its more ambitious scope now extended to offering a series of Leadership Seminars (about twenty-five one- or two-day sessions on various administrative topics) and to housing the ambitious but short-lived Higher Education Management Institute. In 1979 the Center initiated its *Departmental Leadership Program,* supported again by Kellogg; this program provided seminars for academic administrators—deans and department chairs—at various campuses throughout the nation.

Emergence of the Campus-Sponsored Management Institutes

During the 1970s several individual campuses launched institutes predicated on the need to equip administrators with a better understanding of the role and techniques of management. These institutes came in all shapes and sizes. Some, like the Claremont Graduate School's Claremont Higher Education Management Institute (a nine-day institute held for four summers beginning in 1978), flourished briefly and faded away. Others, like Seton Hall University's Higher Education Leadership Institute, established in 1979, have continued to carve out places in a highly competitive market. A perusal of almost any issue of the *Chronicle of Higher Education* will reveal a stunning array of management training opportunities, though few fit the definition of "management institute" set forth earlier. Judged by durability and reputations for excellence, three institutes merit particular attention. They are described in the order that they were founded.

Institute for Educational Management, Harvard University

By any reckoning the Institute for Education Management (IEM) at Harvard's Graduate School of Education stands *primus inter pares* among campus-based management training programs. Discussions beginning in 1965, and financial support provided primarily by the Sloan and Ford Foundations, led to the creation of the IEM. Its first session, in 1970, involved sixty-three participants. Located originally at the Harvard Business School, initially it was staffed almost exclusively by "B School" faculty members. The Graduate School of Education gradually acquired responsibility; first, the IEM administrative offices were relocated there, and then, beginning in 1982, IEM participants were housed in Harvard College residence halls instead of Business School residence halls across the Charles River.

IEM is the most senior and by far the most expensive—at more than $200 per day—of the management institutes. Before its length was scaled back from five and a half weeks to the current twenty-seven-day format, it was indisputably the most comprehensive among them. IEM stresses that it is "designed for executive officers and other senior officials" and that "most participants serve at the president, vice-president or dean level of responsibility" (Institute for Educational Management, 1985). The most prestigious among any of the institutes, IEM attracts a far higher proportion of presidents among its participants (9 percent in 1986) than any of the others.

For years IEM admitted a class of 110 participants, but more recently, at least in part because of a change in facilities, IEM has scaled back. Ninety-two participants attended in 1985, 96 in 1986. To date IEM has "graduated" about eighteen hundred administrators from over five hundred colleges and universities.

A series of core courses, often making substantial use of case studies, comprise the curriculum. These include courses in strategic planning and marketing, human resource management and labor relations, law and politics, institutional advancement and leadership, and financial management and decision analysis. The institute itself is supplemented by an Alumni Workshop (now held every year and a half) to which previous participants are invited.

The 1986 participants' evaluations of IEM reveal a very strong endorsement of the program's effectiveness. Although many participants reported that the work load tended to be too heavy and the class size too large, the overall ratings of IEM's faculty, curriculum, accommodations, and mix of participants were extremely positive (Institute for Educational Management, 1986).

It is particularly relevant to note that in 1986 IEM launched a spin-off, the Management Development Program. A thirteen-day version of the IEM (priced at $2,500 for 1986), the MDP curriculum is very similar to the parent institute. An important aspect of this new development is that the MDP is aimed explicitly at middle management. As the MDP brochure announces, "typically, participants will hold such titles as director, department chair, dean or associate dean" (Institute for Educational Management, n.d.). MDP's initial "class" attracted eighty-five participants, thirty-three of them women; 52 percent of the participants were in academic affairs. Participants' evaluations of the first MDP were very favorable, although there were somewhat fewer rave notices given by MDP participants than by IEM enrollees (Management Development Program, 1986).

Summer Institute, Higher Education Resource Services—Mid-America, Bryn Mawr College

The Higher Education Resource Services (HERS) was created in 1975. Starting the following year, the HERS-MidAtlantic office (since moved to the University of Denver as "HERS-MidAmerica") has operated a Summer Institute for Women in Higher Education Administration, cosponsored by, and held at, Bryn Mawr College. ("HERS-New England," located at Wellesley College, meanwhile has conducted a Management Institute for Women in Higher Education since 1977 using a very different format: five two- or three-day seminars spread throughout the academic year.)

Attracting seventy-six women from throughout North America in 1985 and seventy-four in 1986, the Summer Institute caters primarily to middle-level and entry-level administrators and to full-time faculty members. Few of the 1985 participants (only 4 percent by my count) could be classified as senior-level. A bare majority—55 percent—hold a terminal degree. Designed to boost women's access to significant administrative responsibilities—opportunities until recent years foreclosed to all but a few women—the Summer Institute would appear to be attracting the right kind of eager but relatively inexperienced clientele for the purpose of aiding their budding administrative careers. The comprehensive charge for 1986 was $3,575.

The curriculum is organized into six core areas: academic governance, administrative uses of the computer, management and leadership, financial budgeting, professional development (for example, career planning and networking) and human relations skills. The curriculum places more emphasis on the latter two areas than do the Harvard and Carnegie Mellon institutes.

College Management Program, Carnegie Mellon University

In 1978 Carnegie Mellon University created a College Management Program (CMP). Building on strengths in the management and computer science fields and capitalizing on names of such stalwarts as CMU President Richard Cyert and Economist Herbert Simon, CMP has been administered since 1979 by the Office of Executive Education of CMU's School of Urban and Public Affairs. Twenty-eight middle- to senior-level administrators attended in 1985, a smaller than normal (about thirty-five) but very diverse group. The charge for the 1986 Summer Institute was $3,500.

Spanning four tightly packed weeks, the curriculum is designed to cover a multitude of skill-building and policy-exploration areas. Its objectives are set forth as follows (in "Send the Boss Back to School," 1985):

> Review modern management concepts and techniques.
> Improve curriculum design, academic services, and faculty quality.
> Prepare for shifts in funding from government and private sources.
> Gain insight into political, economic, technical, and demographic trends.
> Obtain hands-on experience with a computer.

The latter emphasis reflects the CMU's preeminence in using computers for instructional and academic purposes.

A review of participants' evaluations of the 1985 program reveals uniformly high praise.[10] All respondents gave the program an overall rating of "excellent" or "good"; there were no meaningful differences in the overall ratings by senior-level and middle-level administrators. All respondents indicated that they would recommend the CMP to a colleague. Almost all (fifteen of nineteen) made favorable comments about the heterogeneous mix of participants; interestingly, of the four who expressed reservations about the mix, three were themselves middle-level administrators.

The Institutes Compared

A cursory review of the three institutes leads to several observations. First, all three have tightly compacted curricula and an intensive pace. The curricula on the whole are more similar to one another than dissimilar; all present essentially the same topics, a rich mix of management skill-building and policy discussion. However, the HERS/Bryn Mawr program appears to place greater emphasis on career development issues. The Carnegie Mellon program, given its stress on computer skills, has a somewhat more technical cast to it.

The institutes run almost exactly the same length, basically four weeks. Although Harvard's IEM is substantially more expensive—about 60 percent more costly than the other two—the IEM material establishes that quite a few "fringes" are included.

Turning to the characteristics of the participants, the most obvious difference is that HERS/Bryn Mawr is limited to women. Perhaps the most striking feature, though, is that HERS/Bryn Mawr and IEM attract dramatically different participants in terms of their administrative seniority: almost three-quarters of the IEM attendees are senior-level administrators (and many of those who are not are minorities and/or women); HERS/Bryn Mawr, on the other hand, draws minimal participation from the senior ranks. It attracts a much less experienced clientele, one that probably can benefit handsomely from the Summer Institute's offerings. Carnegie Mellon is positioned between the IEM and HERS/Bryn Mawr programs in terms of degree of participants' administrative experience. Some basic characteristics of the three institutes and their participants are shown in Tables 11.1 and 11.2.

Although participant evaluation forms were not available for all of the institutes, it is likely that the institute experience is viewed very favorably by participants at all three at the time they complete their training. (This speculation is based on several sources, none highly reliable: conversations with institute staff, chance conversations over the years with participants at all three of the institutes,

TABLE 11.1
Three Leading Higher Education Management Institutes: Selected Characteristics (1986)

1. Name	College Management Program	Institute for Educational Management (IEM)	Summer Institute for Women in Higher Educ. Administration
2. Sponsor	Carnegie Mellon University (School of Urban and Public Affairs)	Harvard University (Graduate School of Education)	Higher Education Resource Services (HERS) & Bryn Mawr College
3. Year Begun	1978	1970	1976
4. Duration	21 days	27 days	26 days
5. Charges*	$3,500	$5,850	$3,575
6. Director	Harry R. Faulk, Associate Dean, Executive Education, School of Urban and Public Affairs, CMU	Lee Bolman, IEM Educatl. Chairman; Sharon A. McDade, IEM Program Dir.	Codirectors: Cynthia Secor, Dir., HERS-MidAmerica; Margaret Healy, Treasurer, Bryn Mawr College

* Charges (including nonrefundable application fees, room, board, computer time) are for 1987.

and the observation that participants in the institute at Claremont, directed for four years by the author, were almost uniformly very enthusiastic about their experience, as reflected in detailed evaluations.) However, this leaves aside two more important issues. Is the institute experience viewed by participants, with several years' hindsight, as having lasting value? And is the institute experience valued in the academic marketplace? While it is likely that the answer to both questions is yes, at present that conclusion is only conjectural.

TABLE 11.2
Three Leading Higher Education Management Institutes: Participants' Characteristics, 1985 and 1986

	College Management Program (Carnegie Mellon)		Institute for Educational Management (Harvard)		Summer Institute for Women in Higher Educ. Admin. (HERS/Bryn Mawr)	
	1985	*1986*	*1985*	*1986*	*1985*	*1986*
1. Number of Participants	28	20	93	96	76	74
2. Percentage of Women	21%	30%	31%	30%	100%	100%
3. Level of Administrative Responsibility*						
A. Senior	15 (54%)	7 (35%)	69 (74%)	59 (61%)	4 (5%)	7 (9%)
B. Middle/Junior	9 (32%)	8 (40%)	24 (26%)	36 (38%)	50 (66%)	51 (68%)
C. Faculty	4 (14%)	5 (25%)	0 (0%)	1 (1%)	22 (29%)	16 (22%)
4. Percentage with Doctorate**	n.a.	15 (68%)	69 (74%)	77 (80%)	42 (55%)	36 (49%)
5. Estimated Median Age†	n.a.	43	43	—	41	43

* Author's classification based on job titles of 1985 and 1986 institute participants. For these purposes, three levels of administrative responsibility were defined (arbitrarily) as follows:

A. Senior-level: president/chancellor; provost; vice president; dean; executive dean; registrar; business manager; treasurer; librarian.

B. Middle- or junior-level: associate/assistant vice president; director; executive director; coordinator; manager; head; associate/assistant dean or director; assistant to, executive assistant to, or special assistant to the same.

C. Faculty: apparent full-time faculty appointee, including department or division chair/head.

For purposes of this item, the job titles that obviously were not as high as "middle-level" (e.g., "admissions officer" or "financial aid counselor") were nonetheless included with the middle-level category.

The comparative figures for IEM's Management Development Program (1986) are: Senior-level, 27 (32%); Middle/junior-level, 52 (61%); Faculty, 6 (7%).

** Includes all doctorates (e.g., J.D., Ed.D., D.B.A., etc.).

† Calculated from age distributions provided by institutes.

Whither Leadership Development?

What works? And what doesn't? After two decades of experimenting with different approaches to management training and leadership development activities, how much is known? Can it be established that certain strategies are more successful, more cost effective, more enduring than others in equipping administrators to grapple with the grinding challenges that face them?

In some respects the answers to these questions may be irrelevant. So decentralized and uncoordinated are the providers of management and leadership training programs that no word from "on high" is likely to influence heavily, much less control, the potpourri of offerings. Even so, the higher education community, facing another decade at the least of very scarce resources, cannot afford to ignore these issues.

Some clues are available about the linkage between successful careers and training programs. One view holds that traditional off-site training is destined to have only a limited impact. A decade ago Kanter, Wheatley, and associates conducted an extensive evaluation of five training programs supported in the mid-1970s by the Carnegie Corporation of New York. Two of the five programs were "institutes": Harvard's IEM and the now-defunct Institute for Administrative Advancement (IAA).[11] The authors argue that training programs—including those two institutes—were not adequately integrated into the participants' own campus settings and accordingly had limited success in boosting career development. This was so, they contend, even though all of the programs they evaluated appeared to them to be of high quality and, on the whole, were valued by those who participated in them (Kanter et al., unpublished, p. 127). The authors conclude:

> There is a striking agreement, both from individual narrations of careers, and research findings, on the key elements to career success: role models, good contacts, sponsorship, visibility, being in the right place at the right time, a job that forces one to learn new skills. Training programs that occur outside of an institution are separated from these real sources of career success: the people and jobs that impede or facilitate individual careers. In some instances, training tried to offer a short-cut approach to further careers; it attempts to teach new skills, create connections among people, promote individual visibility and offer good role models. But training is an extrainstitutional response to a clearly institutional problem. As such, its impact is badly circumscribed (p. 58).

The authors observe further that the value of training cannot be assessed apart from its actual impact on career advancement. At best, they say, training

> provides a spurt of energy, a booster rocket propelling one to a new position. But the long-term effects on careers and the factors that determine career success come not from training, but from the jobs people hold. Certain jobs, because they are on a long mobility track, or because they are important to the institution, involve work with others, and allow for discretion in decision-making, will result in people in those jobs being valued and rewarded with promotion (p. 61).

Training, the authors conclude, cannot assure career success, for "training cannot by itself change the opportunity structure for individuals" (p. 62).

It should be noted, though, that Kanter et al. were evaluating programs conducted a decade and more ago. Too, their evaluation was concerned exclusively with women participants, many of whom may have faced uphill struggles in their careers. Still further, their assessment surely followed too closely on the heels of the training activities they examined to permit them to gauge longer-term career advancement. Those considerations circumscribe, to an unknown degree, the relevance of their findings for training opportunities as the 1990s draw near. Recall that participants in the three contemporary institutes described in the previous section appear to be largely satisfied with their experiences—although, of course, more time will be required to assess the impact of those experiences on their careers.

Five Propositions

Five propositions emerge from the scattered evidence.

One, participants in various training programs tend to express approval, often voiced enthusiastically, about their experiences; participants, at *least* in the short run, value these experiences. These fervent endorsements may well be attributable in some measure to a Hawthorne effect; the heady experience of substantial, intensive, high-quality professional development activities—in handsome settings, often at prestigeful sites, remote from the routines of one's daily responsibilities, amid stimulating peers—is bound to be exhilarating for many participants. The evaluation forms completed at the conclusion of such activities, or the letters that inevitably follow, might be considerably less exhuberant three months or a year later if participants' expectations of advancement do not materialize. However much one might be inclined to discount the validity of "instant evaluations," the enthusiasm of participants for their professional development activities is unmistakable.

Two, the effects of such activities on career success is almost totally unknown. Suggestions that participation in a particular program may have accelerated participants' careers is simply not substantiated by available data. While participants in the sought-after ACE Fellows or IEM programs *may* enjoy enviable promotion rates, evidence of causation is scant to nonexistent. It may well be that many of those participants had already been "fast-tracked" by their home institutions and that their selection to participate in a costly program merely confirms their institution's confidence that they are primed for advancement.

Three, there is no evidence to establish that one kind of program is more efficacious than another. Thus, while logic may dictate that year-long internships or participation in full-blown, four-week management institutes would be richer learning experiences and thereby would provide stronger boosts to careers than, say, participation in less comprehensive, shorter-term activities, such conclusions at this time must be conjectural. In fact, the scant evidence that does exist—this writer is aware of only one study that cuts across types of programs (McDade, unpublished)—suggests that participants tend to value their participation about as much for one kind of management training activity as for another.

Four, however inadequate the evaluative information may be, there is no reason to discredit the instincts of participants that their off-campus learning experiences—via institutes, internships, *or* short-term conferences—are valuable to them. Thus, while better answers are needed about the cost-effectiveness of various types of training programs, all of the programs *appear* to make useful contributions to their participants.

Five, until such time as more compelling evidence may emerge, it is, accordingly, probably important for the higher education community and its patrons—the foundations—to continue to sponsor and support a wide array of both "major" and "minor" training opportunities. However imperfect any of these activities may be, surely the benefits derived from them are substantial; the costs, borne by the institutions and a handful of generous foundations, *likely* are well justified.

In an era in which top- and middle-level administrative jobs are grueling and the pressures relentless, almost any opportunity to escape from "the trenches"—to mix with one's peers in (it is hoped) a nonthreatening environment and to be exposed to an enriching curriculum—is bound to be invigorating. Such activities deserve support.

As it happens, a recent development has the potential for prying the lid partway off the opaque box: the formation of a National Leadership Group by ACE's Center for Leadership Development. The ACE Commission on Leadership Development (a fifteen-member advisory panel) has charged the center with the responsibility of functioning as a "synthesizer and innovator in the field of leadership development." Toward that end, the center has formed a National Leadership Group consisting of some three dozen persons drawn from the directors of leadership and professional development programs, scholars who have addressed issues of professional development, and others (particularly staff members of the Washington-based presidents' associations) with a strong interest in leadership development. This latest ACE endeavor may prove to be useful, for it is designed to cut across the bewildering array of offerings and, if possible, arrive at some conclusions about how best to facilitate professional development.

Conclusion

In his exceptionally helpful 1978 monograph, Robert A. Scott observed that "higher education has not yet realized its responsibility for the professional development of its mid-level staffs" (Scott, 1978, p. 35). Nearly a decade later, even after much frenzied activity to combat "the management crisis," Scott's conclusion probably should not be much altered. Some contemporary judgments have not softened much; two longtime observers recently claimed that "higher-education administrators now represent a vast and teeming laity whose lack of professional training and self-esteem is nothing less than a conspiracy against the effectiveness of our colleges and universities" (Lawrence and Jones, 1985, p. 57). Whether or not so serious an indictment is true, the number and apparent quality of professional development opportunities for administrators has grown over time, and it is likely that some inroads have been made.

Still, on the whole, as suggested at the outset of this chapter, far too little is known; much is left to speculation. The time has come to begin a serious assessment of the field of management and leadership training in higher education in an effort to determine what strategies work best. The American Council on Education's renewed efforts toward that end may help point the way toward sounder strategies.

Recognizing that there are "few if any useful guidelines for assessing the quality of administrative performance" (Hodgkinson, 1981, p. 72), it may yet be that help is on the way.

NOTES

1. The most relevant data flow from a 1981 survey conducted by Pennsylvania State University's Center for the Study of Higher Education in cooperation with the American Council on Education; for example, career paths of presidents and deans are reported in Moore et al., 1983.
2. An extensive listing of programs, along with succinct descriptions, is found in Sharon A. McDade's doctoral dissertation, 1986, pp. 136–57), scheduled to be published in revised form as an ASHE-ERIC Higher Education Report (McDade, forthcoming).
3. Some eighty-six U.S. and three Canadian universities offer programs of graduate study in higher education (Shorr and Hoogstra, 1984). In 1986, 586 doctorates were conferred in "higher education" by American universities (National Research Council, unpublished).
4. Among the many useful sources, for example, is the excellent compendium by Jedamus, Peterson, and associates (1980).
5. "Institutes . . . are programs of at least four to six weeks duration, usually held during the summer. Within several weeks of intensive study, the Institute attempts to provide information on several of the most important administrative skills, e.g., budgeting, law, negotiations, finance and control, organizational behavior" (Kanter et al., unpublished, p. 19).
6. See, for example, *The NCHEMS Newsletter,* No. 92, May, 1986.
7. The estimated annual turnover involved, for example, 13 percent of 3,100 presidents/chancellors, 15 percent of 11,700 senior academic managers, and 20 percent of 66,600 department/division chairpersons (Fisher, 1978, p. 27).
8. The principal benefactor of the ICUA at Harvard was the Carnegie Corporation, which had awarded Harvard $924,000 to operate the Institute (Hefferlin and Phillips, 1971, p. 53).
9. At about the same time, an extensive guide to training programs was authored by JB Lon Hefferlin and Ellis L. Phillips, Jr., and published in book form (1971).

10. The program director made available to the author all completed evaluation forms, numbering nineteen of the twenty-eight participants (68 percent).
11. The IAA from 1973 to 1976 provided a six-week summer program, primarily for faculty women interested in administrative careers. Hosted initially at the University of Michigan, then at the University of Wisconsin, a total of eighty-two women participated in the IAA.

REFERENCES

ACADEMY FOR EDUCATIONAL DEVELOPMENT. "New Unit to Improve Management of Colleges and Universities." News Release, December 4, 1970.

AMERICAN COUNCIL ON EDUCATION. *A Guide to Professional Development Opportunities for College and University Administrators.* Washington, D.C.: ACE, 1979.

DILL, DAVID D. "Teaching in the Field of Higher Education: Management Courses." *Review of Higher Education,* Spring, 1978, pp. 39–44.

FISHER, CHARLES F., ED. *Developing and Evaluating Administrative Leadership.* New Directions for Higher Education, No. 22. San Francisco: Jossey-Bass, 1978.

GREEN, MADELEINE F. Background Paper, Leadership Development Meeting, December 12, 1985. Center for Leadership Development, American Council on Education, unpublished.

HAYNES, L.J. "Skills of the Effective Academic Administrator: Structuring the Curriculum." *Review of Higher Education,* Summer, 1985, pp. 8–16.

HEFFERLIN, JB LON, and PHILLIPS, ELLIS L., JR. *Information Services for Academic Administration.* San Francisco: Jossey-Bass, 1971.

HIGHER EDUCATION MANAGEMENT INSTITUTE. *Management Development and Training Program for Colleges and Universities, Progress Report No. 2.* Coconut Grove, Fla.: HEMI, October, 1976.

HODGKINSON, HAROLD L. "Administrative Development." In Arthur W. Chickering and associates, *The Modern American College.* San Francisco: Jossey-Bass, 1981.

INSTITUTE FOR EDUCATIONAL MANAGEMENT. *Management Development Program.* Cambridge, Mass.: IEM, Graduate School of Education, Harvard University, n.d.

INSTITUTE FOR EDUCATIONAL MANAGEMENT. *Orientation Handbook.* Cambridge, Mass.: IEM, Graduate School of Education, Harvard University, Summer, 1985.

INSTITUTE FOR EDUCATIONAL MANAGEMENT. *IEM Evaluation, 1986.* Cambridge, Mass.: IEM, Graduate School of Education, Harvard University, 1986.

JEDAMUS, PAUL; PETERSON, MARVIN W.; and ASSOCIATES, *Improving Academic*

Management: A Handbook of Planning and Institutional Research. San Francisco: Jossey-Bass, 1980.

KANTER, ROSABETH MOSS, MARGARET J. WHEATLEY, ET AL. *Career Development for Women in Academic Administration: The Role of Training.* Report to the Carnegie Corporation of New York. Unpublished, May 31, 1978.

KELLER, GEORGE. *Academic Strategy: The Management Revolution in American Higher Education.* Baltimore: Johns Hopkins University Press, 1983.

LAWRENCE, BEN and JONES, DENNIS. "The Higher-Education Manager as a Professional." *Journal for Higher Education Management, 1,* no. 1 (Summer/Fall, 1985), 57–62.

MANAGEMENT DEVELOPMENT PROGRAM. *MDP Evaluation, 1986.* Cambridge, Mass.: MDP, Graduate School of Education, Harvard University, 1986.

MCDADE, SHARON A. *Professional Development of Senior-Level Administrators of Colleges and Universities.* Unpublished doctoral dissertation, Harvard University, 1986. (Available through University Microfilms, Ann Arbor, Mich.)

MCDADE, SHARON A. *Professional Education for Senior Administrators of Higher Education Institutions.* ASHE-ERIC Higher Education Report. Washington, D.C.: Association for the Study of Higher Education, forthcoming.

MOORE, KATHRYN M.; SALIMBENE, ANN M.; MARLIER, JOYCE D.; and BRAGG, STEPHEN M. "The Structure of Presidents' and Deans' Careers." *Journal of Higher Education, 54,* no. 5 (September/October, 1983), 501–515.

NATIONAL RESEARCH COUNCIL. Office of Scientific and Engineering Personnel, Doctorate Records File, 1986. Unpublished.

PEARSON, CAROL S., and MARMION, HARRY A. *The ACE Fellows Program: The First Twenty Years.* Washington, D.C.: American Council on Education, 1985.

PHILLIPS, ELLIS, JR. Conversation with the author, March 14, 1986.

ROURKE, FRANCIS E., and BROOKS, GLENN E. *The Managerial Revolution in Higher Education.* Baltimore: Johns Hopkins University Press, 1966.

SCHUSTER, JACK H. "A Word for the 'Blue Plate Special': The Intermediate Professional Development Institute." Paper presented at the annual meeting of the American Association for Higher Education, Chicago, Ill., March 15, 1984.

SCOTT, ROBERT A. *Lords, Squires, and Yeomen: Collegiate Middle Managers and Their Organizations.* AAHE-ERIC Higher Education Research Report No. 7. Washington, D.C.: American Association for Higher Education, 1978.

"Send the Boss Back to School." Brochure describing College Management Program, Carnegie Mellon University, n.d.

SHORR, MARILYN, and HOOGSTRA, LISA. *Directory of Higher Education Programs and Faculty.* Washington, D.C.: Association for the Study of Higher Education and ERIC Clearinghouse on Higher Education, 5th ed., August, 1984.

BIBLIOGRAPHY

Argyris, Chris. "Educating Administrators and Professionals." In *Leadership in the '80's: Essays on Higher Education.* Cambridge, Mass.: Institute for Educational Management, Harvard University, 1980, pp. 1–38.

Benezet, Louis T. "Academic Leadership: Of What or of Whom?" *Management Forum* (Academy for Educational Development), June, 1974, pp. 1–4.

Bonham, George W. "The Stresses of Leadership." *Change,* April, 1979, pp. 12–13.

Glenny, Lyman A. *The Anonymous Leaders of Higher Education.* Berkeley: Center for Research and Development in Higher Education, University of California, 1971.

Green, Madeleine F., and Kellogg, Theodore. "Careers in Academe: Confirming the Conventional Wisdom?" *Educational Record, 63,* no. 2 (Spring, 1982), 40–43.

Kerr, Clark. "Administration in an Era of Change and Conflict." *Educational Record,* Winter, 1973, pp. 38–46.

Poppenhagen, Brent W., and Dunn, Melvin. "Preparing Mid-Level Professionals for the Future of Postsecondary Education," *Review of Higher Education,* Fall, 1979, pp. 31–41.

Secor, Cynthia. "Preparing the Individual for Institutional Leadership." In Adrian Tinsley, Cynthia Secor, and Sheila Kaplan, eds. *Women in Higher Education.* New Directions in Higher Education, No. 45. San Francisco: Jossey-Bass, 1984.

12

Leadership Development: A Participant's Perspective

DANIEL H. PERLMAN

Can leadership be taught? The existence of a number of formal leadership development programs, including several sponsored by major national education associations and by a number of distinguished universities and colleges, and the interest shown by aspiring and established leaders in attending them, attests to the widespread acceptance of the notion that leadership in higher education is susceptible to preparation or to honing. I share this view, albeit with some reservations.

A central question addressed in this book is: "Is it possible to prepare higher education leaders and, if so, how?" When asked from the perspective of someone who aspires to a leadership role, the question becomes: "Is it possible to prepare *to be* an educational leader?" or, somewhat less grandly: "Is it possible to prepare to be a college dean, or provost or president?"

In the preceding chapter Schuster describes several major professional development programs whose purpose is to prepare individuals for leadership roles. Indeed, many of the graduates of these programs have gone on to assume responsible administrative positions, including presidencies. However, one ought not assume a direct causal relationship between attendance at these programs

Daniel H. Perlman is president of Suffolk University.

and subsequent career achievements. *Post hoc est non propter hoc:* that which follows is not necessarily caused by that which precedes.

Asking how these leadership development programs help people prepare to enter and succeed in positions of responsibility is similar to asking about the relationship between the quality of any academic program and the success of its graduates. What is the relationship between the experiences we provide the students who attend our colleges and universities and their achievements as graduates? As with the successful alumni of our colleges who assume positions of influence and responsibility, the success of graduates of leadership development programs, as measured by their upward career mobility, is undoubtedly due to a combination of factors.

1. *Better skills.* To some extent the curriculum of these formal leadership development programs and the learning experiences they provide contribute to the success of graduates who accede to positions of leadership because of improved managerial and administrative skills and better information.

2. *Enhanced self-confidence.* The programs also serve in many cases to empower their alumni by enhancing their self-confidence. The opportunity to evaluate one's abilities against those of participants from various other colleges and universities, including those with greater prestige, can contribute significantly to the participant's opinion of his or her readiness and ability to assume a leadership position. This may be especially true for women and minorities and for people from "invisible" colleges.

3. *Contacts and "networking."* It is sometimes asserted that mobility in higher education is facilitated by a web of personal contacts or networks. If so, perhaps a primary value of these programs is as a source of such contacts. Most of these programs provide an opportunity to meet people from other institutions as well as from state higher education agencies and national associations. Directories of participants past and present and periodic gatherings of alumni make it easy to maintain contact.

4. *Career strategies.* Leadership development programs may facilitate career mobility by helping participants understand how they might shape or influence the course of their career, that is, how they might actively "manage" their career. This knowledge includes a better understanding of how the search process works, a refined sense of the "rules of the game" for career mobility, and what initiative is appropriate for individuals to take on their own behalf.

5. *Prestige.* Another factor related to the success of some graduates of leadership development programs is the weight that may be given by search committees to participation in leadership development activities by a candidate or to a letter of reference from the sponsoring organization or from the program director. The reputation or prestige of a particular program or of its sponsoring organization, coupled with the "weight" given to letters of reference on behalf of an alumnus or alumna, may outweigh the educational content of the program or the network of contacts it produces as a factor contributing to its graduates' success.

6. *Evidence of motivation.* College trustees or search committee members sometimes conclude that participation in these programs is an indication of a candidate's high motivation, determination, and diligence. It should be noted, however, that up to now faculty search committees have reportedly given less credence to formal leadership development experiences than to conventional academic experience as a faculty member, department chair, and dean.

7. *New perspectives.* By providing a break from the routine, these programs give their participants a new perspective on their work, a broadened outlook, or renewed vigor in much the same way that extended travel or a sabbatical leave do.

8. *Momentum.* It is also likely that some people are selected for and attend leadership development programs who are already on career paths that will land them in a leadership position whether or not they participate in an organized leadership development program and irrespective of which one.

It is probably impossible to disentangle the component factors associated with the career advancement of participants in leadership development programs. Probably all eight factors are at work. I suspect that many of them were in my case, as they were in the case of other program participants with whom I have spoken.

As Green elaborates in Chapter 1 and Bennett elaborates in Chapter 3, it has been fashionable in higher education to think of academic administrators as being summoned reluctantly out of the faculty to serve begrudgingly or with a spirit of nobless oblige for a period of years until they could retreat respectably into scholarship. Administrative tasks were regarded as a burden that distracted attention from more meritorious academic pursuits. Wanting to be a department chair or college president was a factor that disqualified a candidate from serious consideration in the view of some. This view or affectation was expressed often by Robert M. Hutchins, chancellor of the University of Chicago during the 1930s and 1940s, whose views on higher education were widely read and respected; and it is still held by many academics.

A Case History

My own experience reflects a more deliberate approach to higher education leadership, perhaps a more typical approach than the folklore would suggest. Leadership development experiences played a significant role in the evolution of my career. While the preparation of college and university leaders is idiosyncratic, my experiences may identify and illuminate common issues.

First, I had the good fortune of attending a small, experimental liberal arts college, Shimer College, then affiliated with the University of Chicago and employing what is sometimes referred to as "the Hutchins curriculum": reading and discussing excerpts from the works of seminal thinkers in the major disciplines, organized into yearlong courses in the humanities, the natural sciences, the social sciences, languages, and integrative studies. The curriculum of the college was prescribed completely, reflecting a conviction that everyone should have the same intellectual equipment and cultural development regardless of any subsequent graduate specialization or occupational preparation. My interest in higher education administration began during my undergraduate years when it occurred to me that to contribute to the world of scholarship and learning by helping to make it all come together and work would be both a noble calling and exciting work.

Although various other aspirations and objectives intervened in the ensuing years, the administration of higher education recurred as a central interest. In reviewing the experiences that helped prepare me for a presidency, it is clear that my education at a college which took the world of ideas seriously and where there was a coherent and integrated concept of what an undergraduate education was all about, was a decisive factor. This experience and the excitement for learning that it instilled were central to my aspirations. Without a strong liberal arts education and a desire to contribute to the world of higher learning, no amount of "leadership development" would have sufficed to prepare me for a presidency.

While a graduate degree in higher education is not the typical path to the presidency, it was an attractive option for me. The University of Chicago higher education program is part of the Social

Science Division and incorporates psychology, anthropology, sociology, and history. The program introduced the emerging literature on higher education (for example, Sanford, 1962) and the applications of social science to the study of colleges, as well as the views of various philosophers—Plato, Whitehead, Cardinal Newman, et al.—on the proper role, organization, and content of higher education. It was intriguing both to study the views of people who had thought deeply about the purpose and content of higher education and to understand how little was then known about how colleges and universities actually functioned as social, economic, and intellectual systems interacting with their constituents and their environment.

The opportunity to study with scholars who were having a profound influence on their respective fields made the program stimulating. Leading intellectuals, such as educational psychologist Benjamin Bloom, psychoanalyst Bruno Bettelheim, educator Norman Burns, biologist-turned-philosopher Joseph J. Schwab, pioneer in adult education Cyril O. Houle, and others, had a profound impact on my interest in and zeal for higher education as a field of study and as an arena for practice.

The opportunity to work under the guidance of a gifted mentor was the next important phase of my professional development. Rolf A. Weil, an able and energetic administrator, has been president of Roosevelt University in Chicago for more than twenty years, through a period that saw sweeping changes in higher education in general and in the Chicago area in particular: the student demonstrations of the 1960s; the increased competition for students and resources brought about by the great expansion of the state colleges and universities in the Chicago area; changing residential and economic patterns in that metropolitan area including the growth of the suburbs and the decline and later revitalization of the Chicago Loop, especially the south loop where Roosevelt University's main campus is located; the adoption by virtually all colleges and universities of the aspects of Roosevelt University's mission that were unique or distinctive at the time of its founding in 1945, namely, an integrated student body and faculty, degree programs for adults, and faculty involvement in governance.

Serving under President Weil's mentorship in a series of positions from assistant to the president to vice president for administration provided a laboratory for learning administration and leadership from a practitioner of great ability. Weil, educated as an economist at the University of Chicago, had been dean of the

College of Business Administration at Roosevelt University before becoming acting president in 1964 and president in 1966. As his assistant, I had the opportunity to see how he handled situations of all types including many, especially in the mid-1960s, that were tense, threatening, uncomfortable, and confounding. Learning about integrity, courage, consistency, perspective, parsimony, resiliency, forthrightness, and humanity from a mentor is an experience that cannot be replicated in a leadership development program. The fact that Roosevelt University was a developing institution with a relatively small administrative staff meant that I had the opportunity to become involved with a very broad range of issues and activities that in a more heavily staffed university might have been parceled out to other offices.

One of my responsibilities during these years was that of secretary to the Board of Trustees, a position providing a rare opportunity for an aspiring administrator to observe from a unique vantage point the interaction between the president and the trustees and also to see how matters progressed through the governance structure of the university.

At that point in my career, formal training and exposure to the experiences and practices of other colleges and to national higher education leaders seemed a useful and interesting addition to my preparation for further leadership responsibilities. I decided to participate selectively in programs that I thought might develop my skills, expand my knowledge, increase my contacts, and further my career objectives. I was concerned that serving at one institution over an extended period, despite growing responsibilities and authority (in all I served at Roosevelt University for nineteen years, of which fifteen involved working directly with the president), would give me a parochial outlook and narrowed vision. Thus, one of my major objectives in participating in national professional development programs was to avoid such parochialism, to gain a sense of how things were done in other places by other people; in short, to experience some of the diversity and variety I knew to be inherent in American higher education. In addition to whatever other objectives they achieved, these programs were useful in that respect. Over a period of nearly twenty years I had an opportunity to participate in several formal leadership development programs.

University of Michigan Seminar, 1966. The first program I attended was a weeklong conference on academic administration conducted by the Department of Higher Education of the University of Michigan. At the time I was assistant to the president, a position virtually unique in higher education administration in having no professional association and therefore little opportunity to meet and learn from professional colleagues. I used the occasion of the trip to Ann Arbor to meet with my counterpart at that institution, an interesting and useful experience. In addition to the academic content of the seminar, I found that the experience of talking with colleagues in the field suggested new opportunities and responsibilities that might come my way.

American Council on Education Fellow, 1972–1973. I became aware of the ACE Fellows Program not long after I had completed my doctorate. I had been in the same position at Roosevelt for six years and was concerned that there was no natural career path that led from being an assistant to the president to something else. The Fellows Program seemed a reasonable way to learn about other options and opportunities and to prepare for them. The condition for my nomination by the president was that I serve a "home campus" internship under his mentorship, since Roosevelt University did not have the resources to pay my salary for a year while I was at another institution. While the experiences of ACE Fellows over the years suggest that an internship on another campus, the "host campus" option, is usually a richer learning experience for the Fellow, my home fellowship was still worthwhile. Weil took seriously his responsibilities as mentor and gave me the opportunity to accompany him on fund-raising calls and to sit in on the e full cycle of budget negotiations, new experiences for me and useful in understanding the finances of an independent urban university.

A strength of the American Council on Education Fellows Program is its ability to convey an understanding of higher education as a national enterprise. Especially valuable to me in this respect were the several weeklong seminars on national issues affecting higher education. In meeting the heads of various Washington-based higher education associations and various congressional leaders and staff concerned with education issues, Fellows develop an awareness of the national issues confronting higher education and the concerns of various sectors and interest groups. They get a sense of how these interest groups and the various professional associations that represent them interact, collaboratively and in competition. Also, the Fellows Program provides participants opportunities to visit other campuses, to meet other administrators, and to see how things are done in other settings—enabling Fellows to see that the other pasture is not necessarily greener, that people struggle or deal with similar problems and issues on virtually every campus.

The ACE Fellows Program is enriched by the requirement that participants submit a publishable paper on some issue studied or worked on during the year, a discipline I found useful and effective, enabling me to write about the application of management information systems to higher education, then just beginning, and about external degree programs, then newly in vogue. The Fellows Program is the only leadership development program I have experienced that has a formal writing requirement. For the preparation of leaders in a field where writing is such an important skill, supervised practice is essential. The absence of a writing component in the other programs is a deficiency, in my opinion.

The Fellows Program has provided continuing professional development opportunities. For many years the alumni have maintained an annual "working reunion," whose participants are required to present to the group a current case study or problem, a description of some issue they are dealing with. These working reunions have provided ongoing opportunities to discuss complex issues and review the outcomes and consequences of various courses of action, proposed and imminent. Although several of the other leadership development programs have periodic "alumni reunions," they are not used as working sessions to the same extent.

The Institute for Educational Management (IEM), 1974. Two years after participating in the ACE Fellows Program and after changing positions and taking on additional responsibilities at Roosevelt University as dean of administration, I had an opportunity to participate in the Institute for Educational Management. The program is described by Schuster in Chapter 11.

More than any of the other formal midcareer development programs in which I have participated, the IEM program conveys an understanding of the various managerial or administrative aspects of higher education involved in running a campus. Participants do not become experts in the various administrative specialities but learn how all the aspects of administration fit together in a well-managed university or college; they learn what questions to ask to monitor the operation of these component units and what results to look for from each of these domains.

The learning environment established by IEM, including a carefully prepared syllabus and study guide, a tight schedule of classes, discussions, and related activities, and voluminous assigned readings of cases and journal articles, is successful in getting participants to prepare conscientiously for each class and to treat the analysis and discussion of each case very seriously. Discussions tend to be intense, probing, focused and cumulative—in which the learning from one course or session is applied to the next. Participants learn that there are many ways to look at a problem or issue, depending on one's background experiences or present context; that it is useful to discuss the issues one confronts in administration with others who have different perspectives; that intense discussion need not be a quarrel; that there are experts in various fields and subfields to whom one can look for advice and suggestions; and that the executive group within a college or university must function as a team to be effective. IEM participants also get a sense of how the various constituent groups on and off campus interact with one another and with the campus leadership, that is, how "the system" works.

If the ACE Fellows Program gives its participants a sense of "the big picture," that is, the national issues in higher education, IEM gives its participants a comprehensive view of how the campus microcosm functions, the differing perspectives of, say, a senator who needs to comprehend regional, national, and global issues, and a mayor who must understand what is happening in each ward.

Probably most IEM participants have their expenses fully paid by their sponsoring college; in my case the costs were shared equally between my university, myself, and an IEM scholarship. Without the scholarship and without some assistance from my university I would have been unable to attend. My own financial contribution to attending this and other leadership development programs intensified my desire to take maximum advantage of these opportunities, and the scholarship was essential to assist Roosevelt University in supporting me.

The President's Executive Exchange Program, 1977–1978. The President's Executive Exchange Program is conducted by a federal commission to provide an opportunity for about forty selected executives from "the private sector" to have the experience of working in management positions inside the federal government for a year, usually in Washington, and to arrange for selected government executives, usually substantially fewer in number, to work in appropriate assignments in the private sector for a year. Similar in many ways to its better-known cousin, the White House Fellows Program, it provides a structured program throughout the year of talks by congressional leaders, cabinet officers, and other key federal executives as well as by corporate CEOs. There is also an international seminar—ours included meetings in Brussels, Paris, Bonn, and Berlin with governmental leaders in those countries, with officials of international agencies, with American embassy personnel, and with overseas executives of multinational corporations—to show how American foreign policy is conducted and provide a better understanding of international issues.

I learned of the opportunity through the American Council on Education's Office of Leadership Development, which for a few years in the mid-1970s coordinated the applications of participants from the higher education community. Higher education was included only for a few years; the President's Executive Exchange Program now serves only people in the business community and government agencies. Since my position at Roosevelt University included managing government relations, the program seemed well suited to help me learn my way around Washington a bit more, to increase my knowledge of the administrative and legislative process, and to provide the opportunity to meet various federal executives and political leaders. Participants from the private sector become temporary federal employees, so although my university granted me a leave of absence for the year, it had no financial outlay. It was an expensive year personally, because I maintained two residences and commuted home frequently. Some of the corporate participants had their additional expenses reimbursed by their companies, but it was not reasonable or feasible to request a university with a tight budget to take on added expenses of that type.

The President's Executive Exchange Program reflects its political, rather than academic, origins. In addition to each person's specific job, the emphasis is on meeting and listening to political and governmental leaders. As an academic I expected more "homework" or background reading assignments in preparation for each speaker. The program's culture differs from the campus culture of research, discussion, and dissent. An objective of the program is for participants to understand the views of the administration on various issues.

My assignment during the year 1977–1978 was with the (then) U.S. Office of Education as a special assistant to the deputy commissioner for higher and continuing education. It was an interesting time to be in the Office of Education because the staff was developing proposals for an imminent reauthorization of the Higher Education Act and because it was the last year in which Education was imbedded in what was then the Department of Health, Education, and Welfare. Five of the forty private-sector participants were from higher education. We organized a higher education subgroup, meeting in Washington and Europe with officials concerned with higher education issues. The program enabled participants to see how higher education policy is formulated and how federal programs are carried out, and to gain the sense of being "inside Washington" that comes from meeting with government leaders. In many ways it was an extended civics class, a midcareer version of the "junior year in Washington" program available to undergraduates. It was also useful to work with corporate executives during the year, most of whom were in fairly senior positions in Fortune 500 firms, and to observe how the goals, style, and temperament of people in the corporate community differs from those in higher education.

Fulbright Lectureship on Higher Education, 1975. Although not conventionally regarded as a leadership development program, the Fulbright Lectureship program provided an exceptional opportunity to get a comparative view of higher education. My acceptance of a three-month lectureship in the Philippines in the field of American higher education enabled me to see how higher education is organized and conducted in another culture, to study a system of higher education that is both similar and dissimilar to ours, and to meet with educators eager to learn about current educational developments in the United States.

I was attracted to the Fulbright program because of a longstanding interest in comparative higher education, including a master's thesis in that area, and a curiosity about how schools influence and are influenced by the history and culture of their country. I learned that higher education in the Philippines is as heterogeneous in its organization and sponsorship as in the United States. I had an opportunity to observe how the various cultural influences left by the Spanish and by the Americans who governed the country from 1898 to its independence following World War II were reflected in different types of colleges and universities; to view the relationship between the government of the Philippines, then under martial law, and higher education; and to see the way its educational system accommodates minority groups and responds to pressures of various kinds. On my return, the information I learned and my impressions became the subject of an article and several talks.

Comparative education is a useful methodology from which to gain a perspective on American higher education, including an appreciation of the differing political, cultural, social, and historical contexts in which colleges operate. One becomes more accepting and tolerant of diversity in higher education when one understands the importance of an institution's origins, its particular circumstances or environment, and the pressures upon it.

In order to accept the Fulbright, I used my vacation period for that year and took a two-month leave of absence from my university. Supplementing the Fulbright with personal funds enabled my wife and children to come along on what proved to be an interesting experience for all of us. My wife lectured to academic audiences in the Philippines and Japan on her field of specialization, the diagnosis and treatment of learning disabilities.

Academy for Educational Development Research Project, 1974–1975. The broadening of one's perspectives, essential to leadership development, can come through a variety of experiences. Contributing to a study on broadly representative campus senates conducted by John Millett, then head of the Management Division of AED, the Academy for Educational Development, enlarged my understanding of governance issues (see Millett, 1978). I prepared a case study on the Faculty Senate at Roosevelt University, one of a group of about twenty colleges and universities with broadly representative senates participating in Millett's study. His conferences for the case study authors were similar to graduate seminars on the organization and governance of higher education. Millett brought to these seminars a vast experience in higher education with AED, as a university president and as chancellor of the Ohio Board of Regents, giving us a perspective on the forms and reforms of campus governance. Later I had the opportunity to participate with Millett and his AED colleagues in a project in college and university planning, funded by the Kellogg Foundation and involving several workshops with the presidents and other representatives of a group of participating universities; this provided a similar broadening experience.

NTL Workshop, 1980. Understanding and improving one's interpersonal skills is another dimension of leadership development. A weeklong workshop for college and university administrators conducted by National Training Laboratories, Inc. (NTL) at their summer "campus" in Bethel, Maine, focusing on interpersonal and group dynamics in professional settings. I attended that workshop during the week that the board of Suffolk University voted on my appointment as president, so my coparticipants were the first colleagues to learn of the board's decision. The group leader, who shortly thereafter himself became a college president, invited the other participants to tell me or enact the things they would want to tell or ask of the president of their own institution, had they the opportunity. Most wanted more of their president's time and attention. They each wanted their president to be interested in them. The experience provided a vivid foretaste of the multiple and competing claims on one's time and attention experienced by an academic president.

Troutbeck Seminar, 1985. Perhaps the least explicit part of leadership development is the examination of values and convictions that govern one's belief system and conduct. While this is the substance of liberal education, administrators rarely have the time or the opportunity to reexamine these important issues at periodic intervals. The Troutbeck Seminar for college and university presidents, sponsored by the Educational Leadership Project of the Christian A. Johnson Endeavor Foundation at the Troutbeck Conference Center in upstate New York, is one such opportunity. Similar to the programs for corporate executives sponsored by the Aspen Institute for Humanistic Studies, the Troutbeck Seminar provides the opportunity for small groups of college presidents to spend a week reading and discussing excerpts from the writings of classical authors and seminal thinkers on the issues of leadership and governance, with the assistance of a skilled discussion leader. The value of this seminar is its focus on great issues and great thinkers, enabling its participants to reaffirm the experience and reinforce the outcomes of a liberal education. Academic administrators no less than faculty should return to the wellsprings of liberal education periodically for refreshment and reaffirmation. The book of readings sent in advance to each participant, some familiar to me, others new, raised key issues in order to present contrasting views and to evoke discussion. The discussions were invigorating. Such experiences are at least as important to leadership development as are seminars on educational management.

ACE Fellows Seminar on Values and Ethics, 1986. The Council of ACE Fellows, the alumni organization of the ACE Fellows Program, sponsored a similar program on values and ethics for the Fellows Program alumni in July 1986. The curriculum included reading and discussion of excerpts from the writings of philosophers and novelists as well as political theorists and men and women of action. Studying great essays and works of literature reaffirms the values and the process of a liberal education. Like the Troutbeck Seminar, the program provided an opportunity to be intellectually refreshed by the wealth of the humanities.

These and other developmental experiences, including conferences by various professional associations, seminars for new presidents conducted by the American Council on Education, significant books on higher education, as well as biographies and autobiographies of successful leaders, especially higher education leaders, played a role in my professional preparation. The various leadership development programs in which I had an opportunity to participate at key points in my career were undoubtedly useful in helping me prepare for broader responsibilities as they came along.

Expectations and Outcomes

So there is support for the notion that leaders can be prepared. It is worth noting, however, that only a small fraction of the people entering college presidencies and other leadership positions in higher education have participated in an organized leadership development program beforehand. While formal leadership development programs are useful in preparing some people for leadership positions, there is no evidence that participation in these programs is either a necessary or an especially efficient route to a leadership position.

It is a mistake for participants to develop or be given unrealistic expectations about their career paths following their involvement with one of these programs. Some participants have an unarticulated hope that the program will transform them into a prince or princess, or a magical belief that being selected is akin to being knighted. Mistaken assumptions and inflated expectations can lead to unnecessary disappointment or frustration; moreover, upward career mobility is only one criterion for the evaluation of these programs, insufficient by itself. Enhancing the professional effectiveness and increasing the personal satisfaction of participants, whatever their level of responsibility within their college or university, are broader but more useful objectives, and they are criteria against which a program's success should be measured. The best of these programs have other merits as well, in addition to fulfilling targeted learning and career development purposes. They attract interesting people with whom conversation about higher education issues can be lively and stimulating; they are sometimes set in interesting surroundings and can be fun as well as intellectually rewarding.

Many Pathways, Many Styles

Different preparatory experiences or leadership development programs may be better for some people, or for some components of the higher education community, than for others. The selection of a specific leadership development program is undoubtedly influenced by the participant's perception of the program's value and prestige in different sectors of higher education. Other factors affecting the choice of a given program include the time involved, the conflicting demands of family and job responsibilities, the cost and whether one's institution is willing to assume all or part of that cost, the availability of scholarship subsidies, the location, the program's fit with one's career objectives, the other program participants, the sponsoring organization, the program leaders, and, for the programs with competitive admissions, the risk of rejection if one applies and is not accepted, especially if the application process on one's campus is in any way public.

It is important to remember that formal programs are only one way to prepare for administrative and leadership positions. It is difficult to advise someone who might wish to prepare for a leadership assignment how to invest his or her time and energy. Is it better for the aspiring administrator to attend leadership development programs or to write a book? Is it better to apprentice oneself to a successful president in a subordinate administrative role or to seek out positions of maximum responsibility and autonomy? What about the value of an additional degree? Should the aspirant study law at night, or business administration, or public policy or higher education? Does it help to be qualified as a J.D. or an M.B.A. as well as a Ph.D.? How important is the prestige of the institution with which one is affiliated or from which one has received his or her degree? Obviously, there is no single answer to these questions. What is prudent and appropriate for one person is not necessarily appropriate for another.

Achievement in one's present position is crucial as one seeks to prepare for broader responsibilities. A reputation for excellence and integrity in one's job is ultimately of decisive importance to search committees and hiring officials. To carry out current responsibilities halfheartedly because one is preparing for the next position by pursuing training that is extraneous, tangential, and diverting to the successful and imaginative completion of those responsibilities will be unsuccessful in the long run. In public life, where one "runs for office," being a good candidate is a necessary career phase; in higher education, one does not ordinarily campaign for office. Holding oneself to the highest standard of performance in one's present responsibilities, participating in and contributing to the intellectual life of one's own institution and of the academy, developing and exercising one's abilities of expression, honing one's sense of judgment and one's ethical standards, guiding the work of others in a collegial setting, and learning how colleges and universities function and the role played by each constituency may be the best way to prepare for assignments of increased responsibility and leadership.

Kerr and Gade (1986) estimate that ten thousand men and women will have been chosen by search committees and boards to serve as college and university presidents during the decades of the 1980s and 1990s out of perhaps a hundred thousand "seriously considered persons" (pp. 3–4). Those who are selected as presidents must have qualifications, credentials, and experience that are attractive to the search committee and governing board of a particular institution. But what is attractive or compelling in one setting or at one time is not necessarily compelling or attractive in another. The candidate's completion of one or more leadership development experiences may or may not seem significant to those making the decision at a particular institution. Kerr and Gade refer to a "prestige scale" among institutions and to the various sectors or "compartments" into which institutions are grouped: public and private, research universities, highly selective liberal arts colleges, doctorate-granting and comprehensive universities and colleges, less-selective liberal arts colleges, and community colleges (p. 20). They observe that movement between sectors is uncommon. There is at least anecdotal evidence to suggest that formal leadership development experiences are more likely to be seen with favor by search committees at institutions of mid-level and lower prestige than at institutions of high prestige.

Some governing boards or search committees may attribute a level of managerial sophistication or awareness to those candidates who have formal preparation that it does not ascribe to others, assuming a cause and effect relationship between preparation and effectiveness. But in fact there is no evidence that those who have prepared for a college presidency by participating in a formal leadership development experience are any more effective than those presidents who have arrived in their positions without such training. Of course, measuring or comparing "presidential effectiveness" is highly problematic, since the situations faced by presidents and the context of presidencies are so different from one institution to another. And to further complicate matters, as Kerr and Gade observe, different constituent groups have different criteria for judging the success of a college president.

The higher education literature, including that written by current and former presidents, is replete with differing views on how to be effective and on what attributes contribute to effectiveness. Fisher (1984), Berendzen (1986), and Walker (1979), among others, emphasize different and often contradictory personality styles, temperament, and manner as necessary or desirable qualities for effective presidents. Fisher describes a regal or aloof president; his metaphor is the president on a pedestal. Walker describes a "democratic" president who behaves as a colleague rather than as a remote figure on an elevated perch. Berendzen describes a style dominated by public relations activities where virtually all academic decisions are delegated to the provost and much time is spent in public appearances and media events away from the campus. His metaphor is a suit of armor. Kerr and Gade (1986), Riesman (1980) and others speak of the academically involved president who is the intellectual leader of the institution, who is sufficiently involved with students to know them by name and sufficiently involved with the faculty to know the research interests of each and the salient issues in each discipline.

These contradictory recommendations and descriptions suggest that different styles, personalities, and temperaments are effective for different people in different settings or contexts. The only generalization that emerges is that the personality and style of the president must be congruent with the expectations and needs of the institution and its constituents. Activities and characteristics that are regarded with favor and produce effective results in one context may fall flat or be regarded as antithetical in another. Kerr and Gade (1986) make this point when they observe how "enormously diverse college [presidents are] in their abilities, in their characters, in their motivations, in their personalities" and when they conclude: "Four axioms follow from this discussion: (a) the presidency is context-bound; (b) contexts vary greatly; (c) there is no single best, or even possible, strategy for all contexts; (d) the president should be evaluated within the possibilities and limitations of the context" (pp. 170–71).

There is an assumption in the literature on the college presidency that personality styles, temperaments, and "strategies" can be controlled. But there is a compelling argument that people's basic personalities and their manner of interacting with others are relatively stable by the time they are old enough to be considered for a presidency or other major administrative position, barring major situational changes or substantial psychotherapeutic intervention. Most leaders would agree that it is more important to be true to one's own personality and at ease with oneself and with others, than to try to assume a personality style recommended by someone else; such an attempt is usually perceived as an affectation.

Recommendations about particular leadership styles may be valuable to search committees trying to clarify the particular type of personality they would like to have fill the deanship or presidency at their institution. For people preparing for leadership positions the more useful studies are those which, while emphasizing the diversity of personalities and styles of people who become leaders, identify common tasks and strategies. After interviewing ninety people in positions of leadership in business, public life, academia, and other settings, Bennis and Nanus (1985) observed that they had found

> a wildly diverse group. . . . There seemed to be no obvious patterns for their success. . . . They were . . . articulate and inarticulate, assertive and retiring, dressed for success and dressed for failure, participative and autocratic. There were more variations than themes. Even their managerial styles were restlessly different. . . . For those of us interested in pattern, in underlying themes, this group was frustratingly unruly" (pp. 25–26).

Nonetheless, they identify four "strategies" or qualities that they believe are characteristic of effective leaders regardless of their personality or leadership style: gaining the attention of an organization through establishing a vision or creating a focus that is responsive to the needs of the organization; providing meaning by communicating; establishing trust by being reliable and "all of a piece"; "deployment of self through positive self regard" by creating in others a sense of confidence and high expectation and by recognizing one's own strengths and compensating for one's weaknesses.

John Gardner (1986) also emphasizes that there are many styles and kinds of leaders. For Gardner, leaders are those who envision goals, affirm values, motivate, manage, achieve a "workable level" of unity, explain, serve as a symbol, represent their group externally, and renew the purposes and spirit of their group. Managing, which he further differentiates into component skills, is, for Gardner, but one aspect of leadership.

Specific to the higher education context is Kerr and Gade's (1986, p. 60) inventory of the abilities and skills it takes to be a college or university president:

1. "The ability to work upward with a board (or boards) and, in public institutions with a governor and key legislators. This requires careful preparation of materials, a reputation for integrity, an attitude of respect, and a willingness to concede to higher authority."
2. The ability "to administer a staff through good choice of subordinates, clear and careful instructions, a balanced program of rewards and punishments, and a fair evaluation of results."
3. "The ability to work laterally with independent colleagues, particularly faculty members. This demands expertise at negotiation, high sensitivity to personal feelings, and great patience in awaiting results."
4. "The ability to handle confrontations. . . . This requires strategy and tactics in making and resisting demands . . . and willingness to be personally combative."
5. "The ability to work with a whole series of individuals and small groups in give-and-take conversations that fan out in many directions."
6. The ability to "appeal to faculty or students or alumni or the public at large."

Kerr and Gade acknowledge that these six skills are "very complex and, to a degree, contradictory." They observe that these skills "never come equally in the same individual" and that "presidents [and one might add, prospective presidents] too often think in terms of acquiring specific skills such as understanding budgets and accounts or contract law, or dealing with the media [that] can be supplied at the staff level."

Organized leadership development programs can help participants think about those six skills and about similar lists of skills formulated by others, and such programs can provide case examples in writing and *in situ* in which the exercise of those skills—or the failure to exercise them—can be observed. But classroom discussion and short-term observation lack the emotional intensity of the real thing. Long-term observation and learning close-up, with the feel of what it is like to be an actor rather than an observer, can take place only with a mentor on a job of increasing responsibility and complexity over an extended period.

Teaching and Learning Management and Leadership

It is commonly accepted that management skills are teachable. Academic programs in business administration, public administration, hospital administration, and school administration are all based upon this premise, as are many of the formal programs of leadership development that focus on management skills and tasks. Because management skills are more concrete, they are easier to teach and to learn than are the other leadership skills. Indeed, management skills provide the substance of the curriculum in most leadership development programs.

A systematic and intensive residential program with a formal curriculum, such as the Institute for Educational Management (IEM), can provide its participants with a detailed awareness and appreciation of various managerial and administrative tasks. This awareness, while not sufficient to make the participants experts in any specific area of administration, is enough to enable them to locate, understand, appreciate, and evaluate the experts. Participants who come with a range of specialties and qualifications enhance each other's learning by sharing their knowledge in class and outside. The experience of working intensively with a heterogeneous group of administrators who do not all share the same experiences and assumptions is especially valuable. Learning to work effectively with such a group on common tasks is one of the most valuable aspects of these programs.

What about the other aspects of leadership? Bennis and Nanus assert that the "major capacities of leadership can be learned . . . at least if the basic desire to learn is there. . . . Nurture is far more important than nature in determining who becomes a successful leader." But only a limited amount can be learned ahead of time through classes or books. "For those who are ready, most of the learning takes place during the experience [of exercising leadership] itself" (Bennis and Nanus, 1985, pp. 222–23). Indeed, a number of the most effective of the leadership development programs limit participation to people who are already in positions of responsibility. Several programs enable participants to simulate the experience of leadership, either by working closely with a mentor, as in the case of the ACE Fellows Program, or vicariously through case studies, as in Harvard's IEM.

Values are harder to impart than are specific skills. There are certain essential and necessary values that leaders in higher education must have if they are to be successful and effective. Paramount among these is a commitment to higher education, a belief in the importance of the work performed by colleges and universities. Henry W. Wriston, former president of Lawrence College and of Brown University, made the same point when he described his "conviction that a college president should be a scholar . . . but that there [is] a prior and still more important quality: a commitment to higher education which no discouragement [can] shake—indeed, which with nothing [can] successfully compete" (Wriston, 1959, quoted in Kerr and Gade, 1986, p. 192). This fundamental and underlying commitment to higher education is essential to leadership. A deep and unshakable commitment evolves over many years; it cannot be acquired by training.

Some qualities and abilities are learned, if at all, by observing and emulating respected supervisors, role models, or mentors over fairly sustained periods of time. The studies in moral and ethical development by Harvard psychologist Lawrence Kohlberg and others suggest that there are levels of ethical development (although probably somewhat different for women than for men; see Carol Gilligan [1982]) and that ethical development can be learned by observing and working with others who are at a "higher stage" in their own development. In this respect the right mentor is invaluable. Some qualities are acquired over a lifetime, including one's early childhood. These qualities include courage, conviction, ethical standards, integrity, sensitivity to the needs of others, rationality, and the ability to modulate one's interaction with others.

Conclusions

A Developmental Process. Formal leadership development programs should be seen as one part of an ongoing lifetime of learning and career development rather than as a onetime leadership experience. If they are good, they are effective incrementally. They do not transform nonleaders into leaders or bestow instant charisma or wisdom or verve. By focusing attention on particular issues or values or skills they can help participants nurture, hone, or refine those faculties. They also broaden one's contacts and networks.

It is not possible to prepare college and university leaders in the sense that it is possible to prepare lawyers or accountants or physicians, a substantial proportion of whom will pass the appropriate certifying examinations and enter the profession upon completion of a specific program of studies. But it is possible to prepare oneself for leadership positions if one has adequate motivation, ability, and good fortune. Such preparation can take many forms of which certain leadership development programs are one. The reasons for the apparent success of these programs are complex and include various factors in addition to the curriculum, just as attendance at certain universities seems to facilitate the career mobility of its graduates making it easier for them to open certain doors. No single set of experiences constitutes the "right" preparation. There is no prescribed preparation that is both necessary and sufficient.

People accept leadership positions at various ages, but preparation to be an effective educational leader must be continuous throughout one's professional life. The skills necessary to be an effective president or senior administrator can differ from situation to situation. The people who remain effective over time, or at different institutions, are able to develop and exercise new skills as each context requires. There is no shortcut or royal road to leadership, no way to circumvent the development of one's abilities or character, including patience. For leadership development to be successful, participants must have a fundamental conviction of the importance of higher education, an ability to convey that conviction with enthusiasm and sincerity, and a capacity to guide the work of others.

The Role of Leaders in Leadership Development. Educational leaders have a responsibility to encourage members of their faculty and staff to fulfill their own potential. Those of us in a position to do so should sponsor candidates to participate in leadership development programs, serve as mentors, organize training experiences, and foster a climate of personal growth and development among the staff and faculty of our institutions.

Sponsoring leadership development does entail certain costs and risks: the costs of sponsoring participants and the risks that competent people may want to move on to greater responsibility and new challenges elsewhere. But these are costs and risks we must assume to maintain a sense of openness and opportunity in our institutions.

Although most of the focus of this chapter is on leadership development from the perspective of an individual participant, it should be recognized that developmental programs can be organized and conducted as group training and intervention to improve the leadership team on a given campus. If a college or university is dependent upon the effective functioning of a leadership team including the president as well as senior administrators, key faculty leaders, and others, and if this group must learn to function effectively together as a team, it follows that the development of skills in the leadership team as a group may be a more successful strategy than sending individual administrators to different programs where they will work with people they may not see again. While the beneficial impact on a campus of having an administrator participate in a leadership development program may increase significantly with each additional member of the leadership team who participates in the experience and comes back to reinforce the spirit of openness and change, the benefit might be even greater if a developmental program of team-building and skill-building were developed and conducted for the entire team.

The identification, encouragement, and preparation of the best and most dedicated people to become leaders, whether done as part of a team or individually, can help foster both their personal growth and fulfillment and the betterment of the institutions they serve. In a world of increasing complexity, higher education takes on ever-greater importance. Leadership development programs that recruit and prepare outstanding and committed people of all races, both genders, and diverse backgrounds to be the deans, the provosts, and the presidents of tomorrow are essential to helping our colleges and universities surmount the challenges they confront and fulfill their missions of teaching students, expanding knowledge, and serving the public.

REFERENCES

Bennis, Warren, and Nanus, Burt. *Leaders: The Strategies for Taking Charge.* New York: Harper & Row, 1985.

Berendzen, Richard. *Is My Armor Straight? A Year in the Life of a University President.* Bethesda: Adler & Adler, 1986.

FISHER, JAMES L. *Power of the Presidency.* New York: American Council on Education/Macmillan Publishing Company, 1984.

GARDNER, JOHN W. *The Tasks of Leadership.* Leadership Papers/2. Washington, D.C.: Independent Sector, 1986.

GILLIGAN, CAROL. *In a Different Voice: Psychological Theory in Women's Development.* Cambridge: Harvard University Press, 1982.

KERR, CLARK, and GADE, MARIAN L. *The Many Lives of Academic Presidents: Time, Place and Character.* Washington, D.C.: Association of Governing Boards of Universities and Colleges, 1986.

MILLETT, JOHN D. *New Structures of Campus Power: Success and Failures of Emerging Forms of Institutional Governance.* San Francisco: Jossey-Bass, 1978.

RIESMAN, DAVID. *On Higher Education.* San Francisco: Jossey-Bass, 1980.

SANFORD, NEVITT, ED. *The American College: A Psychological and Social Interpretation of the Higher Learning.* New York: John Wiley & Sons., 1962.

WALKER, DONALD E. *The Effective Administrator: A Practical Approach to Problem Solving, Decision Making and Campus Leadership.* San Francisco: Jossey-Bass, 1979.

WRISTON, HENRY W. *Academic Procession: Reflections of a College President.* New York and London: Columbia University Press, 1959.

Conclusion: An Action Agenda

Even though no formula exists for developing leaders, we know that organizations and individuals can take a number of steps to find new leaders and help them to be effective. Higher education has recognized the importance of good management in the last twenty years, as well as—with some hesitation—the benefits of providing administrators with the necessary skills and knowledge.

In spite of the growing recognition of the importance of good management and of the usefulness of professional development efforts, the higher education community still does not think of leadership development as an investment in the long-range health of an institution or of the entire enterprise. Efforts are still fragmented and responsibility still lies disproportionately with the individual to tend to his or her own professional development. The burden of change still is on the individual, though considerable institutional change will be needed if we are truly to develop new models of leadership and new ways of functioning. The recommendations that follow indicate the work that lies ahead.

Leadership development must be the responsibility of leaders. Every administrator has a responsibility to develop new talent. The stakes are too high to let leaders flounder and make mistakes that could be avoided. Administrators in colleges and universities ought to be especially sensitive to their obligations as educators beyond the classroom as mentors and teachers of future administrators. The commitment to provide a positive climate for professional development must begin with the board, by encouraging the president to participate in professional development activities, be they seminars, professional meetings, a sabbatical, or teaching. Boards must recognize that even in tight fiscal times, expenditures on professional development by the president and others will improve the performance of administrators on many fronts. While knowledge and skills acquired through seminars and workshops can have a clear payoff in terms of money saved and lawsuits avoided, the personal renewal of administrators will also contribute to the health and vitality of the institution. Presidents have an obligation to educate their boards about the importance of leadership development as well as to set the tone for other administrators and to encourage participation in professional development activities.

All institutions should have policies concerning human resource development and should allocate funds for this purpose. Such policies might cover sabbaticals for faculty and administrators, inhouse development programs, and provision for participation in external professional development opportunities. All of these activities have the potential to contribute to the development of individuals and to the effectiveness of the institution. Just as institutional leaders invest in equipment and the physical plant, so must they invest in people.

Leadership development should be an institutional concern, not simply a personal one. Leadership development should improve the institution, as well as individuals. Professional development is generally thought of in terms of the individual's agenda, but far better use of scarce resources could be made if the organizational agenda came into play as well. For example, sending individuals to national seminars and workshops is useful in itself, but if the gains do not spill over into the institution, that usefulness is limited. Most often, individual professional development is not integrated into an institutional game plan. Administrators should ask themselves how a person attending a workshop or engaged in another professional development activity can use that learning to contribute to the campus. What particular skills or knowledge would help the institution? How can we arrange to have others benefit when that individual returns to campus?

There are various other ways of linking individual and institutional development. Involving key people in a development experience that involves colleagues on campus as well as an institutional agenda benefits both the individuals and the campus. For example, some presidents send their entire group of senior administrators to Harvard Institute for Educational Management, not only for the training provided, but also to develop a common language and common approach to problem-solving. Or, a workshop on campus involving faculty leaders, department chairs, and deans has the dual benefit of enabling individuals to think about the demands of their roles as well as to highlight campus issues that can form a common agenda. Similarly, staff retreats enable decision-makers to focus on issues confronting the institution as well as their roles as team members. Process and substance, individual and organizational development are parts of a whole.

It must be recognized that leadership is found at many levels in the institution and must be shared. Too often, leadership is considered to be a function of administrative rank. This notion suppresses the development and exercise of leadership at various levels and in different areas of the institution. Colleges and universities are too complex and too unruly to be led by a single individual or even the "senior management team." Presidential leadership must be reinforced by good leadership by faculty, department chairs, and nonacademic administrators. A crucial job of the president is to assemble an effective "team" of senior administrators, complementing his or her own strengths and interacting in a healthy and productive manner. This does not happen spontaneously, but by carefully selecting the team and investing time and energy in its functioning, the president can multiply his or her own effectiveness. Further, all administrators are dependent on their subordinates and on good leadership at every level to be optimally effective. Thus, leadership is not only important at the top. The first line of academic management is at the department chair level. These "leaders among peers" as John Bennett suggests, have a highly ambiguous and therefore difficult role. Good department chairs are vital to the institution.

The same is true of many less-visible individuals throughout the institution. Colleges and universities have recently begun to attend to the professional development of administrators outside the academic arena. Professional development for this latter group is in fact less of a problem than for academic administrators. Large institutions may have a staff person whose job it is to attend to their development, and workshops for first and mid-level management are accepted and plentiful. But the distance separating the academic and nonacademic sides of the institutional house is great, and there is often too little communication between one area and another.

Efforts must be strengthened to ensure the full participation of women and minorities as leaders. Although women and minorities have made small gains in assuming leadership positions, progress has been painfully slow, and higher education has a great deal of work yet to do. Affirmative action laws and required procedures have virtually put illegal discrimination to a halt, but subtle discrimination and attitudinal obstacles to full participation of women and minorities are still very much with us. The problems of women are different from those of minorities, and their advancement will require some different strategies. Women are more than half the undergraduates and a rising proportion of graduate and professional students; minority representation is declining as a proportion of the eligible pool in both levels. They share the problem of the "chilly climate" (Sandler, 1986) that is slow to recognize the legitimacy of their presence and the importance of their contributions.

The work to be done now is to continue to educate campus constituents about the importance of affirmative action and the benefits that will be reaped from diversity in leadership. An equally important agenda is institutional change, the need to develop an environment that truly values diversity and that reflects this value in its curriculum and its cocurriculum, as well as in its policies and procedures. Administrators must communicate this message with conviction to search committees and ensure procedurally that the message is heard. The challenge is even greater now, for the problem is more subtle and more elusive. Higher education is shortchanging itself by excluding some first-rate talent from leadership positions. The real work is just beginning, and the success of affirmative action ultimately depends on the commitment of institutional leaders and their ability to mobilize others to make it happen.

The search process must encourage new models of leadership. The search process as it has evolved over the last fifteen years has enabled many campus constituents to have a meaningful voice in the process and to open up opportunities for many. As Green points out in Chapter 10, the remedies to make the process more democratic, more open to women and minorities, and simply more fair, has created a whole new set of problems. Searches are often distressingly slow, encumbered by excessively large committees whose members bring various agendas to the search. Satisfying the various constituents represented may lead to the appointment of an individual who is acceptable to all but inspiring to none. Those who are ultimately making the decision—boards, presidents, or vice presidents—must exert leadership over the search process, which includes selecting the committee, clarifying the job specifications, and maintaining the pressure for affirmative action. Many of the pitfalls of the search process can be avoided by a hiring official who stays close to the search and sees the selection process as an opportunity to improve the institution.

Hiring people who have potential and good track records at what they have done, but who lack the experience that might naturally be considered a prerequisite (such as the position of associate dean or department chair as a prerequisite for a deanship), is one of the few ways of really opening up the pipeline. As long as the search process perpetuates the catch-22 that one must have experience to get experience, or be in the pipeline to get into the pipeline, we are unlikely to bring in new blood. In short, committees and institutions must take risks in hiring individuals if they are to break any new ground.

Leadership development is a continuous, lifelong process. We too often think of leadership development as an episode, an annual workshop or a onetime leave. In reality, leadership development occurs through a variety of experiences continuously throughout one's career. Mentors, project assignments, new jobs, volunteer work, professional development programs, all contribute to leadership development. This is especially important to note in connection with the obligations that all leaders have to foster the development of others. Leaders must think broadly about how to go about doing this: serving as mentors, enriching the jobs of their subordinates through meaningful delegation, structuring opportunities for faculty and administrators throughout the institution to function in a leadership capacity. The continuation of one's liberal education, opportunities to consider thoughtfully one's values and belief system and to assess one's interpersonal skills are also aspects of leadership development. It is especially important in an educational setting to attend to the continued personal and professional development of students, faculty, and administrators. Considering leadership development a continuous process will facilitate that development.

Change is always slow in the academy. Traditions and strong belief systems anchor us in the past while we struggle to adapt to the present and anticipate the future. But the collective awareness of higher education can be heightened and through a process of point and counterpoint, pushing and pulling, taking two steps forward and one step backward, change does happen. It happens through debate and dialogue, through the endless repetition and reworking of recurring themes. Leadership is one such theme, fashionable once again in education, and a term on the lips of many prominent individuals. The notion that new models of leadership are needed is both an old one and a new one. It is old in the sense that every new period in history produces calls for change and adaptation in its social institutions; this one is no exception. It is new in the sense that many of the structures, practices, and traditions in colleges and universities have been in place for a good part of this century, and the changes needed to produce shared leadership, to disperse leadership throughout institutions, and to diversify leadership are fundamental ones. But in its own peculiar way, higher education is dynamic, and we can hope that new ways of doing business and new models of leadership are indeed forthcoming.

REFERENCE

Sandler, B., and Hall, R. *The Campus Climate Revisited: Chilly for Women Faculty, Administrators, and Graduate Students.* Washington, D.C.: Association of American Colleges, Project on the Status and Education of Women, 1986.

Index

Academic Administration Internship Program, ACE, 208
Academy for Educational Development, 32, 206, 210, 236
ACE. *See* American Council on Education
Adams case, 120
Administrative Development Program (Ohio State University), 130
Administrators
  burnout, 26–27
  career elements, 160–162
  career mobility, 170–174
  career profiles, 162–166
  careers vs. positions, 161
  and faculty, 91–92
  as faculty, 159–160
  -faculty conflict, 15–16
  geographic mobility, 173
  interdisciplinary teams, 139
  interviewing, 192, 194–195
  job searching, 168–169
  marketplace, 167–170
  and mentors, 169–170, 177
  minority, 191
  professional development programs, 201–224
  and search process, 176, 183–199
  selecting, 181–200
  training of, 17
  types, 160–162
  women, 169–170, 191, 203
  see also Department chairs; Leaders; Presidents
Adolphus, S.H., 120
AED. *See* Academy for Educational Development
Affirmative action, 99, 168–169, 188, 252
Age
  administrators', 165–166
  faculty, 66–67
Age Discrimination in Employment Act of 1967, 99
Allerhand, M.E., 146
American Association for Higher Education, 183, 203
American Association of State Colleges and Universities, 134
American Association of University Administrators, 202–203
American Association of University Professors, 76, 77
American Association of Women in Community and Junior Colleges (AAWCJC), 102

American Council on Education (ACE), 21, 26, 32, 82, 134, 221
  Center for Leadership Development, 210, 220
  Commission on Leadership Development, 220
  department chairs survey, 61–62
  Department Leadership Institute, 70, 210
  Fellows Program, 20, 22–23, 44, 112, 203, 208, 209, 219, 237–238, 245
    described, 231–232
    minority participation in, 128–129
    women in, 104
  Office of Leadership Development in Higher Education, 209, 210, 234
  Office of Women in Higher Education, 102–103
American Management Association, 203
American Society for Training and Development, 203
Ames, E., 86
Anarchy, 14
Andrew W. Mellon Foundation. *See* Mellon Foundation, Andrew W.
Argyris, C., 17
Asian-Americans, 119, 121
Aspen Institute for Humanistic Studies, 237
Association of American Colleges, 22, 35
Authoritarianism, 4

Barnard, C., 140
Bass, B.M., 2
Beer, M., 145
Belbin, R.M., 142
Belles, A.G., 119
Bennett, J.B., 60, 68, 73 *n*.2, 148, 227, 251
Bennett, W., 35
Bennis, W.G., 2, 13–14, 16–17, 18, 242, 244
Berendzen, R., 241
Bettelheim, B., 229
Birnbaum, R.F., 171
Blacks. *See* Minorities
Bloom, B., 229
Bogart, K.L., 113, 114
Bolman, L., 215
Booth, D.B., 73 *n*.2
Bower, H.R., 147
Brooks, G.E., 206
Brown, D., 26
Brown, D.G., 147, 167
Brown University, 245
Brown v. Board of Education, 120
Bryn Mawr College. *See* HERS
Burnout, 26–27, 72
Burns, J.M., 4, 17, 149
Burns, N., 229
Bush Leadership Fellows Program, 203
Business-Higher Education Forum, 123

California State University, Administrative Fellows Program, 203
Campbell, A., 123
Caplow, T., 167
Carnegie Corporation, 100, 203, 217
Carnegie Council on Policy Studies in Higher Education, 171
Carnegie Mellon Program. *See* College Management Program
Cavanaugh, J., 137
Center for Creative Leadership, 18, 48, 115
Center for Faculty Evaluation and Development, 70
Chater, S.S., 68
Cheever, J., 86
Chibucos, T., 104
Christian A. Johnson Endeavor Foundation, 26, 237
Chronicle of Higher Education, 32, 183, 210
Civil Rights Act of 1964, 99, 120
Claremont Higher Education Management Institute, 210

Claremont Summer Institute, 22, 214–215
Claremont Women Administrators Program, 203
Cleveland, H., 18, 25, 43, 45–46, 49–50, 107–108, 138, 139, 141
Coalition builders, 39–41, 47
Coercive power, 4, 15
Cohen, M.D., 13–14
College and University Personnel Association, 202
College Management Program (Carnegie Mellon University), 213–214, 215*t.*, 216*t.*
Commission on Strengthening Presidential Leadership, 14, 33, 112, 137, 141–142
Columbia University, 67
Communication, 42, 143, 190–191
Conflict
  faculty-administrators, 15–16
  resolution, 40, 42
Consultants, 183–184, 197–198
Council for the Advancement and Support of Education, 202
Cronin, T.E., 123
Cultural barriers, 123
"Custodian of standards," 65–66
Cyert, R., 17, 33, 143–145, 213

Danforth Foundation, 131
Departmental Leadership Program, ACE, 210
Department chairs, 54, 57–73, 251
  description, 57–59
  developing, 68–72
  leadership opportunities, 65–68
  mentors, 71
  problems, 58–59
  rewards and frustrations, 61–63
  role ambiguity, 59–61
  transitions, 63–65
  workshops, 70–71
  see also Faculty; Leaders
Department Leadership Institute, ACE, 70
Department of Health, Education, and Welfare, U.S., 234–235

DeVries, 123
Different Voice, A (Gilligan), 108
Dill, D.D., 203
Dingerson, M.R., 164
Dinsmore, P.C., 146
Discrimination. *See* Affirmative action; Sex discrimination
Doctoral degrees
  administrators', 164–165
  minorities, 125, 126–128, 126*t.*, 131–133
Drucker, P.F., 107, 204–205

Edwards, R., 143
Elementary/Secondary Act of 1972, 99
Ellis L. Phillips Foundation. *See* Phillips Foundation, Ellis L.
Epstein, J., 76
Equal Opportunity Commission, 125, 126*t.*
Estler, S.E., 160, 161, 171
Ethics. *See* Values
Eurich, N.P., 20
Executive Orders 11246 and 11375, 99
Exxon Education Foundation, 207

Faculty
  -administrator conflict, 15–16
  as administrators, 159–160
  aging problems, 66–77
  alienation, 89
  developing leadership, 87–97
  encouraging shared leadership, 82–86
  evaluation, 68
  as leaders, 54, 74–86
  and minority students, 123
  obstacles to leadership, 75–76, 91–92
  pitfalls in developing leadership, 78–82
  recruitment and interdisciplinary teams, 67, 139
  responsibility for leadership, 91
  rights, 15
  see also Department chairs

Federal agencies, 100
see also specific names
Feedback, 48
Financial control, 31
Fisher, J.L., 15, 33, 137, 141, 148, 241
Fiske, E.B., 67
Focus on Minority Women's Advancement (FMWA), 103
Followers. *See* Leadership
Ford Foundation, 100, 131, 132, 208–209, 211
Fortune 500, 235
French, J.R.P., 15
Friedan, B., 108
Fulbright Lectureship, 235–236
Fuller, S.E., 142–143
Fund for the Improvement of Postsecondary Education, 100, 130

Gade, M.L., 14, 15, 30–31, 33, 37, 40, 51 *n*.1, 137, 174, 240, 241–242, 243, 245
Gardiner, J.J., 51, 55, 139, 140
Gardner, D., 204
Gardner, J.W., 37–38, 40, 107, 123, 140, 149–150, 242–243
Generalist. *See* Knowledge executive
Gerth, H.H., 16
G.I. Bill, 120
Gilligan, C., 108, 245
Glickman, A.S., 21
Goals congruence, 4
Graduate Education for Minorities, 132
Granovetter, M., 167
"Great man theory," 3–4
see also "Man on the white horse"
Green, M.F., 104, 137, 145, 155, 157, 210, 227, 252
Greenleaf, R.K., 140, 148, 149
Gross, E., 162
Groups. *See* Teams
Guide to Professional Development Opportunities for College and University Administrators, 209–210

Hackman, J.R., 145–146
Hall, R.M., 108, 113, 114
Handlin, O., 77
Harvard Business School, 209, 211
Harvard Institute for Educational Management (IEM)
comparison with other institutes, 214, 215*t*., 216*t*.
described, 211–212, 232–233
evaluation, 217, 219
inception, 22
minority participation, 129, 130
program and method, 244, 245, 250–251
women in, 104, 130
Haynes, L.J., 203
Haynes, L.L. III, 120
Hazen Foundation, 208
Healy, M., 215
Hefferlin, J.B., 6, 209
Hellwig, B., 108
HEMI. *See* Higher Education Management Institute
HERS (Higher Education Resource Services), 102, 103, 130, 212–213, 214, 215*t*., 216*t*.
Hesburgh, T.M., 137, 141, 142
Hesse, H., 148
HEW. *See* Department of Health, Education, and Welfare, U.S.
Higher Education Act, 234
Higher Education Management Institute (HEMI), 207–208, 210
Higher Education Resource Services. *See* HERS
Hispanic Journal of Behavioral Sciences, 133
Hispanic Leadership Fellows Program, 129–130
Hispanics, 119, 120, 121, 129–130, 131, 169
Hodgkinson, H.L., 118, 149, 221
Holloman, C.R., 16
Holmes, D.R., 160
Houle, C.O., 229
Humor, 144
Hutchins, R.M., 227–228

IAA. *See* Institute for Administrative Advancement
ICUA. *See* Institute for College and University Administrators
IEM. *See* Harvard Institute for Educational Management
Ikenberry, S., 204
Indians, American, 119, 129, 131
Information
application limitation, 138–139
inherent characteristics, 138
leadership and, 42–43, 140
Institute for Administrative Advancement (IAA), 101–102, 217, 222 *n.*11
Institute for College and University Administrators (ICUA), 21, 209
Institute for Educational Management (IEM). *See* Harvard Institute for Educational Management
Intellectual development, 49–50
Interdisciplinary collaboration, 138–139
Interviews, of administrative candidates, 187, 192, 194–195

Job market, 167–169
Johnson, L.B., 120
Johnson Foundation. *See* Christian A. Johnson Endeavor Foundation
Jones, D., 220
Journal for Higher Education Management, 203
Journal of the National Association for Bilingual Education, 133
Journey to the East (Hesse), 148

Kakabadse, A., 21
Kamm, R.B., 141
Kansas State University, 70
Kanter, R.M., 107, 108, 161, 217, 218
Kaplan, S., 113
Kauffman, J.F., 33, 161, 171
Kearns, K.P., 215
Keller, G., 206
Kellogg Foundation, W.K., 206, 210, 236
Keohane, N.O., 124, 143, 144
Kerr, C., 14, 15, 30–31, 33, 37, 40, 51 *n.*1, 77, 137, 174, 240, 241–242, 243, 245
"Knight on the white horse" (leadership concept). *See* "Man on the white horse"
Knowledge executive, 43–46, 47, 49–50
Kohlberg, L., 245
Kram, K.E., 20

Lao-Tse, 148
Lawrence, B., 220
Lawrence College, 245
Leaders
attributes of, 143
as coalition builders, 39–40, 47
department chairs, 54, 57–73, 251
development of, 10–11, 13–29, 47–50
effective, 16
entrepreneurial, 34
faculty, 54, 74–86, 87–97
and followers, 4, 140
future, 36–38, 43
as future agents, 46–47
identifying, 22–23
as knowledge executives, 43–46, 47, 49–50
symbolic, 38–39, 42
team, 41–43, 145–147
women, 98–117, 251–252
Leaders for the '80s Project, 102
Leadership
and challenge, 18–19
and changing concepts, 30–52
constraints, 14
and context, 9–11
defined, 4, 16–17
development, 49, 225–248, 249–251, 253
development programs' effectiveness, 226–247
dialogue, 140

enhancement, 24–26
information processing and, 138–139
and intellectual development, 49
lack of consensus, 9
limiting, 36
literature on, 2–4
and management differentiated, 16, 17
managerial era, 32–34, 41
"man on white horse" concept, 137, 148
minority, 118–136, 251–252
new models development, 4–7, 11, 53–55, 252–253
postmanagerial era, 34–36
presidential, 141
resistance to, 14–16
search process, 252–253
shared, 55, 251
styles, 242–243
tasks, 37
team building, 137–151
training, 20–21, 204–220
as transaction, 3
women's, 98–117
Leavitt, H.J., 139, 140, 141
Lee, J., 119
Legislation, 99–100
Legitimate power, 15
Lehner, C.J., 131
Lester, V., 143
Levine, A., 142
Liberal arts education, 45–46
Lilly Endowment, 209

Maccoby, M., 4, 18, 25, 46, 143, 149
Magrath, C.P., 141, 147
Management
aversion to, 17–18
and delegation, 147
development, 24
effective, 31, 34, 36
institutes, 204–220
and leadership differentiated, 16, 17
skill teaching, 244–245
training programs, 20–21
"Management Crisis," 206
Management training institutes. *See* Professional development programs
Managerial era. *See* Leadership
Managerial Revolution in Higher Education, The (Rourke and Brooks), 206
Mandel, R., 98
"Man on the white horse" (leadership concept), 137, 148
March, J.G., 13–14
Margerison, C., 21
Marital status, administrators', 166
Marlier, J.D, 162
Marmion, H.A., 209
Marshall, S.A., 101
Martorana, S.V., 165, 172
Mayhew, L., 17, 143
Mays, B.E., 121
McCabe, R.H., 141, 143, 147
McCann, J., 162
McCauly, C.D., 18–19, 20, 21
McDade, S.A., 104, 202, 215, 219
McGee, R., 167
McGrath, P., 144
McKnight Black Doctoral Fellowship Program, 131–132
McMillen, L., 110
Megatrends (Naisbitt), 107
Melendez, S.E., 121, 124
Mellon Foundation, Andrew W., 209
Mentors, 19–20, 71, 123, 169–170, 177
Merry, U., 146
Miller, W.F., 147
Millett, J., 236
Mills, C.W., 16
Miner, A.S., 160, 161, 171
Minnich, E., 112
Minorities, 35, 191
administrative career positions, 163–164
cultural barriers, 125
developing leadership in, 118–136, 251–252
in educational institutions, 119–122
-focused scholarship, 124, 133

mainstreaming, 124–134
and mentors, 169–170, 177
obstacles to advancement, 122–124
reference checks, 198
search process and, 196
women's programs, 103
see also Affirmative action; Women
Minter, W.J., 207
Models, new leadership, 4–7, 11, 53–55, 252–253
Moore, K.M., 19, 156, 157, 163, 165, 170, 171, 172, 175
Moral development. *See* Values
Morrison, A.A., 115

Naisbitt, J., 107
Nanus, B., 2, 16–17, 18, 242, 244
Nason, J.W., 143, 144, 183
National Aeronautics and Space Administration, 139
National Association of College and University Business Officers, 202
National Association of Student Personnel Administrators, 202
National Center for Educational Research and Development (U.S. Office of Education), 207
National Center for Higher Education Management Systems (NCHEMS), 206–207
National Conference of Academic Deans, 203
National Consortium for Educational Access, 127
National Endowment for the Humanities, 100
National Identification Program for the Advancement of Women in Higher Education (NIP), 102–104
National Institute for Leadership Development, 102
National Institute of Education, 35, 100, 207
National Institute of Mental Health, 100
National Institutes of Health, 100
National Training Laboratories, Inc., 203, 236–237
Native Americans. *See* Indians, American
NCHEMS. *See* National Center for Higher Education Management Systems
Ness, F., 33
Nettles, M.T., 123
Networking, 107, 109–110, 114, 124, 128, 226
New Jersey Department of Higher Education, 129
New Jersey Minority Doctorate Program, 132
Newman, F., 35
NIP. *See* National Identification Program for Women in Higher Education

Office of Education, U.S., 207, 234
Ohio State University. *See* Administrative Development Program
"Old boy network," 124, 128
Olin Corporation Charitable Trust, 206

Pearson, C.S., 113, 209
Peck, R.D., 34
Pell grants, 120
Persuasion, 143
Peters, T.J., 107
Petrovich, J., 124
Philips, A.M., 144
Phillips, E.L., Jr., 209
Phillips Foundation, Ellis L., 208
Plante, P.R., 90–91
"Polycentric" authority, 14
Postmanagerial era, 34–36
Power, 14–15
Pratt, J.H., 120
Pregnancy Discrimination Act of 1978, 99
Presidents, college/university, 53–54, 137, 141
ability/skills inventory, 243
autocratic, 14

consensus building, 148–149
leadership team questionnaire respondents, 150–151
personality and style, 240–242
as servants, 147–149
team building, 144–147
teams, 141–145
women, 98, 103, 110
President's Executive Exchange Program, 233–234
Professional development programs, 201–224, 225–228
Public policy, 99–100
Pusey, N.M., 145

Raven, B., 15
Recruitment. *See* Search process
Rehabilitation Act of 1973, 99
Rehnke, M.A.F., 73 *n.*3
Relationships
mentor-protégé, 19–20
trusting, 48
Riesman, D., 33, 137, 142–143, 149, 241
Rivera, T., 121
Rockefeller Foundation, 209
Rodman, J.A., 164
Role prejudice, 101
Roosevelt University, 229–230, 231, 234, 236
Rosenbach, W.E., 15
Rourke, F.E., 206

Sabbaticals, 72
Salimbene, A.M., 172
Sandler, B.R., 108, 113, 114, 196
Schein, 146
Scholarship, minority-focused, 124, 133
Schuster, J.H., 204
Schwab, J.J., 229
Scott, R.A., 160, 220
Search process
assumptions and bias, 195–196
basic principles, 182
consultants and, 183–184, 197–198
improving, 175–176, 195–198
new leadership models, 252–253
problems in, 183–189
steps in, 189–195
team aspects, 139
Secor, C., 113, 215
Self-awareness, 47–48
Self-study process, 95
Seton Hall University Higher Education Leadership Institute, 210
Sex discrimination, 108–109
see also Affirmative action; Role prejudice
Shared governance, 90–91
Shavlik, D.L., 181
Simon, H., 213
Sixteen College Administrative Intern Program, 203
Sloan Foundation, 211
Smolansky, B.M., 171, 173
Spilerman, S., 167
Stodgill, R.M., 2
Students, competition for, 36
Sturnick, J., 106
Suffolk University, 236–237
Summer Institute for Women in Higher Education Administration. *See* HERS
Symbolic leader, 38–39, 42

Taylor, E., 103
Taylor, R.L., 15
Teams
advantages, 139
building leadership, 137–151
interdisciplinary, 138–139
leaders, 41–43, 145–147
leaders' dialogue, 139–140
organizational advantages, 139
presidential, 141–145
Tinsley, A., 113
Title VI, 99
Title VII, 99
Title IX, 99
Touchton, J.G., 181
Training programs, 20–21, 204–220
see also Professional development programs
Transaction, 3
TRIO programs, 120, 121

Troutbeck Seminar, 237, 238
see also Christian A. Johnson Endeavor Foundation
Trust, 48, 143–144
Tucker, A., 73 *n*.2
Twombly, S., 162, 165, 171, 172, 175

University Associates, Inc., 203
University of Chicago, 227, 228, 229
University of Denver, 212
University of Michigan, 101, 222 *n*.11, 230–231
University of Wisconsin, 222 *n*.11

Values and ethics, 143, 237–238, 245
Van Alstyne, C., 162
Van Belsor, E., 115
VanderWaerdt, L., 73 *n*.1
Veiga, J., 167
Vision, institutional, 142–143

Wade, J.F., 164
Waggman, J.S., 17
Walker, D.E., 14, 15, 241
Waterman, R.H., Jr., 107
Weber, M., 16
Webster, R.S., 146–147
Weil, R.A., 229–230, 231
Wellesley College, 212
Western Interstate Commission for Higher Education. *See* WICHE
Wheatley, M.J., 217
White, H.C., 161
White, R.P., 115
White House Fellows Program, 233
WICHE Management Information Systems, 207
Wilson, R., 121
Wilson Foundation, Woodrow, 129
Withers, J.S., 162
W.K. Kellogg Foundation. *See* Kellogg Foundation, W.K.
Women, 35, 166, 169, 191
administrative career profiles, 163–164
administrator programs, 203
and family roles, 108, 110–111
and federal agencies, 100
forces shaping leadership, 99–105
as leaders, 98–117, 251–252
leadership development, 105–115
leadership programs, 101–104
leadership strengths, 107
and mentors, 169–170, 177
minority programs, 103
networks, 107, 109–110, 114
search process and, 196
sex discrimination, 108–109
see also HERS
Women in Higher Education Administration, Summer Institute for. *See* HERS
Women's Educational Equity Act Program (WEEAP), 100
Woodrow Wilson Foundation. *See* Wilson Foundation, Woodrow
Working Woman (publication), 108
Wriston, H.W., 245

Zaleznik, A., 16

[redacted]